Winks and Daggers

Books by Thomas Hauser

General Non-Fiction

Missing
The Trial of Patrolman Thomas Shea
For Our Children (with Frank Macchiarola)
The Family Legal Companion
Final Warning: The Legacy of Chernobyl (with Dr. Robert Gale)
Arnold Palmer: A Personal Journey
Confronting America's Moral Crisis (with Frank Macchiarola)
Healing: A Journal of Tolerance and Understanding
Miscellaneous
With This Ring (with Frank Macchiarola)
A God To Hope For

Boxing Non-Fiction

The Black Lights: Inside the World of Professional Boxing
Muhammad Ali: His Life and Times
Muhammad Ali: Memories
Muhammad Ali: In Perspective
Muhammad Ali & Company
A Beautiful Sickness
A Year At The Fights
Brutal Artistry
The View From Ringside
Chaos, Corruption, Courage, and Glory
The Lost Legacy of Muhammad Ali
I Don't Believe It, But It's True
Knockout (with Vikki LaMotta)
The Greatest Sport of All
The Boxing Scene
An Unforgiving Sport
Boxing Is . . .
Box: The Face of Boxing
The Legend of Muhammad Ali (with Bart Barry)
Winks and Daggers

Fiction

Ashworth & Palmer
Agatha's Friends
The Beethoven Conspiracy
Hanneman's War
The Fantasy
Dear Hannah
The Hawthorne Group
Mark Twain Remembers
Finding The Princess
Waiting For Carver Boyd

For Children

Martin Bear & Friends

Winks and Daggers

An Inside Look at Another Year in Boxing

Thomas Hauser

The University of Arkansas Press
Fayetteville
2011

Manufactured in the United States of America

ISBN-10: 1-55728-970-0
ISBN-13: 978-1-55728-970-4

14 13 12 11 10 5 4 3 2 1

⊗The paper used in this publication meets the minimum requirements of the American National Standard for Permanence of Paper for Printed Library Materials Z39.48–1984.

Library of Congress Cataloging-in-Publication Data

Hauser, Thomas.
Winks and daggers : an inside look at another year in boxing / Thomas Hauser.
p. cm.
Includes bibliographical references.
ISBN 978-1-55728-970-4 (pbk. : alk. paper)
1. Boxing. I. Title.
GV1133.H3449 2011
796.83--dc23

2011021059v

Dedication

This is the eighth book that I've published with the University of Arkansas Press. The staff there is a joy to work with. My thanks to:

Mike Bieker
Carolyn Brt
David Scott Cunningham
Katy Henriksen
Brian King
Melissa King
Thomas Lavoie
Larry Malley
Sam Ridge
Charlie Shields
Julie Watkins
Kathy Willis

Contents

Author's Note

Winks and Daggers contains the articles about professional boxing that I authored in 2010. The articles I wrote about the sweet science prior to that date have been published in *Muhammad Ali & Company; A Beautiful Sickness; A Year at the Fights; The View From Ringside; Chaos, Corruption, Courage, and Glory; The Lost Legacy of Muhammad Ali; I Don't Believe It, But It's True; The Greatest Sport of All; The Boxing Scene; An Unforgiving Sport;* and *Boxing Is. . . .*

Round 1

Fights and Fighters

In recent years, Manny Pacquiao has been the best story in boxing.

Manny Pacquiao and the Essence of Boxing

"Boxing," Hugh McIlvanney has written, "is a sport in which two men try to batter each other senseless. No matter how you dress it up, the basic objective is to render the opponent unconscious. You can say that more people are killed in motorcycle racing, that more people are killed in mountaineering. But in neither of those two activities is the fundamental objective to knock the other guy out. Motive, not statistics, will always separate boxing from other sports."

On the night of March 13, 2010, Manny Pacquiao readied for battle in the futuristic city known as Cowboys Stadium. The gate that divides the visiting team's dressing room had been lowered, cutting the room in half. Eight "red corner" undercard fighters were on the other side of the gate. Pacquiao's opponent and the "blue corner" fighters were in smaller quarters.

Pacquiao had arrived at the stadium at 7:50 PM. The earliest he would be called to the ring was ten o'clock. For the better part of an hour, he talked on his cell phone and sent text messages to friends. Then he readied for battle.

One day earlier, Manny had weighed in at 145¾ pounds. His opponent, Joshua Clottey, had tipped the scales at the maximum contract weight of 147. The assumption was that Clottey now weighed at least 160. Pacquiao weighed 150. His body was sculpted without an ounce of superfluous fat. It was hard to imagine that, less than two years before, he'd fought after weighing in at 130 pounds.

Football, like boxing, is a violent game. In this same dressing room, gridiron warriors had suited up for battle. Forty-five players on each team that confronted the Dallas Cowboys had donned rib protectors, shoulder pads, arm pads, knee pads, hip pads, thigh pads, and helmets with face masks. When the competition began, they'd protected each other and helped teammates off the turf after they'd been knocked down.

Pacquiao would enter the ring for combat naked from the waist up. A protective cup to safeguard his genitals would be his only shield. There would be no one to block for him. His head would be completely exposed.

The rules of football are designed to minimize direct blows to the head. Boxing requires them.

Pacquiao knows that there's a dark side to his trade. Before each fight, he asks the people closest to him to "pray for me."

Two centuries ago, William Hazlitt wrote of the hour before a fight begins, "It is then the heart sickens as you think what the two champions are about and how a short time will determine their fate."

As the clock ticked down, Pacquiao shadow-boxed, moving around the center of the room.

There were final instructions from trainer Freddie Roach.

Then it was time. Manny left the dressing room and walked through the subterranean depths of the stadium. A tunnel of humanity lined by Dallas Cowboys cheerleaders—sexual icons of our time—lay ahead. The inside of the stadium was bathed in a silver otherworldly glow. Spotlights moved back and forth. Forty thousand fans were screaming.

A smile played across Pacquiao's face. He seemed to be without fear. In many respects, this fight in this stadium was about the future of boxing. But boxing is timeless. The essence of the competition he was about to engage in was the same as John L. Sullivan experienced on a barge towed upriver to avoid New York law enforcement authorities in 1881. After the bell rang, it would be no different, really, from what Joe Louis and Max Schmeling did at Yankee Stadium or the encounter between Muhammad Ali and George Foreman in the heart of Africa. It was the same as the competition among unarmed combatants at the first Olympiad in Greece thousands of years ago. A boy who once fought on the streets of the Philippines for pocket change also knew it well.

* * *

2010 began with the collapse of the proposed mega-fight between Manny Pacquiao and Floyd Mayweather Jr. Then, on January 10th, Bob Arum (Pacquiao's promoter) announced an alternative plan. Manny would fight Joshua Clottey of Ghana at Cowboys Stadium in Arlington, Texas.

Thereafter, Bart Barry observed, "We come to the end of our Pacquiao-Mayweather mourning season. Fun as it is to gnash teeth and tremble at the future of prizefighting, the sun has risen anew, men still don gloves to resolve conflicts in manly ways, and a major venue awaits a major event."

Pacquiao-Clottey was for Pacquiao's World Boxing Organization 147-pound championship. Three themes were central to the promotion. The first, of course, was the persona of Manny Pacquiao.

Manny came to Dallas on fire, both as a fighter and as an attraction. Three times during the previous fifteen months, he had moved up in weight to challenge bigger men. Each time, there was widespread doubt as to what the outcome would be. And each time, after the fight, it looked as though the result had been preordained.

"It's not just about beating opponents," former featherweight champion Barry McGuigan, now a television commentator, observed. "It's the way that you beat them. Pacquiao went through Oscar de la Hoya like a sparring partner. The way he knocked out Ricky Hatton was staggering. He just pole-axed him. Then he systematically took apart Miguel Cotto in a way none could have predicted."

Pacquiao's journey from abject poverty in an impoverished land to iconic status and wealth beyond his imagination has captivated his followers. "The broad outlines of his legend," *Time Magazine* declared, "have made him a projection of the migrant dreams of the many Filipinos who leave home and country for work. Some spend decades abroad for the sake of the ones they love. Everyone in the Philippines knows a person who has made the sacrifice or is making it. Pacquiao gives that multitude a champion's face of selflessness; the winner who takes all and gives to all."

The second promotional story line revolved around Freddie Roach.

Roach turned pro at age eighteen and began his career with ten consecutive wins. After losing a decision, he ran his record to 26-and-1. The legendary Eddie Futch was his trainer.

"I look at old tapes of myself now," Roach says, "and I know I could have been better. In the gym, I listened to what Eddie taught me and I could do it. But then the fight would come and I'd fight instead of box. I'd get hit and I had to hit back, which wasn't always good. And I was stubborn. If something wasn't working, instead of adjusting to something else, I'd keep trying the same thing. There's a line between being courageous and being foolish. But when I was young, I was too aggressive to see it."

There's an old adage that says, if a fighter isn't getting better, he's getting worse. Roach peaked young. He was 13-and-12 after the age of twenty-two. By the end of his career, he was an opponent. He retired at age twenty-six, never having made more than $7,500 for a fight.

"I remember when Eddie took me to his office and told me that I was taking too many punches and my performance wasn't what it used to be and I should retire," Roach says. "I started to cry. I had no idea what I was going to do with my life."

Then life got tougher.

"All the people who said to me when I was winning fights, 'You're a great guy; when you finish boxing, come to me and I'll give you a job,' all of a sudden, they weren't around."

Roach worked for a telemarketing company and drank heavily for the better part of a year. Then, at Futch's suggestion, Virgil Hill (who Eddie trained) asked Roach to work with him because Futch was focusing heavily on his more-established fighters.

"When Virgil asked me," Roach recalls, "the first thing I said was, 'I don't know how to train fighters.' But he and Eddie talked me into it. After that, Eddie, grew me as a trainer, step by step, the same way he grew me as a fighter. I remember when he let me go to a rules meeting alone for the first time. It was when Virgil fought Leslie Stewart [in 1987] and won the light-heavyweight championship. I felt so good, that Eddie trusted me like that."

Roach, like his mentor, can take a good fighter and make him better. "You have to have patience," he explains. "You have to be a psychiatrist. You have to be a problem solver. You have to know boxing. And you need a good fighter. That part about having a good fighter is the key."

"Over time," Roach continues, "I realized that I could be a better trainer than I was a fighter. Now my goal is to make as many world champions as possible. It's not as good as being a champion myself would have been, but that's the way life is. There are still times when something is difficult and I say to myself, 'Boy; I wish Eddie was around.' But someone told me not long ago, 'Eddie would be proud of you.' And I said, 'I know.'"

Roach has risen to the top of his profession. "There are a lot of people who blew me off who are very nice to me now," he notes. "I don't hold grudges, but I remember. A couple of years ago, Bob Arum called me an idiot."

Freddie smiles. "It comes and it goes. I like Bob. Everything is good between us now."

Pacquiao-Clottey was marketed as "The Event." That led to the third promotional hook. This was the first fight card ever in Cowboys Stadium.

In late 2009, Dallas Cowboys owner Jerry Jones had offered a $25,000,000 ticket-sale guarantee for Pacquiao-Mayweather that was rejected out of hand by Golden Boy (Mayweather's promoter). "I wanted that fight between those two fighters worse than my next breath," Jones acknowledged.

From Jones's point of view, Pacquiao-Clottey was branding for his stadium. "I'm certainly a fan of boxing," he explained. "But that's not what this fight is about. This is a very logical way to introduce our stadium to the world and lift its aura."

In other words; Jones wasn't in boxing to be in boxing. He was in the sport to build his stadium as a venue. Just as the Dallas Cowboys style themselves as "America's Team," he wants Cowboys Stadium to become "America's Stadium."

Toward that end, Jones hosted the 2010 NBA All-Star Game. A record 108,713 fans attended. Cowboys Stadium will also be the site for the 2011 Super Bowl and the 2014 NCAA Men's Basketball Championship Final Four.

The stadium is awesome. Built at a cost of $1.2 billion, it seats 80,000 fans for football with space for additional standing-room attendees and can accommodate twenty thousand more for boxing. There's a retractable roof and a four-sided HDTV video board that's 160 feet long, 72 feet high, and weighs 600 tons. The video board, Jones is fond of saying, is the largest in the world.

Ticket prices for Pacquiao-Clottey ranged from $700 down to $35 (for standing room "party passes"). On fight night, 41,841 fans filed into Jones's palace.

Bob Arum spent most of fight week walking around with a smile on his face like the proverbial cat that had swallowed a canary. "This is going to be one of the biggest events in the history of boxing," he proclaimed.

"If you think the Dallas Cowboys cheerleaders are pretty, wait until you see them on that forty-million-dollar video screen."

There was a buzz to the promotion. Jones radiates intensity and he said it like he meant it when he told the media, "This will be a fight to remember. We're going to promote this like it was the Super Bowl."

The National Football League is an entity unto itself. It goes to great lengths to preclude other sports from poaching on its cachet and marketing power. Jones acknowledged as much on a March 9th teleconference call, saying, "The NFL is reluctant to cross over with other sports." But then he added, "In a very obvious way, people will recognize there is a crossover in interest for this fight. I'm not trying to be presumptuous about boxing and the NFL. But we all know how popular the NFL is right now. It raises all boats and it will raise boxing."

HBO got a taste of the Jerry Jones style during production planning when the discussion turned to whether or not the pay-per-view telecast would include live overhead shots of Cowboys Stadium on fight night. The cost was beyond HBO's budget. Jones indicated he would see to it that the cost would be covered. "I'm not known for following budgets," he said.

Thereafter, Arum noted, "Don King and I are lucky this guy didn't get in boxing when we did. He would have run us both out of the business."

Freddie Roach, for his part, took one look at the inside of Cowboys Stadium and told Jones, "You've got a lot of balls, building this place."

Meanwhile, there was a fight to be fought, although it began as a fistic rendition of the old Broadway song "Mutual Admiration Society."

Clottey told the media, "Pacquiao is my favorite fighter. He has been for a long time. He is a very nice guy and I feel comfortable around him."

Pacquiao responded in kind, saying, "Clottey is a very good boxer. He is big and strong. I like this match because both sides, there is no trash talk. We are setting a good example for everybody."

That said; for most of the promotion, Team Clottey was treated by the media as an afterthought. Pacquiao was a 6-to-1 betting favorite. Clottey's manager (Vinny Scolpino) and trainer (Lenny DeJesus) went almost unnoticed during fight week as they strolled around the Gaylord Texan Hotel, which served as event headquarters.

Still, within the boxing community, Clottey was considered a live underdog. "I'm not a flyweight," he reminded people, referencing Pacquiao's climb up the ladder through seven weight divisions. "I am not a bantamweight. I am a welterweight. I can throw shots that land and cause damage."

"We have the perfect game plan," Roach countered. "Clottey is a big strong guy and we respect him. But he is what he is. He fights the same way whether he fights southpaws or right-handers. He's predictable. He's good at what he does, but he does the same thing over and over again. I feel that Manny is going to overwhelm him with speed and combinations. Clottey has a good chin but he doesn't protect his body that well. I think Manny will break him down with body shots. I don't know if Manny can knock him out. But I think he can make Clottey quit or take things to a point where the referee or Clottey's corner stops it."

On the day of the weigh-in, Roach elaborated on that theme, saying, "I'm not worried about Clottey's size. Manny weighed 144 pounds when he woke up this morning. That meant he could eat breakfast and a small lunch. He's happy and strong, and Clottey is starving himself to make weight. I know Clottey will go into the ring ten pounds heavier than Manny. But size doesn't win fights. Skill does. And I've got the better fighter."

Roach might have added that boxing's traditional "tale of the tape" doesn't measure the size of a fighter's heart.

On fight night, Pacquiao proved Roach right. The biggest problem that Team Pacquiao faced came in the dressing room before the fight. When it was time for Manny to hit the pads in his final warm-up prior to leaving for the ring, Freddie realized that there were no pads.

Roach brings two sets of mitts from his home base in Los Angeles to out-of-town fights. The night before Pacquiao-Clottey, he'd worked the corner of Jose Benavidez (a promising young prospect in his stable) on a FoxSportsNet telecast. After the fight, he gave the pads he'd warmed Benavides up with to a friend as a memento. He forgot that, earlier in the week, he'd donated the other pair of mitts to a charity auction.

The solution was simple. At age fifty, Freddie warmed Pacquiao up by catching the punches of the best fighter in the world on his bare palms.

As Pacquiao walked to the ring to face Clottey, the atmosphere was electric. But whether a boxing ring is in Cowboys Stadium, the MGM Grand in Las Vegas, or a small union hall in Pennsylvania, it's still a boxing ring.

Two fighters doing their best to win are necessary for a great fight. The early rounds established the pattern of this one. Clottey stood with his hands held high, both fists in front of his face, elbows protecting his body. Pacquiao attacked, getting off first, darting in and out, looking for openings. His speed intimidated and befuddled Clottey. Joshua was reluctant to abandon his defensive posture. When he did, Manny responded with pinpoint violence, firing straight lefthands that came at their target as fast as jabs. That's the way it was all night. The fifth round was Clottey's best. Other than that, Pacquiao pitched a shutout.

As the fight progressed, round after round, Lenny DeJesus implored his charge, "Come on, we gotta take chances. What are you waiting for? . . . The kid's ahead. Let's throw punches. Hurt this guy . . . Let's create openings now, okay? Let's take a chance . . . Let's be creative. Let's throw punches. We're losing every round, so get to it . . . We're losing every damn round. Come on. You're taking a whipping, baby . . . What's going on? Come on. We haven't won a round, baby. We've got to do something."

When it was over, Pacquiao had thrown 1,231 punches to Clottey's 399. He outlanded Clottey in every round, highlighted by a 232 to 82 edge in power punches landed.

The judges were on the mark with a 120–108, 119–109, 119–109 verdict. Clottey managed to avoid winding up as a featured attraction on Pacquiao's highlight reel. But a fighter in a championship bout should have a loftier goal.

"Clottey didn't come to fight," Roach said afterward. "He came to survive. I know it was hard for him. Most fighters can't adjust to Manny's speed. They see him on television and say, 'Oh, he looks fast.' But you don't really know how fast he is until you're in the ring with him. And once you're there, when you feel his power and his punches are coming from all angles . . ."

Roach's voice trailed off, then picked up again. "An opportunity like this comes along for a fighter once in a lifetime, if he's lucky. If Clottey was my fighter, I'd be very upset with him. I'd rather get knocked out trying to win a championship than do what he did."

A half-century ago, A. J. Liebling wrote, "The desire to punch other boys in the nose will survive in our culture. The spirit of self-preservation will induce some boys to excel. Those who find they excel will try to turn a modest buck by it. It is an art of the people, like making love."

In rare instances, the best practitioners of the art of boxing are embraced by their country, an entire ethnic group, or believers in a given religion. Once in a generation, if that generation is fortunate, a fighter is embraced by the world.

Pacquiao is ascending to the summit. It's ironic that he practices the most unforgiving of sports. Cruelty seems foreign to his nature. Like Joe Louis and Muhammad Ali before him, he has come to symbolize caring and compassion.

Meanwhile, it's a joy to watch Pacquiao ply his trade. He's the most exciting fighter in the world today and everything that an athlete should be: awesomely talented, a great competitor, respectful toward opponents, and appreciative of his fans. He's also the best show in boxing.

Where Pacquiao goes from here is an open issue. His immediate priority is a run for Congress in the Philippines against the scion of a wealthy political family. It's an uphill battle with the odds against him; more so than for any of his fights in the ring.

Win or lose, Pacquiao is likely to return to the sweet science before the end of the year. When he does, he will remind us all once again of the essence of boxing.

"Life," Matthew Wells wrote several years ago, "rarely comes at you in short bursts of wild mayhem. More often than not, it is a long drawn-out grind that forces you to make thousands of small adjustments in order to keep pointed in the right direction. Boxing, more than any other sport, is emblematic of this struggle. It reminds us that life can be hard and even unfair, but with hard work and dedication, you can, once in a while, achieve something truly brilliant."

The underside of boxing was on display in Las Vegas on April 3, 2010.

Hopkins-Jones II: Better Never Than Late

This is a column I'd rather not write. But I chronicle the contemporary boxing scene, and I'd be less than honest if I didn't write it.

Roy Jones is one of my favorite people, in or out of boxing. When he was young, he was a great fighter. And I've always been impressed by his generosity of spirit. Roy might blow off production meetings and promotional press conferences. But time and again, I've seen him get on a plane and fly across the country to speak with students at inspirational forums or attend charitable ventures.

That brings us to the matter at hand.

Seventeen years ago, Jones fought Bernard Hopkins for the IBF middleweight championship. Roy was 21-and-0 with 20 knockouts and clearly a superstar in the making. Bernard was 22-and-1 with 16 KOs; good but not yet considered great. Jones hurt his hand early in the fight, but won eight of twelve rounds on each judge's scorecard.

Thereafter, both men journeyed to ring greatness. Jones made James Toney look like a novice, dominated the light-heavyweight division for years, and outclassed John Ruiz to win the WBA heavyweight crown. Bernard established hegemony over the middleweight ranks after Roy moved up in weight.

Hopkins is now forty-five years old. Jones is forty-one.

For seventeen years, the loss to Roy has stuck in Bernard's craw like broken glass. Jones is the only man to have decisively beaten him. When Roy was at his peak and dominating the light-heavyweight division, Hopkins said little about moving up in weight to challenge him. But as Roy's skills deteriorated, Bernard grew bolder. With increasing frequency, he suggested that a rematch was in order. On several occasions, they seemed close to finalizing a deal. Each time, it fell apart.

Ten days before Jones fought Joe Calzaghe, Roy told the media, "Bernard Hopkins can talk about whoever he's going to fight next. I couldn't care less. I already beat Bernard Hopkins, so why would I want to fight him again? He can do all he wants to try and tie himself to my career, but I'm not tied to his."

On November 8, 2008, Calzaghe exposed Roy as a once-great fighter who had become a shell of his former self.

Three days later, Hopkins declared, "I don't want to fight Roy; not after Saturday night. What's the point? The things that he was able to do because he was Superman; he can't do them anymore. Physically, he looked old. His face was shrunken. He didn't look strong. It wouldn't be right."

But Naazim Richardson (who trains Hopkins) sounded a prescient note, saying, "If Roy calls Bernard to fight and Bernard is seventy-five years old, Bernard will take his teeth out of the jar and go fight. If I was advising Roy, I'd say, 'You don't need that fight. Let it be. Leave it as it is and the history books will say you beat Bernard Hopkins.' But I got a feeling that Roy is like someone who robs the junkyard when the dog is asleep. Now you tell him that the dog is awake, and he's foolish enough to go back again."

Hopkins-Jones II is now scheduled for April 3, 2010, at Mandalay Bay in Las Vegas. Square Ring is a promotional partner, but Golden Boy (Bernard's promoter) is controlling the venture.

Within the boxing community, there's more dread than interest in the fight. Over the past seven years, Jones has posted five wins against five losses with three "KOs by." In his most recent outing, he was knocked out in the first round by Danny Green.

Like Jones, Hopkins has suffered defeat. His record over the past five years is 4-and-3, with losses to Jermain Taylor (twice) and Joe Calzaghe. But each loss was by a razor-thin margin and he has never been knocked out.

HBO (which has a synergistic relationship with Golden Boy) considers Jones so far over the hill that it refused to produce the fight as a *World Championship Boxing* or pay-per-view telecast. Instead, it will quietly distribute the show without HBO branding on pay-per-view. Larry Merchant speaks for many at the network when he says, "It's a free country. They can fight if they want to. And I don't have to watch it if I don't want to. I'd rather not see it."

Golden Boy has now hired an independent production company.

Adding insult to expected injury, it's possible that Jones will come out of the venture making no money at all.

Sources say that the bout contracts call for promotional expenses (e.g. the cost of television production, distribution fees, and publicity costs such as the pre-fight press tour) to be paid off the top. Golden Boy and Hopkins will receive the next $3,500,000. In theory, Jones and Square Ring will get the following $3,500,000, with a fifty-fifty split thereafter.

The problem with this math in terms of Jones's financial well-being is that the fight is unlikely to generate $7,000,000 in profits. It might not even generate $3,500,000.

Golden Boy has a "four-wall" deal with Mandalay Bay. The site has guaranteed a relatively small number of ticket buys. April 3rd is Easter Eve and, more significantly, the same night as the semifinals of the NCAA men's championship basketball tournament (which could kill pay-per-view buys). Golden Boy CEO Richard Schaefer has made a point of telling the media that the main event won't begin until after the basketball games are over. That's another way of saying that the undercard won't be worth watching.

At the February 9th kick-off press conference in New York, Schaefer said that he expected the fight to generate between 300,000 and 350,000 buys. Most industry analysts consider that number to be wildly optimistic.

During the initial pre-fight build-up, Oscar De La Hoya declared, "As a fan, I'm excited that the fight is finally happening."

As a promoter, Oscar might be excited. As a fan, he should be disgusted.

I've been wrong before. I was one of those guys who thought that Evander Holyfield would be destroyed by Mike Tyson the first time they fought.

Also, the attribute in an opponent that gives Hopkins the most trouble is speed (think Jermain Taylor and Joe Calzaghe). Jones's hands are still fast, although not as fast as they once were.

That said; I'm dismayed by the thought of Hopkins-Jones II. My mind keeps drifting back to a moment in time thirteen years ago.

I'd been traveling around the country with Muhammad Ali, speaking to students about tolerance and understanding. On February 26, 1997, our travels took us to Pensacola, Florida. That afternoon, we visited the Square Ring Gym, where Roy was training.

Ali was suffering noticeably from Parkinson's syndrome by then, but he was still physically strong. Roy invited him into the ring. Muhammad obliged. They engaged in a mock sparring session.

That night, over dinner, Roy told me, "I feel better about Ali now. When we got in the ring, I could see right away that he was looking for the flaw in my jab. He found it. And he signaled to me by doing the same thing with his jab that I was doing."

"And?"

"I know it's there," Roy said. "But I'm so fast, I can get away with it."

Roy isn't that fast anymore. Everything changed for him when his reflexes became a split second slower. He was never a technically sound fighter in the traditional sense. He was great because of his preternatural physical gifts, including the ability to see things as, or even before, they unfolded and react instantaneously to them. Now that his athleticism is diminished, he's no longer "Roy Jones" in the ring and hasn't been for a long time.

Hopkins knows that he fought the wrong fight the first time around against Roy. Instead of trying to box, he should have mauled and brawled. Now he can do either.

Hopkins-Jones II has the look of Larry Holmes against Muhammad Ali. Roy knows how to beat Bernard, but his body can no longer do what has to be done. His reflexes and chin are likely to betray him.

How apt is the parallel between Jones and Ali?

Larry Holmes sees it.

"I'm not a doctor," the former heavyweight champion says. "I'm just Larry Holmes. But I'll tell it to you straight. Roy Jones shouldn't fight no more. People told me to stop fighting before I did, and it took a while for me to listen to them. But I wasn't taking punches upside the head and getting beat up like Roy is now."

"Roy Jones can't do his thing in the ring anymore," Holmes continues. "He's getting hit and he's getting hurt. Everyone but Roy sees it. It's like Ali. When Ali was young, he almost never got hit. If Ali had quit at the right time, he'd be healthy and talking well now. But he fought too long; he started getting hit in the head a lot; and look at him now. So I'd say to Roy, 'You did your thing. You were great. You proved yourself. But you can't keep getting hit in the head and not wind up with problems of a bad kind. Don't be stupid. Don't fuck up your life. Get real with yourself.

There's lots of things you can do to feel good about yourself besides being a fighter."

Medical experts are in accord.

Flip Homansky once served as a commissioner and chief ringside physician for the Nevada State Athletic Commission. He's one of the most respected and knowledgeable voices in the United States with regard to the medical aspects of boxing.

"I prefer to not get involved with boxing matters anymore," Homansky says. "I haven't commented publicly on a fight since I left the commission. But this fight troubles me so much that I will."

"I believe that, if it's at all possible, regulators should act before a serious injury occurs," Homansky continues. "Having worked with fighters for many years, I can tell you that there's no magic bullet to use in determining whether or not a fighter should be licensed. CT-scans, PET-scans, and MRIs can be helpful. But too often, testing doesn't tell you what you need to know until it's too late. The key is having all of the available data on a fighter, including his past performances, reviewed by good doctors who understand boxing. If you do that with Roy Jones, you start with the fact that, when Roy was young, he never got hit; and now he can't do anything but get hit. Then you compare how Roy responded to blows when he was young and how he responds now. Something in Roy's brain no longer works like it should. Common sense tells you that this fight shouldn't happen. It's a farce, and it's a farce that endangers Roy's well-being beyond the normal risks that a fighter takes."

Margaret Goodman (who succeeded Homansky as chief ringside physician for the Nevada State Athletic Commission) concurs, saying, "Out of all the fighters I worked with when I was with the commission, the one I felt the most privileged to work with was Roy. This makes me so sad. It's not whether or not Roy can pass the medical tests. I'm sure he can. All that will mean is that they're giving him the wrong tests. This isn't just a medical decision. It's a boxing decision. Roy's ability to avoid punches and handle punches when they land has deteriorated to the point where this fight shouldn't be allowed to happen. Roy is a fighter at risk. Red warning lights are flashing. Roy will take punishment in training and he'll take more punishment in the fight. To think that this could happen in Nevada, which once prided itself on having the highest medical standards in the country for boxing, is a travesty and an embarrassment."

Sometimes, a once-great fighter with courage and heart has to be protected from himself. The ultimate responsibility for saying "no" to Hopkins-Jones II rests with the Nevada State Athletic Commission. The NSAC should have refused to grant Muhammad Ali a license when he wanted to fight Larry Holmes. But greed triumphed over sound medical judgment in the decision-making process. The whole world now sees the results.

Eight years ago, the Nevada State Athletic Commission acted on principle when it denied Mike Tyson a license to fight Lennox Lewis. Lewis-Tyson wound up in Memphis. Las Vegas survived. Now the NSAC should again act on principle and refuse to allow Hopkins-Jones II. But the assumption is that the promotion wouldn't have reached the point it's at now unless Golden Boy had been assured by commission personnel that Jones would be licensed.

Roy Jones was a special fighter. He's still a special person. I hate to see him put himself in harm's way like this. Hopkins-Jones II is bad for Roy and bad for boxing.

Thirteen years ago, after sparring with Roy, Muhammad Ali said, "He reminds me of me when I was young."

Now Roy reminds people of Ali as an aging fighter. It would be tragic if he were to remind people of Ali outside the ring when he gets old.

AND A NOTE AFTERWARD

I didn't watch last Saturday night's fight between Bernard Hopkins and Roy Jones. Like most people who've followed boxing in recent years, I knew how it would end.

I gather it was ugly and that the crowd booed a lot. Michael Rosenthal of *The Ring* called it "painful to watch" and "one of boxing's worst nights in recent memory." He said that Jones fought "barely at all" and "the fight dragged on until the final bell put everyone out of their misery."

Dan Rafael of ESPN.com called it a "depressing mess" and added, "When the most action in the fight comes from fouls, you know it's not good."

What no one knows—and no one will until down the road—is how the repeated blows to the head that Jones is taking now in the gym and in fights will affect him in the future. Oscar De La Hoya touched on that issue last December when he urged Roy to retire after Jones was knocked out in the first round by Danny Green. But there was blood money to be made from Hopkins-Jones II. Oscar and Golden Boy CEO Richard Schaefer wanted to make it. The enablers around Roy got in on the act. And the Nevada State Athletic Commission abandoned its leadership role with regard to the health and safety of fighters a long time ago.

Hopkins is in the revenge business. He got what he wanted on Saturday night; a twelve-round decision victory over a once-great fighter who's now an empty vessel in the ring. Given the opportunity, Bernard would probably fight Jermain Taylor again too. That way, he could avenge his two losses to Taylor (who withdrew from Showtime's super-middleweight tournament after suffering a brain bleed).

Meanwhile, Hopkins's win over Jones proves nothing with regard to the relative greatness of either fighter. If Muhammad Ali and George Chuvalo fought a rematch today, one assumes that, unlike their earlier fights, Chuvalo would win.

If Roy Jones winds up talking like Ali, will the people who pushed this fight on him in the manner of a supplier giving heroin to an addict feel guilty?

They should.

Pavlik-Martinez marked the fifth time that I was in Kelly's dressing room in the hours before and after a championship fight.

Kelly Pavlik and the Hard Road of Boxing

Most professional fighters have struggled with demons. That's one of the things that impelled them to become fighters. They're faced with the constant reality of being punched by men trained in the art of hurting. And if a fighter becomes The Man, it seems as though everyone wants a piece of him.

Kelly Pavlik has been a fighter through much of his childhood and all of his adult life. No matter how many challenges he confronts in and out of the ring, there's always another dragon to slay on fight night.

Pavlik moved into the spotlight three years ago when he knocked out Edison Miranda in seven rounds. On September 29, 2007, he duplicated that feat against Jermain Taylor to become middleweight champion of the world. A victorious rematch against Taylor and third-round demolition of mandatory challenger Gary Lockett followed.

Pavlik was the pride of Youngstown, Ohio. There was talk of his being the successor to Arturo Gatti as Atlantic City's flagship fighter. But boxing is an insecure business. There's no such thing as security in boxing.

On October 18, 2008, Pavlik went up in weight to fight Bernard Hopkins. If he'd won, it would have elevated him to superstar status. Instead, he suffered the first loss of his career. And even though he was still middleweight champion of the world, things weren't quite the same.

In most sports, an athlete can lose and come all the way back within a short time frame. Boxing is different. Every loss impacts significantly on a fighter's career.

Pavlik's first fight after losing to Hopkins was in Youngstown against Marco Antonio Rubio on February 21, 2009. The Chevrolet Centre was sold out.

"That's the first time I ever saw Kelly nervous before a fight," Michael Cox (a Youngstown police officer, who's Pavlik's friend and one of his cornermen) said afterward. "He didn't want to disappoint all those people and he knew that he needed to put on a dominating performance."

Pavlik knocked Rubio out in nine rounds.

Promoter Bob Arum wanted Kelly's next fight to be in Cleveland. But the 8 percent city tax on top of a 5 percent state athletic commission tax made that impractical. Thus, Arum began planning for a June 27th date in Atlantic City against Sergio Mora.

But there was a problem. Pavlik's promotional contract with Top Rank ran until May 31, 2010. One of the clauses provided that, if Kelly won a world championship, Top Rank would be entitled to promote his next five fights. The Pavlik camp took the position that, once those five fights were held, the contract would terminate even if that occurred before May 31, 2010. Pavlik-Mora would be Kelly's fifth fight subsequent to winning the title.

Arum said that Team Pavlik's interpretation of the contract was ridiculous. Moreover, he maintained that he was entitled to a seven-month contract extension (through December 31, 2010) because of time that Kelly had been unable to fight due to injury.

Pavlik-Mora fell through. Then Kelly signed a contract extension that unites him with Top Rank through May 2011. After that, Arum closed a deal for an early-October bout between Pavlik and Paul Williams. But a staph infection that began in Kelly's left hand forced postponement of Pavlik-Williams until December 5, 2009.

Even then, Pavlik-Williams was in doubt. At a September 29th press conference announcing the new date, dead skin was flaking off Kelly's hand. Eventually, the fight was cancelled. That led to the sort of bombastic idiocy that plagues boxing; to wit, claims that Pavlik was ducking Williams. The truth was more serious than that.

In early March, while Kelly was playing basketball, the skin over a knuckle on his left hand (where he'd received a cortisone injection several months earlier) burst and began oozing puss. A doctor prescribed antibiotics, but the infection persisted; even after surgery to clean the area out. Further tests revealed the presence of MRSA (methicillin-resistant *Staphylococcus aureus*), a sometimes fatal infection that resists most antibiotics.

Pavlik was given new medication and had an allergic reaction to one of the antibiotics. That coincided with an overdue visit to a hand specialist in Cleveland.

"As he was looking at me," Kelly later recalled, "I got the shakes and the shivers and I started swelling up. My face was turning purple. The doctor said, 'Look, we'll worry about the hand afterward. Go upstairs to the infectious specialist now.'"

Kelly's temperature rose to 104.5 degrees. His heart rate was 150 beats per minute. His blood pressure was rapidly dropping.

"I'm not a medical man," Mike Pavlik (Kelly's father) said afterward. "But he was really close to the edge that day."

Kelly was hospitalized for four days. After two surgeries on his left hand, he needed physical therapy to regain full use of his finger.

"The kid was injured," Arum said afterward. "He couldn't make a fist. It wasn't some fear of Paul Williams. To hear morons talk like that when they have no basis for what they're saying really makes me sad."

Meanwhile, the once-adoring local media was turning on Pavlik. In today's culture, athletes lose their privacy. Some, like Floyd Mayweather Jr, revel in that and act in a way that's calculated to make their personal life a public spectacle. Others, like Kelly, don't. They just want to be regular guys.

But in Youngstown, Pavlik isn't just a regular guy. If he'd left home and moved to a large urban area where he isn't a local hero, he could enjoy relative anonymity. Loyalty to, and a comfort level with, Youngstown have kept him where he is. That makes him a standard bearer for the entire city and a packhorse for other people's hopes and dreams.

Larry Holmes (another fighter who stayed close to home) recently noted, "Fighters are human beings. Just because we're fighters doesn't mean that we don't have feelings. And sometimes, people forget that."

The media acknowledges few boundaries and shows little respect in covering an athlete's personal life. Nobody dissects the private lives of sports writers. Nobody writes about how many drinks a reporter had at the bar before filing his story or how many pancakes an overweight scribe ate at breakfast.

But in Pavlik's case, there were reports of heavy drinking and blaring headlines in *The Vindicator* (Kelly's hometown newspaper): "Pavlik Fights Off Rumors About His Personal Life" one headline read. Among the rumors: "Pavlik was pulled over for a DUI. He was arrested for carrying a gun. He stabbed someone."

As Kevin Iole wrote on Yahoo.com, "The rumor mill has worked overtime in Youngstown. Pavlik's career has taken a hit. A whisper campaign has suggested that he's hanging with the wrong crowd; that he's on the verge of financial collapse."

"It's been a tough year," Mike Pavlik said as 2009 drew to a close. "First, Kelly had his health problems. Then there was a turn in the way some of the newspapers wrote about him. There were a lot of rumors. We went day to day, not knowing what to expect. I don't care that much about the boxing part of it. I've come to understand that the boxing business is a terrible business. It's the selling of human flesh. People don't even care about what you've done for them lately. It's all about what you can do for them now. I don't care that much about what other people say. But I care a lot about Kelly's feelings and the young man inside."

"It has been a hard summer and fall; for Kelly and for all of us," Michael Cox added. "It's very hard to watch someone you care about have to struggle and go through this craziness. The rumors and stories got completely out of control."

"I honestly wouldn't wish fame on anybody," Kelly said. "There are a lot of perks that come with it. I'm well aware of that and I'm thankful for it. But there's a lot of bad and a lot of stress that comes with fame, too."

On December 19, 2009, Pavlik returned to the ring and scored a fifth-round knockout over journeyman Miguel Espino in Youngstown. That raised his record to 36-and-1 with 32 knockouts.

Then Kelly made a decision to address some of the personal issues in his life; most notably, his drinking.

Many fighters don't take care of themselves the way they should. They train for eight weeks and then, between fights, let themselves go. But the work ethic of a good fighter is far more demanding than the work ethic required of most conscientious men and women. And that work ethic extends to a fighter's lifestyle. He might fight as few as two or three times a year. But the truly great fighters are always on the job. The demands of their trade would overwhelm ordinary people.

"I realized that I'd worked too hard for too long and come too far to let it all slip away from me," Kelly said. "I decided to do what I had to do to make things right."

On April 17, 2010, in Boardwalk Hall in Atlantic City, Pavlik's journey through boxing placed him in spotlight again; this time against Sergio Martinez.

The thirty-five-year-old Martinez is a remarkable phenomenon. Born in Argentina, he moved to Spain and now lives in Oxnard, California. The first time he stepped into a boxing gym, he was twenty years old. Two years later, he turned pro.

Over the years, Martinez had compiled a 44–2–2 record with 24 knockouts. The blemishes on his ledger are deceiving. One of the draws came twelve years ago in Sergio's third pro fight. The other was last year against Kermit Cintron in a bout that virtually everyone in attendance thought he won.

As for the losses; Martinez was stopped by Antonio Margarito ten years ago. And last December, he was on the short end of a majority decision after a hotly contested encounter with Paul Williams. No less an authority than Kelly Pavlik thought that Sergio won that fight.

Pavlik-Martinez was a crossroads bout for both men and Kelly's first big test since losing to Hopkins. Sergio was confident, ready, and strong; a superbly conditioned athlete; fast with a solid chin, and a southpaw to boot.

"Kelly will have to be at his best to beat Martinez," Jack Loew (Pavlik's trainer) said. "And he will be. Ever since we signed for this fight, I've heard people say that Martinez is the wrong style for us. He's too fast; he's a left-hander. Let me tell you; Kelly hits harder than anyone Martinez has ever fought. And Kelly has never lost to a lefthander; not in the amateurs or the pros. I don't care what Martinez does. He doesn't have enough to beat us."

"Southpaws that move are tough," Pavlik acknowledged. "Martinez is a dangerous fighter. But a lot of the time, he's off-balance. He leaves himself open to get hit. And he's not as fast as people think he is."

Pavlik looked good in the days leading up to the fight. There was a glow about him that hadn't been there since his first outing against Jermain Taylor almost three years ago. He'd been eating better; no red meat, very little fat. Even his voice sounded different.

"This is a huge fight for me to prove a lot of things to a lot of people," Kelly said.

The belief was that he'd done what he had to do outside the ring to get back on track in it.

"Kelly has been very motivated and focused," Michael Cox said. "He really dedicated himself in training camp. There was no complaining. He did everything he had to do. He knows that his star has fallen, and he's determined to make the next part of his career even better than the first part. He's aware that, the same way the Miranda fight set the stage for what followed, this fight will go a long way toward determining what happens in the next part of his career."

"Kelly fought so hard for so long that it took a lot out of him," Mike Pavlik added. "The last few months, I've see a burning desire in him that I hadn't seen in a while. He wants to fight again."

Pavlik arrived at Boardwalk Hall and entered his dressing room at 8:30 on Saturday night. The arena was the scene of his greatest triumph (seizing the championship from Jermain Taylor) and also his loss to Bernard Hopkins.

The members of Team Pavlik unpacked their bags. No one had brought Kelly's socks. There was a call to the hotel, asking a friend to bring them over.

Light conversation between Kelly, his father, and Jack Loew followed. The Cleveland Browns were the first subject of discussion.

"I don't think they gave [recently traded quarterback] Brady Quinn a fair chance," Mike Pavlik offered.

"He had nothing to work with," Loew added.

The conversation turned to Tiger Woods.

"I thought sex therapy was to teach you how to do it; not how to stop . . . There's a new DVD out. Tiger Woods talks about his best eighteen holes."

HBO production coordinator Tami Cotel came into the room and asked if she could check Kelly's weight on an HBO scale. At three o'clock the previous afternoon, each fighter had weighed-in officially at 159½ pounds. Martinez now weighed 167. Kelly stepped on the scale. Since the weigh-in, he'd gained eighteen pounds.

The conversation resumed. Kelly fired a series of one-liners about a Youngstown legend named Bear Cabelli, who has a reputation for being tougher than the average guy.

"Bear Cabelli is so tough that he sleeps with a pillow under his gun . . . Bear Cabelli is so tough that he won a staredown with the sun . . . Bear

Cabelli is so tough that he slammed a revolving door shut . . . Bear Cabelli is so tough that he killed two stones with one bird . . . When Bear Cabelli puts milk on his Rice Krispies, he's so scary that Snap, Crackle, and Pop shut the fuck up."

Loew began taping his fighter's hands. When he was done, Kelly did some light stretching exercises and shadow-boxed briefly in the center of the room.

There was a quiet moment.

"How do you feel?" Mike Pavlik asked his son.

"Good."

At ten o'clock, Kelly put on his trunks, socks, and shoes. Top Rank photographer Chris Farina, who'd come into the room, memorialized the moment.

"I'm glad I'm not a fighter," Mike said. "I don't want anyone taking photos of me when I'm getting dressed."

Referee David Fields came in and gave Kelly his pre-fight instructions.

At 10:22, Lucian Bute vs. Edison Miranda (HBO's first televised fight of the evening) began. Miranda is a different fighter from what he was when he fought Pavlik. Back then, the Colombian was a feared and ferocious puncher. A disputed loss to Arthur Abraham was the only blot on his record. He has now lost five of his last twelve fights.

All eyes turned toward a television monitor in a corner of the room.

"Miranda is shot," Jack Loew said.

"He doesn't even fight back anymore," Mike noted.

Round one ended. Loew began gloving Kelly up.

Kelly kept an eye on the television monitor. "Bute is a sneaky fighter," he said. "And he's a good body puncher."

Miranda was knocked out in the third round.

Loew warmed Kelly up on the pads.

"Remember; back him up . . . Tight punches . . . Don't reach with the right hand . . . He might come out firing to make a point. If he does, fire back . . . If he turns, turn with him . . . That's it . . . Be patient. You'll catch him."

Then it was time for battle. "What's meant to be will be," Mike Pavlik said.

Every fight is a self-contained drama. Pavlik-Martinez played out in three distinct acts.

Rounds one through four saw Sergio circling elusively, darting in and out as Kelly moved forward. During those rounds, Martinez outlanded Pavlik 61-to-38 and opened a small cut on Kelly's left eyelid. It was not unlike a matador sticking banderillas into a bull.

In round five, the tide turned. Pavlik had kept the pressure on and it started to pay dividends. Over the four middle rounds, he outlanded Martinez 75-to-57, punctuated by a righthand to the top of the head in round seven that knocked Sergio down. It was more of a balance shot than a hurting one. Still, it gave Kelly a 10–8 round. After eight stanzas, he was ahead by a point and had taken control of the fight.

In round nine, Martinez regained control. A straight lefthand opened a gash over Pavlik's right eye. Sergio was all over him like a swarm of bees.

From that point on, the challenger put a beating on the champion. Kelly's face was a gory mask with blood streaming down both cheeks. Over the final four rounds, he absorbed 112 punches while landing only 51.

This writer scored it 115–112 in favor of Martinez. The three judges turned in similar cards.

Sergio fought a magnificent fight. But several self-inflicted wounds contributed to Kelly's defeat.

First, Pavlik didn't use his advantage in weight as effectively as he could have. He was neglectful of Martinez's body for long periods of time and was too passive when he got in close. He should have leaned on Sergio, pumped punches into his side, and roughed him up. Instead, he landed only twenty-two body blows.

Second, Kelly tired down the stretch. Part of that was due to the demands of the fight. And part of it was because, while he worked hard and lived a disciplined life in the months leading up to April 17th, Martinez had worked hard and lived a disciplined life in the years leading up to the fight. There's a difference.

If a fighter hasn't taken care of his body properly for several years, he can't put everything together in three-and-a-half months. Not if he's fighting Sergio Martinez.

A better cutman also would have helped. For most of Kelly's career, Miguel Diaz was in his corner. But according to a source in the Pavlik camp, Diaz demanded excessive fees for fights after Pavlik-Hopkins. That and a reported personality conflict led to Miguel being let go. There are other excellent cutmen in boxing. Sid Brumback (who was in Pavlik's corner against Martinez) has not proven himself to be one of them.

Against Martinez, the cutwork in Kelly's corner was ineffective and the flow of blood was a factor. A big one.

"I was having a hard time seeing," Pavlik said in his dressing room after the fight."

Kelly was sitting on the same chair he'd been on a little more than an hour earlier when Jack Loew gloved him up.

His body was streaked with blood.

Mike Pavlik stood by his son. The preceding hour had been particularly painful for Mike. He hadn't just watched Kelly lose an athletic competition. He'd seen his son get beaten up.

Kelly bowed his head.

"Shit! I hate losing."

"It's part of the game," Mike said. "Nobody stays champion forever."

"A fucking punching bag. That's what I was tonight."

"I'm still proud of you."

Kelly shook his head.

"For eight rounds, I fought a good fight. The last four rounds, I was a fucking punching bag. They should have put 'Everlast' on my forehead."

"Not many people in history have been middleweight champion of the world," Mike told his son. "Hold your head high."

One at a time, family members and friends came over to Kelly, offering hugs and words of consolation. Then he rose from his chair, dressed without showering, and started for the door with Mike at his side.

"I'm going to the hospital to get sewn up," he said. "I'll see you guys back at the hotel."

A SEPARATE NOTE ON THE AFTERMATH OF PAVLIK-MARTINEZ

Kelly Pavlik sat on a folding chair in his dressing room at Boardwalk Hall in Atlantic City. Blood seeped from ugly cuts above both eyes. Twenty minutes earlier, he'd lost a hotly contested battle to Sergio Martinez and, with it, the middleweight championship of the world.

Kelly was physically and emotionally spent. Leaning forward on his chair, he spat a gob of bloody saliva onto the floor.

World Boxing Council executive secretary Mauricio Sulaiman (the son of WBC president Jose Sulaiman) and Ed Pearson (the WBC's on-site supervisor for Pavlik-Martinez) entered the dressing room.

"The handwraps," Mauricio said.

Over the years, the WBC has industriously collected boxing memorabilia. Much of this memorabilia, according to Mauricio, has been joyously given by fighters as a sign of respect for his father.

On occasion, fighters have been less joyful about it. On the night that Pavlik won the middleweight championship from Jermain Taylor, Mauricio left Kelly's dressing room with the new champion's trunks.

Pavlik was not pleased.

"It was a misunderstanding," Mauricio later explained. "I was led to believe that Kelly wanted the trunks to be presented as a gift to my father because of his respect for my father and the WBC. When it was brought to my attention that Kelly wished to have the trunks back, I arranged quickly to return them."

As was pointed out to Mauricio that night, federal law provides, "No officer or employee of a sanctioning organization may receive any compensation, gift, or benefit, directly or indirectly, from a boxer [other than a sanctioning fee]." Violation of this law is a crime punishable by up to one year in prison and a fine of $20,000.

Earlier this year, the WBC added a new wrinkle to its way of doing business. It instituted a rule requiring that the on-site supervisor at a WBC-sanctioned fight inspect each fighter's handwraps after the fight for evidence of wrongdoing.

According to Joe Dwyer (a member of the WBC Board of Governors), this was done in response to the much-publicized incident in which Antonio Margarito's hands were found to have been improperly wrapped.

Well and good.

Then things get not so good.

According to Dwyer, "After the on-site supervisor inspects the handwraps, he sends them to WBC headquarters in Mexico City for further inspection. Then, if necessary, they're sent to the lab for further study."

To Dwyer's knowledge, there has never been a need for the WBC to send any of the handwraps to the lab for further study.

The WBC policy only makes sense if one believes that the opposing fighter's camp (which observes the handwrapping process), the governing state athletic commission (which regulates the handwrapping process), and the on-site WBC representative (who examines the handwraps after the fight) are all incapable of doing their job.

One might also note that the WBC policy destroys the chain of custody that would be essential to any court or governmental administrative proceeding. Indeed, Dwyer (a former New York City police detective who knows something about the preservation of evidence) acknowledges that he examines handwraps after fights on behalf of the WBC but does not take them from the fighters. "If I don't find anything wrong with the handwraps, there's no reason to take them," he says.

And if he did find something wrong?

"I'd report the irregularity to the WBC because it could affect the WBC's recognition of the winner of the fight," Dwyer answers. "But the right place for the handwraps would be with the district attorney's office or the police in the jurisdiction where the fight took place."

Of course, there's another factor to be considered. The handwraps that are sent to WBC headquarters in Mexico City are important pieces of boxing memorabilia. They have sentimental value and are sometimes worth a lot of money.

Craig Hamilton is the foremost expert on boxing memorabilia in the United States. How much does he think the handwraps from Pavlik-Martinez are worth?

"They're nice pieces," Hamilton answers. "With proper authentication, which you have here, I could sell the Martinez and Pavlik handwraps together for a minimum of a thousand dollars. And they might bring considerably more."

When asked what the WBC does with the handwraps after they're inspected in Mexico City, Dwyer answers, "I would assume they're discarded."

It's hard to imagine Jose Sulaiman throwing a thousand dollars worth of boxing memorabilia in the garbage.

As 2010 progressed, Manny Pacquiao and Floyd Mayweather Jr remained on parallel tracks.

The Myth and the Reality of Floyd Mayweather Jr

In today's society, Patrick Kehoe observes, "hyperbole tends to replicate itself as an electronic echo, transmitting the desired information as truth logged into infinite memory. Just keep talking, and something aggrandizing will affix to the culture at large."

One might cite Floyd Mayweather Jr in support of that theory.

Mayweather is an extremely talented fighter who wants to be superstar famous and mega-rich. His record stands at 41-and-0 with 25 knockouts. In recent years, he and Manny Pacquiao have been vying for the right to be called the best pound-for-pound fighter in the world.

Mayweather lives alone in a 23,000-square-foot house in Las Vegas. "When I was growing up," he says, "seven of us lived in one bedroom. I got a closet now that's bigger than that bedroom was."

Floyd has never been married and has four children by two different women. A seven-man security detail that conjures up images of PEDs accompanies him at public functions. He takes pride in his appearance and has no tattoos. "I like the way I look without them," he notes. "And I'm not a follower."

Mayweather is obsessed with money to the point of having changed his sobriquet from "Pretty Boy Floyd" to "Money Mayweather." When asked to name his heroes, he cites Bill Gates, Steve Wynn, Carlos Slim, Mark Cuban, and Warren Buffet; all hugely successful entrepreneurs. He's often draped in expensive bling and brags about his winnings at Las Vegas sports books. The probability is that, like most gamblers, he loses more than he wins.

Mayweather can be seductively charming. He's also very much into control. When he says "jump," the people in his inner circle tend to ask, "How high?"

"I call the shots," Floyd says. "Everything that goes my way isn't always the right way. I know that. But I like things the way I like them."

Asked for more in the way of self-description, Mayweather offers, "I don't like to be lied to or disrespected. I ain't never gonna punch a clock for nobody. I was born to be a winner. I'm happy with my life. I don't hate on people. Some people say I'm an asshole, but I don't hurt nobody. I got a heart. God must love me, because look where I'm at."

The public feuding within Mayweather's family has been referred to as boxing's version of *The Jerry Springer Show.*

The most notable estrangement was between Floyd and his father and lasted for nine years. Floyd Sr fought professionally in the 1970s and '80s and later spent five-and-a-half years in prison for cocaine trafficking. During the chill between father and son, Floyd Sr lobbied to train fighters who would be facing Floyd Jr and declared, "Floyd thinks he's bigger than boxing, and he ain't. No one is bigger than boxing."

They reconciled in May 2009. Now Floyd Sr says, "My son is bigger than boxing."

Floyd has been trained by his uncle, Roger Mayweather, for most of his pro career. Roger was imprisoned in 2007 for assaulting his son's maternal grandmother. Last year, he was indicted on charges of battery and coercion. The police report on the latter incident states that Roger punched a woman named Melissa St. Vil in the ribs several times and wrapped his hands around her throat, causing her to nearly pass out. When the police arrived, St. Vil was coughing and spitting up blood. Trial on these charges is scheduled for later this year.

Floyd Jr has had his own issues with women and the criminal justice system. In 2002, he pled guilty to two counts of domestic violence. Two years later, he was found guilty on two counts of misdemeanor battery for assaulting two women in a Las Vegas nightclub.

The other core members of Team Mayweather are Leonard Ellerbe and Al Haymon. Ellerbe is Mayweather's friend and business manager. Haymon masterminds Mayweather's fight contracts.

In most sports, a fighter has to beat the best in order to reach the top. Corrupt world sanctioning organizations and HBO's outsized marketing power have deprived boxing of that legitimacy.

Within this environment Mayweather has combined careful matchmaking and a cautious ring style with an attention-grabbing persona and superb boxing skills to build a brand name.

Floyd craves celebrity status. He understands what it can do for him financially, not to mention his ego. As Carlo Rotella wrote in the *New York Times,* "He wants to be bigger than boxing can make him; kind of like what The Joker has in mind in *Batman* when he says he wants his face on the dollar bill."

Thus, Mayweather has expended considerable time and energy to turn himself into a magnet for media attention and build his profile outside the ring. In 2007, he appeared on *Dancing with the Stars.* One year later, he faced off against Big Show on *WrestleMania.* Truth and the business of combat sports rarely go hand in hand, so Floyd can be forgiven for boasting that he was paid $20,000,000 for his wrestling foray. Golden Boy promoter Richard Schaefer puts the number at "about $3,500,000." Still, that's a staggering sum for a one-night acting gig.

The bulwark of Mayweather's image-making has been HBO's TV "reality" series, *24/7.* The show has been used to promote eight pay-per-view fights, including Floyd's outings against Oscar De La Hoya, Ricky Hatton, Juan Manuel Marquez, and Shane Mosley.

24/7 has propagated the view that everything Mayweather touches turns to gold and given him a platform to craft his outside-the-ring persona. To some, Floyd symbolizes crass materialism and conspicuous consumption. But as Lou Duva once noted, "Nobody goes into boxing to be loved. You're in this game to make money."

Mayweather has made money. His 2007 fight against Oscar De La Hoya engendered a record-breaking 2,446,000 buys. Oscar was the driving force behind that promotion. But Floyd's seven pay-per-view fights have averaged close to one million buys.

"What's this fight going to do for my legacy?" Floyd asked before squaring off against Ricky Hatton two-and-a-half years ago. "I got no fake answer. It's not going to do nothing for my legacy. I'm fighting because I'm a businessman. I'm like Bob Barker. 'Come on down.' If the price is right, let's make it happen."

"People love controversy, and I'm controversial," Mayweather offers. "If you see Tom Cruise in a movie, that's not really him. It's a character he's playing. Some of what I do in public is me, and some of it is playing a character. You figure out which is which. At the end of the day, it don't matter whether the media likes me or not. People love me. When I go places, I get a lot of love."

It might be that Mayweather confuses love with the attention he gets for being a celebrity. Either way, love isn't central to his image. The pillars of his public persona are money and his ring prowess.

Mayweather's skill as a fighter is a matter of record, and he's boastful when it comes to extolling his place in the sweet science. Among his claims: "I'm the face of boxing . . . I can make anybody look like a nobody . . . When fighters are facing me, they're facing the best. When I'm facing them, I'm just facing fighters . . . Some fighters do different things good. I do everything great . . . There's no remedy on how to beat Floyd Mayweather. It's like a difficult math problem that no one can solve . . . I'm the king of the throne. I do what I want to do . . . All roads in boxing lead to Floyd Mayweather."

Mayweather also maintains, "I'm the reason people don't watch heavyweights no more. I made the world pay attention to the smaller man in boxing."

That will come as a surprise to Sugar Ray Leonard, Thomas Hearns, and Roberto Duran, whose internecine warfare captivated the world several decades ago. Fans of Manny Pacquiao might also take issue.

Then there's the claim, "I'm the best fighter ever. Muhammad Ali? He lost to Leon Spinks, a guy who had seven pro fights. Sugar Ray Robinson? He didn't win a championship after just one year like I did."

In truth, Mayweather won his first world title belt after two years, not one. Robinson had to wait six years and fight 75 fights before he was given an opportunity to fight for the championship. In his first 131 fights, Robinson lost once. During that time, he beat Sammy Angott (twice), Fritzie Zivic (twice), Tommy Bell (twice), Kid Gavilan (twice), and Jake LaMotta (five times).

As for Ali; he had the toughest inquisitors of any champion ever and won five of six fights against Sonny Liston, George Foreman, and Joe Frazier. His greatness is untouched by what happened when he got old.

That said; even Mayweather's critics acknowledge that he's a formidable fighting machine.

The foundation of Floyd's success in the ring is preparation. He knows how to do things right in the gym and trains his ass off. Getting ready for a fight, he always pays the price.

"You got to be ready every time you step in the ring," Floyd says. "You got to be mentally ready before you can do the things you have to do to get ready physically. Then, when you're physically ready, you can take the final mental steps. The mind tells the body what to do, but it's all tied together. I've never been in a fight where my mind said something and my body wouldn't do it."

Those looking for a hole in Mayweather's discipline point to his penchant for fast food. In response, Floyd notes, "Fast food is better than drinking. Fast food is better than drugs. Nobody works harder than me in the gym. That's one of the reasons why, in fights, I don't get tired."

Mental burn out is another matter. On October 23, 2007, an uncharacteristically somber Mayweather told the media, "It's not like it used to be. I think I liked this sport better when I was fighting for free. When you're young, you don't have concerns, so you're not worried about nothing. I mean, you never know what can happen in boxing. A lot of times, you worry about certain things like, if I die in the ring, what's going to happen with your family? When I didn't have no kids to live for, I really wasn't worried about nothing. I was like, I don't care what goes on. I'm just going there to fight. If I die, so be it. Now that I'm a lot older and a lot wiser, it's more like I've got something to live for. I've got some people who love me. So that worries me a lot, because I feel like my job is like a cop. One shot can end your whole career."

Seven weeks later, Mayweather knocked out Ricky Hatton. Then, on June 6, 2008, he announced that he was "permanently retiring from boxing."

"I needed a rest, physically and mentally," Floyd says. "I was burned out."

Few people in boxing took Mayweather's retirement seriously. The assumption was that he'd be back in the ring, sooner rather than later.

The return came against Juan Manuel Marquez on September 19, 2009. Maybe Floyd missed the spotlight and the competition. Just as likely, he needed money. On July 3, 2009, the Associated Press reported that the Internal Revenue Service had filed tax liens against him totaling $6,170,000 and that he owed another $193,000 pursuant to a New Jersey Superior Court judgment.

There were also persistent rumors, denied by Leonard Ellerbe, that Floyd had been swindled out of millions of dollars in a financial scam.

Equally important, Mayweather thought at the time of his retirement that he could make a fortune without boxing; through endorsements, investments, and business ventures. That was easier said than done.

"He wasn't broke," Floyd Sr says. "But he had a money problem."

Against Marquez, Mayweather showed that he was still a superb fighter. The one sour note in the proceedings came when Floyd blew off the agreed-upon contract weight of 144 pounds (nine pounds above Juan Manuel's previous high) and weighed in at 146 pounds. The contract was hastily amended. Mayweather paid Marquez an additional $600,000 out of his reported $10,000,000 guarantee, and the bout took place as scheduled. Floyd won a lopsided decision.

Eight weeks after Mayweather decisioned Marquez, Manny Pacquiao annihilated Miguel Cotto. That set the stage for Mayweather-Pacquiao, which, it was presumed, would be the largest-grossing fight in boxing history.

Not.

Mayweather-Pacquiao fell through to the dismay of the boxing community. Depending on one's point of view, that was because Floyd made unreasonable demands with regard to PED testing that he knew would interfere with Manny's training (a/k/a "the Pacquiao avoidance program") or Pacquiao had something to hide.

Either way, Floyd needed a name opponent to counterbalance the fallout from Mayweather-Pacquiao falling out. Meanwhile, Shane Mosley was scheduled to fight Andre Berto (who, like Mayweather, is managed by Al Haymon) on January 30, 2010.

On January 12th, Berto's ancestral home of Haiti was devastated by a catastrophic earthquake. Six days later, citing concern for members of his family and the fact that he was mentally and physically exhausted, Andre withdrew from the Mosley fight. That same day, Richard Schaefer of Golden Boy (which promotes Shane and co-promotes Mayweather) announced that he was working to put Mayweather-Mosley together for May 1st.

A decade ago, Mosley and Roy Jones vied for pound-for-pound honors, although the consensus was that Jones reigned. Then Shane lost to Vernon Forrest and the debate ended.

Mosley is now thirty-eight years old and had fought only twice since 2007. In one of those fights, he struggled on old legs against Ricardo

Mayorga before knocking the Nicaraguan out in the twelfth round. Then, on January 24, 2009, Shane scored an impressive knockout victory over Antonio Margarito to capture the WBA welterweight crown.

Margarito-Mosley was the platform on which Mayweather-Mosley was built. Shane has a name. Unlike many elite fighters, he really will fight anyone. And Mayweather felt that beating Mosley convincingly would legitimize his own claim to greatness.

Shane had the same agenda as Mayweather, but hoped for a different outcome. "Everybody has Manny Pacquiao and Mayweather on their mind," he said. "I'm going to make sure that they know that I'm here. I want to make a point that I'm the best welterweight fighter right now. I'm not just going to talk about it. I want to be about it. There's no welterweight out there who can beat me."

The marketing theme for Mayweather-Mosley was "who R U picking?" That rang a bit hollow, since virtually everyone in the know was picking Mayweather. The odds opened at 3-to-1 and rose as high as 9-to-2 before settling at 7-to-2.

At the March 2, 2010, kick-off press conference in New York, Schaefer proclaimed, "This is one of the best fights in the history of boxing" and predicted three million pay-per-view buys. Later in the promotion, when Mayweather was referenced during a tele-conference call as "the greatest fighter in boxing today," Schaefer corrected, "Not of today; the greatest of all time."

One hopes that, in his previous career as a banker, Richard fulfilled his fiduciary obligation to clients with more acumen and/or candor.

Mayweather has the habit of demeaning his opponent in the build-up to a fight, and Mayweather-Mosley was no exception. After calling Shane a "dumb motherfucker," Floyd opined, "He's desperate, so he has no choice but to fight me. His career is coming to an end; and before he goes, he wants that last big payday. I don't really like to speak on people's personal business, because his personal life is his personal life. But he just went through a divorce, and sometimes going through a hard divorce can be very excruciating. It can cost a lot of money."

"This is our legacy on who's the best fighter," Shane responded. "It's a challenge that I'm ready to take. It's nothing personal. I'm ready to go into the history books as the guy to beat Floyd Mayweather and the guy that beats everybody out there. The last man standing; I'm into that. I don't bark. I bite."

But when pressed, Shane added, "He wants to talk about my suit. He's talking about the curls in my hair and if I'm getting a nose job. Is he gay or something? You know, all of these different things about my personal stuff. I mean, you've got to watch out. There's different things that don't sound right."

Then there was the issue of performance-enhancing drugs.

The contract for Mayweather-Mosley gave Floyd the right to dictate the terms of drug testing. Anything he wanted would be put in place as long as each fighter was subject to the same testing requirements.

Mayweather might be sincere in his claim that he wants elaborate PED testing for all of his fights as a way of ensuring "a level playing field for clean athletes." Or he might be avoiding a showdown with Manny Pacquiao (whose phobia for giving blood is genuine). For the moment; let's give Floyd the benefit of the doubt on that one.

Golden Boy appears to be less committed to PED testing. How else to explain the fact that it never raised the issue in conjunction with Hopkins-Jones II, Haye-Ruiz, or any of the other high-profile fights that it promoted recently?

Regardless, drug testing was in place for Mayweather-Mosley. During a March 18th conference call, Travis Tygart (CEO of the United States Anti-Doping Agency) advised the media, "Both athletes have agreed to USADA's testing protocols, including blood and urine testing, which is unannounced, which is anywhere and anytime. There is no limit to the number of tests that we can complete on these boxers. Any positive tests will be published following a thorough legal process provided under our protocols."

Initially, Tygart said that a positive test could result in a two-year suspension of the athlete and cancellation of the fight. But it was later acknowledged that punishment could come only after "a full legal process." That would include, among other things, an arbitration proceeding before the American Arbitration Association to be conducted under restrictions of confidentiality, which would delay punitive action until after the fight. Tygart also admitted, "We have no direct control to enforce compliance." In other words, the Nevada State Athletic Commission would have to impose the suspension.

Judd Burstein (Mosley's lawyer) elaborated on that theme, saying, "There is no provision one way or the other in the contract for public disclosure of the test results; although I would think that the parties would be bound to report a positive test result to the Nevada commission."

Meanwhile, Mosley was in the embarrassing position of having to acknowledge yet again that he'd used banned performance-enhancing drugs prior to his 2003 victory over Oscar De La Hoya. That much was clear from Shane's own testimony before a grand jury that investigated BALCO and its founder, Victor Conte.

Mosley claims that he took the drugs unknowingly, although circumstances suggest otherwise. He also notes that he never tested positive for PEDS and, during an April 21st conference call, told the media, "I don't feel that I should be condemned for something that I never tested positive for."

Of course, one reason that athletes sought Conte's services was because he put them on regimens that would allow them to avoid testing positive for PEDs.

Mayweather, for his part, expressed the view that Mosley knew what he was putting into his body before he fought De La Hoya. "Marion Jones lied under oath and she went to jail," Floyd trumpeted. "So what's supposed to happen to Shane? We know what he's done. He lied under oath."

Then again; Mayweather repeatedly ducked questions about his own use of xylocaine to ease the pain in his hands during fights. Xylocaine is now legal under the rules of the Nevada State Athletic Commission if administered under the supervision of a doctor. That wasn't always the case. USADA did not test the fighters for xylocaine.

When fight week arrived, Team Mayweather was in full bloom. Uncle Roger dismissed the media with the thought, "You guys don't know shit about boxing so it don't make no difference what you say."

Floyd did his part for good media relations by refusing to attend the HBO fighter meeting on Friday and declaring "I created *24/7*."

Floyd also proclaimed, "I'm doing Shane Mosley a favor. I'm letting him share the ring with greatness . . . Shane Mosley is an HBO fighter. Floyd Mayweather is a mega-superstar . . . He's good at what he do. I'm great at what I do . . . Shane has checker pieces on the board. I'm playing with chess pieces. Most fighters have checkers pieces. And if they have a few chess pieces, they can't move them as well as me . . . My game plan is to be Floyd Mayweather."

One refreshing aspect to the promotion was that the sanctioning bodies were largely ignored. Mosley was the WBA welterweight champion. But Mayweather refused to pay the WBA sanctioning fee, noting," There should be just one belt in each division. The way things are now, anyone can get to be a champion." Shane followed suit on the theory that, if he lost, the title would be declared vacant; and if he won, he wouldn't need the WBA belt to make money.

The WBC tried to get into the act by offering its "diamond championship" belt to the winner for a 1 percent sanctioning fee. That was rejected as a bad joke, after which WBC president Jose Sulaiman offered the belt "at cost." That offer was turned down on the theory that Mayweather-Mosley would be a happier occasion with $45,000 less in expenses and without a WBC presence.

Ticket sales were a bit disappointing. Ultimately, the attendance on fight night was 15,117, which meant that a thousand tickets went unsold. But during fight week, the buzz was that Mayweather-Mosley would do huge pay-per-view numbers. HBO believed that Floyd had developed an "anchor fan base" among urban African-Americans. And Mayweather-Marquez (which drew poorly at the gate) had engendered 1,080,000 pay-per-view buys.

No one took Schaefer seriously at the final pre-fight press conference when he said, "Our goal is to break four million buys." But 1,500,000 seemed like a realistic number, which would have pushed Mayweather-Mosley past De La Hoya-Trinidad into second place on the all-time buy list for non-heavyweight fights. In the end, the announced total was 1,400,000; good for third place.

The most popular figure in the media center during fight week was Mosley's trainer, Naazim Richardson. Brother Naazim (as he likes to be called) is part philosopher, part storyteller, and all trainer. "Verbally, I can dance with you," he says.

Richardson dismissed Mayweather's mouth as "playing to the barbershops" and expressed dismay at the "Money Mayweather" persona. "You can have a guy who's an idiot," Brother Naazim elaborated. "But he can look at your car and fix the carburetor in a minute, so you got to respect what he does on the cars. I respect Floyd's genius as a fighter, but I don't like the way Floyd handles himself outside the ring sometimes."

Asked for more, Richardson observed, "This is a battle for greatness. You have fighters. You have champions. And you have guys who are special. These guys are special . . . Shane is tenacious. You can't be cute against Shane Mosley for twelve rounds . . . I had an old guy [Bernard Hopkins] who fought a young guy from Puerto Rico [Felix Trinidad] who was undefeated and knocking everyone out. We all remember how that one ended . . . Shane has to start fast. When you have a slow start against a fast rabbit; that story about the tortoise and the hare is bullshit. We all know the rabbit is going to win."

Mosley's partisans took hope in the fact that this was the first time Mayweather would be facing someone his own size since he fought Oscar De La Hoya three years ago. Ricky Hatton and Juan Manuel Marquez were much smaller men.

Shane voiced optimism, declaring, "Floyd says a lot of things that are out of bounds. But I don't care about what Floyd says. I care about what I believe and do. He has good hand-speed, but my hand-speed is good, too. I'm just as fast as him, just as slick as him. I'm going to beat him at his game. I won't spend the whole fight trying to outbox Floyd, but I'll do it from time to time. My power will be the icing on the cake. I pretty much know his thinking process, what he's going to do. He's a counterpuncher. He only strikes when he knows he's got you beat. I'm not worried about that. Floyd fights fighters at what he thinks is the right time. But this time, he made a mistake."

When Mosley was young, he radiated energy and strength. During fight week, that no longer seemed to be the case. At a Thursday sitdown with a group of writers, his face was puffy. There was no sparkle in his eyes. He looked tired. At age thirty-eight, he was the oldest opponent that Mayweather has ever fought.

"As you get older, your body changes," Shane told the writers. "Things stop working the way they used to. You can't work out all day and come back and train the same way the next day. You can't spar every day."

That reinforced the view that boxing has seen the best it's going to see of Mosley. At the weigh-in on Friday, he looked good. But Mayweather had a glow about him.

"Mosley can't beat me," Mayweather said. "He beat Margarito. So what? Margarito got beat by Paul Williams. Margarito got beat by Daniel Santos. Margarito lost six times. Mosley lost five times. Mosley got outboxed by Cotto. Mosley is dreaming when he says he can outbox me. He may be stronger when it comes to lifting weights. But this is boxing, not a weightlifting contest. I got too much for Mosley to compete with me."

On fight night, Chris Brown sang the National Anthem. Given Mayweather's history of criminally abusing women, it wasn't a wise choice. Last year, Brown was charged with felony assault against his then-girlfriend Rihanna. He pled guilty and was sentenced to five years probation plus six months of community service.

Mosley was the first man in the ring. Mayweather kept him waiting before making a well-choreographed entrance punctuated by loud simulated gunshots.

Round one of the fight was even and tactically fought. Fifty-five seconds into round two, Mosley did what he wasn't supposed to be able to do. He whacked Mayweather with a hard right hand that had Floyd holding on.

Earlier in the week, Naazim Richardson had said, "The opportunities will be few and far between. Shane will have to take advantage of them when they're there because the window will close pretty quickly."

The window closed. When Mayweather's head cleared, he didn't run. He fought back. From that point on, he was the aggressor, controlling when and where exchanges took place. When Shane got inside, Floyd roughed him up, pushing down hard on the back of Mosley's head and neck and using his elbows to maximum advantage. He outboxed Shane and he outfought Shane.

Meanwhile, Mosley couldn't let his hands go when the opportunities were there.

"The muscle twitch fiber goes first," Richardson had said. "In your head, you're making the move the way you used to, but the other guy is getting off first."

By round five, Mosley was tired and discouragement was etched on his face. Mayweather's jab was like a snake's tongue and his right hand like the lash of a whip. In the second half of the fight, he beat Shane up.

Mayweather outlanded Mosley 208-to-92 with a 123-to-46 edge in power punches. Those numbers become even more lopsided in light of the fact that thirteen of Mosley's power punches landed in the second round.

The outcome was determined by the variables that most people thought would dictate the result. Mosley was too old and too slow. Mayweather was too fast and too good. The judges were on target with a 119–109, 119–109, 118–110 verdict.

"I tried," Shane said afterward. "I couldn't pull the trigger when I wanted to."

Mosley has now had fifteen fights since 2001. His record in those fights is 8-and-6 with one no contest.

So . . . How good is Mayweather?

Smoke and mirrors don't work in the ring. A fighter can be hyped before; he can be hyped afterward. But those three-minute intervals are unscripted and real. During that time, he's alone, exposed, and fully reliant upon his skills for survival.

Mayweather is a great technical fighter. He wastes no energy. Every move he makes is purposeful. Over his last six fights, he has landed 47 percent of his punches compared to a connect rate of 17 percent for his opponents. That's a 30 percent differential; far superior to that of any other active fighter tracked by CompuBox.

Floyd knows his own abilities and has a keen awareness of what each opponent brings to the table. "A good boxing mind," he says, "means instinct, understanding strategy, being tough, and knowing the right moves to make." He has all of that and more.

In the ring, Mayweather is risk-averse. "You got to be cautious in boxing," he says. "I don't have to be bloody and knocked down and getting beat up to prove that I'm great. There's something greater than that, and that's not getting hit. There's nothing cool about taking punishment. What's cool is dishing it out."

But Floyd can fight rough. Anyone who doubts that should look at DVDs of his bouts against Mosley and Ricky Hatton.

"In the ring, I'm the predator; never the prey," he says. "I've always felt that way. You need killer instinct to be a great fighter, like an animal in the wilderness."

Mayweather has the respect of his fellow fighters. They know how good he is. It would be nice if he showed them more respect in return.

Right now, he's a great athlete, but not a great sportsman. And more important, if Floyd wants to prove himself in the eyes of history, he'll have to be more consistent in seeking out the best available competition.

When people talk about why Sugar Ray Robinson was great, they don't mention his win over an aging Henry Armstrong. No one says that Muhammad Ali was great because he beat an elderly Archie Moore. Robinson and Ali proved their greatness against the toughest opponents imaginable, as did Sugar Ray Leonard by conquering Wilfredo Benitez, Thomas Hearns, Roberto Duran, and Marvin Hagler.

Mayweather hasn't had the inquisitors that those men had. He doesn't seem to want them. That might be a good marketing decision, but it makes it harder to consider Floyd an all-time great.

History judges fighters by what they did in the ring; not by whether they were on *Dancing with the Stars* and how much money they made.

If one were to make a short list of fighters who belong in a boxing hall of fame, Sugar Ray Leonard would be on it.

Sugar Ray Leonard: Behind the Smile

I met Ray Leonard for the first time on July 14, 1984. I know the date because it was the night before Billy Costello defended his 140-pound championship against Ronnie Shields. I was tracking Costello for a book that I was writing about the sport and business of professional boxing. *The Black Lights* was my first foray into the sweet science. I had no idea at the time that I would spend decades of my life as a boxing writer.

Billy and I were in his room at the Ramada Inn in Kingston, New York, with his wife and fifteen-month-old daughter.

Leonard was on site as an expert analyst for CBS, which would televise Costello-Shields the following afternoon. Two months earlier, Ray had knocked out Kevin Howard in his first fight after a two-year layoff occasioned by a detached retina. His record as a pro was 33-and-1 with victories over Wilfredo Benitez, Roberto Duran, and Thomas Hearns to his credit.

Leonard came by Costello's room to say hello. We chatted briefly. Ray picked up Billy's daughter, carried her to a mirror where she looked at her own reflection, and told her, "You're adorable. My wife and I want one just like you someday to go with our boys." A few minutes later, he left.

I wasn't in boxing in 1987, when Ray came back to fight Marvin Hagler. Nor was I at ringside for any of his great fights. My appreciation of him at that time came as an informed fan. Later, I returned to the sport; first as Muhammad Ali's biographer and then as a columnist. After Ray's retirement, we crossed paths a half-dozen times at press conferences, awards dinners, and fights. The exchanges between us were cordial but brief. We never talked in-depth.

On May 1, 2010, I was in the media center at the MGM Grand in Las Vegas. Floyd Mayweather Jr and Shane Mosley were scheduled to fight the following night. Golden Boy (which was promoting the fight) had brought Leonard and Thomas Hearns in for a mid-morning media sit-down to engender pay-per-view buys.

Ray has moved gracefully into middle age. He still has star power and is a magnet for attention. When he walks into a room, heads turn and power brokers gravitate to his side.

Speaking with the assembled media, Leonard and Hearns did their thing. When they were done and Ray was readying to leave, I approached him.

"We've never had the chance to really talk," I said. "I'd love the opportunity to sit with you sometime and discuss things in-depth."

"How about now?" Ray suggested.

Sugar Ray Leonard is boxing royalty. He turned pro in 1976 and was the first ready-made star to come out of the Olympics.

Ray had it all. A gold medal, good looks, the sparkling smile.

And in the ring . . ."Oh, Jesus! What a fighter," trainer Don Turner says.

"I knew from the beginning that I wanted to be different, in and out the ring," Leonard recalls. "Right after I turned pro, a writer asked me what I wanted to be. I'm sure he expected me to say 'a champion.' And I told him, 'special.' It just popped into my head."

Ray was special. Outside the ring, he was dedicated to self-improvement. Early in his career, he would search for the grammatically correct syntax during interviews and, if necessary, correct himself on the spot.

In the ring, he was a complete fighter. He could box. He could punch. He had hand-speed. He had heart. He could take a punch.

"And he was smart," Turner adds. "Bill Russell smart. Ray did whatever he had to do to win, and he won fights in so many different ways. Look at how he conned Hagler."

Leonard won his first world championship in 1979 when he knocked out Wilfredo Benitez. Benitez was a true champion with a 38–0–1 record; not a mediocre alphabet-soup beltholder.

Then Leonard fought back-to-fights against Roberto Duran, who had 72 victories in 73 bouts. Ray suffered the first loss of his career in his initial encounter with Duran. Defying the conventional wisdom that a fighter doesn't come right back and beat the fighter who beat him, he fought an immediate rematch and forced Duran to say "no mas."

"People don't realize how tough Leonard was and how hard he hit," Duran says. "I do because I fought him."

On September 16, 1981, Leonard fought Thomas Hearns. Hearns was undefeated, a ferocious puncher, 32-and-0 with 30 knockouts. The match-up had everything a promotion could want. Two great fighters; a mega-fight build-up. Contested today, it would likely top 3,000,000 pay-per-view buys.

Leonard-Hearns was a time-capsule fight. Ray dug deep, fought through adversity, showed every quality that a fighter needs to be great, and stopped Hearns in the fourteenth round. That night, he entered the ranks of boxing immortals.

Looking back on that historic evening, Leonard says, "Courage is the ability to reach down and find something more inside yourself when it feels as though there's nothing left; and to do it in a way that's poised, not desperate." Then he adds, "It's not what people think it is when you get in the ring. Believe me; it's harder than people think. Every second, you're on the edge. But there are times when you're at your best and; how do I say this? In those moments, you zone out."

Six years later, Leonard cemented his legacy with a split-decision triumph over Marvin Hagler. Prior to that bout, Hagler had won eleven consecutive middleweight championship fights and hadn't lost in eleven years.

"I keep waffling back and forth between Marvin and my first fight with Tommy on which fight means the most to me," Ray says. "I'd say it's Tommy, but Marvin is close. I was blessed that I had those guys to test myself against; Benitez and Duran too."

Like many great champions, Leonard fought too long. The end of his career was marred by losses to Terry Norris and Hector Camacho. "I shouldn't have fought the last few fights," Ray says. "It was a combination of ego, stupidity, and being in limbo; not knowing what else to do with my life. You can train all you want. But when you get to fight time, either you have it or you don't. When it leaves you, it's scary."

Still, the bottom line is that Leonard in his prime fought the toughest available competition. He was a combatant in seven of the twelve fights contested amongst Hagler, Hearns, Duran, Benitez, and himself. Decades after the fact, these fights have a special place in boxing lore. Ray's record in those seven fights was five wins, one loss, and one draw.

"Most people who are serious about boxing understand that Sugar Ray Robinson was the best fighter ever," fabled matchmaker Bruce Trampler says. "But as time goes by, more and more people are starting to believe that Ray Leonard was the best fighter since Robinson. People knew he was good, but not how good. His charisma overshadowed his talent."

Leonard and I talked for the better part of three hours in Las Vegas on May 1st. Part of that time was spent driving to and from an AT&T store, where he made a personal appearance. He was casually but impeccably dressed, wearing an elegant watch and world-championship ring. At age fifty-four, he's still trim. He works a room well. "People come to me like they know me," he says. "I try to be nice. I'm sociable; but believe it or not, I'm a bit shy."

During his superstar years, Ray benefited from a carefully crafted public image. But the reality of a person's life is always more complicated than his public persona. In truth, he battled demons outside the ring in confrontations that were as savage as his wars in it.

"I'm in a good place right now," Leonard says. "I've worked through a lot of things. I was with good people; then bad people. Now I'm back with good people. When I finished boxing, I didn't know what direction my life would go in. I have balance now between privacy and my public life. There are things that are private that are nobody's business but mine. But I'm content; I'm happy. I have an incredible life. My mind is never at rest, but it's at peace."

Leonard is still intense and driven to succeed in everything he does. There are speaking engagements, product endorsements, and business ventures. He oversees the Sugar Ray Leonard Foundation, which supports diabetes research and seeks to combat childhood obesity.

His journey has been remarkable. He has dined with Nelson Mandela in the great man's home and played golf with Bill Clinton. He has hobnobbed with Muhammad Ali, Magic Johnson, and other great athletes of our time. Sometimes he shakes his head in wonder, reflecting on how far he has come. And in the next moment, he can reflect on events of far greater importance that have transpired around him as the years have gone by.

"When Barack Obama was elected," Ray says, "I shed a tear. For real; I shed a tear. My dad is eighty-eight. His grandparents were slaves. He never dreamed of anything like Barack Obama when he was growing up. I know, I never thought I'd see that in my lifetime. It meant that opportunity has opened wide for everyone. If that's not inspirational, nothing is."

Leonard is a boxing success story. Thomas Hearns is broke, talks slowly, and would still put on gloves if the price were right. Wilfredo Benitez exists in a hellish dementia, blind and unable to understand. Roberto Duran is as overweight and affable as George Foreman, but without the financial cushion of a grilling machine. Marvin Hagler has money, but lives abroad and is a recluse as far as the American public is concerned.

Ray came out of boxing financially secure and with his faculties intact. In many respects, he's the sport's best ambassador to the world.

"It's greatly satisfying to me to believe in my heart that I was a great fighter and to know that there are other people who feel that way about me," Leonard says. "I worked hard for that. I strived for that. The best thing about being a fighter is that it's all about you. When the world stops to watch; that feeling is everlasting. I appreciate it even more now than I did before."

I remember sitting with Paulie Malignaggi in the Brooklyn Diner in June 2001, several weeks before he turned pro. Time goes by.

Paulie Malignaggi: A Fighter's Code

Paulie Malignaggi sat on a folding chair in his dressing room one floor above The Theater at Madison Square Garden. He'd just been stopped in the eleventh round of his bid to wrest the WBA 140-pound title from Amir Khan. There had been no knockdowns. Paulie was on his feet when referee Steve Smoger intervened in the eleventh round to save him from further punishment.

Malignaggi's face was bruised and swollen. A New York State Athletic Commission doctor sat beside him.

"Do you have a headache?"

"No," Paulie answered.

"Is there any pain?"

"I feel bad that I lost, but I don't feel that bad physically."

"Are you sure?"

"Believe me; I've been through worse."

"You'll need some ice on those bruises so your face doesn't swell up."

"I know."

The doctor left.

Cutman Danny Milano moved to Paulie's side and pressed an iced towel against the fighter's face.

Paulie looked at the people around him. His brother Umberto, trainer Sherif Younan, co-manager Anthony Catanzaro, and longtime friend Pete Sferazza.

"I felt old tonight," he said. "It's the first time in a fight that I felt like the older guy. I had a good training camp. I'm only twenty-nine. But he was moving around, getting off first. I said to myself, 'That used to be me.'"

"You're not one of the kids anymore," Catanzaro told him. "You're still a young man, but it's different in boxing."

Paulie smiled ruefully. For a fighter with pride, each loss is a bit like death.

"It's a long way from KeySpan Park," he said. "That's for sure. I remember coming out of the tunnel that night. My pro debut; I had all these dreams. My whole career was ahead of me. Sometimes that seems like a long time ago, and sometimes it seems like it was yesterday."

Paulie took a deep breath and let it out slowly.

"Did anybody talk to Grandpa? Could someone call Grandpa and tell him I'm all right."

Paulie Malignaggi was the kid who couldn't, who did. Abandoned by his father, mistreated by an abusive stepfather; he moved in with his maternal grandparents at age fifteen and turned to boxing for self-esteem. Three years later, he won a national amateur championship. He turned pro on July 7, 2001.

Malignaggi was good-looking (still is). He had a big mouth (still does). And he could box (still can). Throughout his career, his weakness as a fighter has been a lack of punching power. Five knockouts in thirty-one fights. The last time that Paulie knocked an opponent out, LeBron James had yet to play in the NBA and Barack Obama was representing portions of the south side of Chicago in the Illinois state legislature.

Paulie won his first twenty-one professional fights. On June 10, 2006, he challenged Miguel Cotto for the WBO 140-pound crown. Cotto was at his peak. Malignaggi fought heroically and went the distance in a losing effort, absorbing a brutal beating in the process. After the fight, Arturo Gatti commended Paulie for his courage. "I'm proud that you're Italian," Gatti told him.

One year later, Malignaggi got another title opportunity. This time, he won every round and seized the IBF 140-pound championship from Lovemore N'dou.

"After I beat N'dou," Paulie says, "I thought the gates of heaven would open up for me."

He was wrong. Victorious but unimpressive title defenses against Herman Ngoudjo and N'dou followed. Then Paulie got another shot at the stardom that had eluded him when he lost to Cotto. On November 22, 2008, he fought Ricky Hatton in Las Vegas.

"If I'd fought like I'm capable of fighting," Paulie declares, "Hatton wouldn't have been able to hit me in the ass with a handful of rice."

But Paulie wasn't Paulie that night. He hadn't been for a year. Whatever else was going on in his life, the chemistry between him and Buddy McGirt (who'd replaced Billy Giles as Malignaggi's trainer) wasn't right.

"They say a fighter gets better when he wins a world title," Paulie notes. "I got worse. Buddy teaches all his fighters to fight the same way. He wants you to fight out of a box, a defensive shell, and move your head a lot. It's okay to fight in the pocket if that's the kind of fighter you are. But I use a lot of movement. Buddy was trying to change everything that I was about as a fighter and he took away my main asset, which is my legs."

Against Hatton, Malignaggi did virtually nothing right. "I stunk out the joint," he admits. "That fight cost me my dreams. If I beat Hatton, I become a star. I might even have made it to the Hall of Fame. The way I fought that night will bother me till the day I die. It was like God gave me a gift when they made that fight and I fucked it up."

Malignaggi's purse for fighting Hatton was $1,200,000; far and away his largest payday ever. For his next bout (an off-TV contest against journeyman Chris Fernandez), he was paid $10,000. He changed trainers, moving from McGirt to Sherif Younan. Then, on August 22, 2009, he journeyed to Houston to fight Juan Diaz.

"I knew what the deal was," Paulie says. "Diaz had just been knocked out by Juan Manuel Marquez. HBO and Golden Boy were trying to build him back up. I'm a light-punching guy who's a former world champion, so HBO and Golden Boy and the Diaz people said, 'Let's get Malignaggi. We'll put the fight in Texas, in Juan's hometown. Paulie won't stand a chance.'"

Paulie made just under $200,000 for the Diaz fight. "The judges robbed me," he says. "They didn't take my money, but they stole the fight. And there's no telling how much money that cost me."

Most observers agreed. Gale Van Hoy's scorecard (118–110 in favor of Diaz) was particularly egregious. "Nobody is that stupid," Paulie says. "It was worse than incompetence. It was corrupt."

The pain and frustration ran deep.

"It's easy to throw your hands in the air and say, 'Why do I bother working so hard?'" Malignaggi raged after the fight. "Why do I leave my family and friends and go to training camp and make all the other sacrifices I make to get ready? When the fight comes, I get screwed anyway.

That's what makes boxing so hard. It's not just the physical part. It's trying to motivate myself to train hard at the same time I'm wondering if I'm going to get fucked all over again. If Juan Diaz is a man, he'll fight me again. If I got a decision like that in my favor, I couldn't live with myself unless I fought the other guy again."

On December 12, 2009, they fought again; this time in Chicago, a neutral site. Paulie won a unanimous decision.

Every fight has the potential to derail a world-class fighter's career. A handful of fights have the potential to be career-altering wins.

After the second Diaz fight, Malignaggi had entered the ring for five watershed fights. He'd lost to Cotto; beaten N'dou to become a world champion; lost to Hatton; lost a disputed decision to Diaz; then triumphed over Diaz in a rematch. Against all odds, he had scraped and clawed his way back into the spotlight and was poised to reach for the brass ring again.

The obstacle to success was England's Amir Khan.

Khan turned pro one year after winning a silver medal as a seventeen-year-old prodigy at the 2004 Athens Olympics and started his career with eighteen consecutive wins. Then, on September 6, 2008, he was knocked out in the first round by Breidis Prescott.

Following the loss to Prescott, Khan moved his base of operations to Los Angeles and began training with Freddie Roach. After a comeback fight against Oisin Fagin, he won a five-round technical decision against a badly faded Marco Antonio Barrera in a fight cut short by an accidental headbutt. Next, on July 18, 2009, he decisioned Andreas Kotelnik to win the 140-pound WBA belt. In his first title defense, he knocked out Dmitry Salita in seventy-six seconds.

Khan is being groomed for stardom by Golden Boy Promotions (which spirited him away from Frank Warren). He wanted to make a splash in the United States, preferably at Madison Square Garden. And he viewed Malignaggi as the sort of opponent a champion faces when he's taking another step up the ladder toward elite status.

From Malignaggi's point of view, the match-up was equally enticing. This was a title fight. But the belt was incidental to the fact that it was a high-profile bout against a "name" opponent that Paulie thought he would win.

"This fight is redemption for me," Paulie said.

Khan-Malignaggi shaped up as an interesting confrontation between two luminescent personalities. Initially, the fighters evinced respect for one another.

"Malignaggi is a tough character," Khan said. "He's a clever boxer. We're both quick; we both have heart; and we both don't quit."

Paulie responded in kind, although he did fan the flames a bit when asked if he thought that Amir was using performance-enhancing drugs. That question came about because Khan and Manny Pacquiao are both trained by Freddie Roach and work with physical conditioner Alex Ariza. In the past, Malignaggi had voiced suspicions about Pacquiao's training regimen.

"Amir is in the same stable," Paulie offered. "I'm not saying he's dirty. It's just, he's got the same team around him. Other than that, I don't suspect Amir Khan of anything. But because he's part of that stable, how is it not going to cross my mind?"

Roach responded by calling Malignaggi an "asshole." Things went downhill from there, with insults flying back and forth.

"Paulie needs shutting up," Khan declared. "I'm going to properly shut him up. I don't think he'll last more than a few rounds. I know for a fact that it won't go the distance."

"I don't know what the big deal is with Khan," Malignaggi countered. "I find it comical that this guy is suddenly in his mind going to take a former world champion like me and stop him. I'm not a big puncher. But let's face it; if you blow on Khan's chin, you might hurt him. He hasn't been tested against a fighter who knows what he's doing. This will be his welcome to bigtime boxing. He has no idea what he's getting himself into."

As the trash talking escalated, Khan found himself faced with quotes attributed to him that were markedly unfamiliar. "One of my friends was responding for me on Twitter," he explained. "I would read something in the newspaper and say to myself, 'Wait a minute. I never said that.' So now I've taken that over myself."

Then Amir experienced a more embarrassing moment. In early May, the *News of the World* reported a claim by a Los Angeles model named Leanne Crow that Khan had sent her sex-text messages and nude photos of himself.

"The exchanges between us were very very explicit," Crow maintained. "I admit I was attracted to him and, at the time, quite enjoyed the banter and gave as good as I got. It was just that I felt a bit cheap afterwards. Everyone knows Amir is supposed to be a clean-cut lad who lives for boxing. But Amir loves to talk dirty and act dirty. The picture messages he sent me were obscene. One was of his face; one was of his torso; and one was of himself aroused. He also asked me to send 'filthy' pictures back. I'd heard he was a strict Muslim."

That led Malignaggi to declaim, "Tell that pervert to stick to sending photos to models, because this boxing game is a real sport."

"I guess I went over the line with that one," Paulie later acknowledged. "You say that sort of thing sometimes in the heat of the moment. But that's the way I am. Talking is what I do. I talk in my sleep."

Underlying Malignaggi's talk was a large dose of resentment born of the belief that Amir was being given what Paulie had been forced to fight for throughout his professional life. Khan, in Malignaggi's eyes, walked around on a red carpet.

The official storyline for Khan-Malignaggi was Amir's debut in the United States. "Amir Khan is here to become a global superstar," Golden Boy CEO Richard Schaefer proclaimed at the final pre-fight press conference.

HBO vice president Kery Davis followed Schaefer to the podium and poured more salt into the wound, saying, "Paulie has the skill sets to help us determine whether Amir Khan is the good marketable fighter we hope he is."

In other words; Paulie was a measuring stick, a prop, a stepping-stone for someone else.

"Arrogant" was one of the more polite adjectives used within the Malignaggi camp to describe Davis's remarks and HBO's abandonment of any pretense of neutrality.

Then things got uglier. At the weigh-in on Friday, the fighters were brought together for a staredown (the publicity-seeking ritual that has become an idiotic incendiary part of boxing). Security was poor. Khan's fans had been allowed to spill onto the stage and were shouting insults. The insults escalated, both ways. Amir and Paulie stood nose to nose, leaning into each other. Golden Boy matchmaker Eric Gomez moved to separate them.

Khan, thinking it was Malignaggi who was laying hands on him, shoved Paulie.

Paulie shoved back.

Suddenly, fists were flying.

"The pressure is getting to Amir," Paulie said afterward. "He can't take it anymore. I'm a better fighter than anyone he's ever fought, and he knows it."

That was true to the extent that Malignaggi would have been favored over each of Khan's previous opponents. Throughout his career, Paulie has been a consummate boxer. "I can make you miss in a lot of ways," he says. "I can make you miss with my legs, with my upper-body movement, by moving my head. It's not just speed. You have to know what to do with it."

Indeed, when Floyd Mayweather Jr was asked recently to name a current fighter other than himself whose "boxing brain" he respected, the first fighter he mentioned was Malignaggi.

Freddie Roach also admired things about Paulie. "He's a top-ten fighter," the trainer said five days before Khan-Malignaggi. "He's resilient and tough. He showed a lot of balls against Cotto. He can make you look bad because he's elusive, and he's coming off a good win."

"But I don't rate Juan Diaz that high," Roach continued. "Diaz is slow and comes right at you. Anyone with boxing ability can beat Diaz. And Paulie has some bad habits that Amir will take advantage of. Paulie keeps his hands low and doesn't throw a straight punch except for the up-jab. So if you're fast, which Amir is, you can beat him down the middle. Paulie has a habit of pulling straight back from punches, which works against a lot of guys. But it won't work against Amir, who's taller, has a longer reach, and is faster than Paulie."

"Amir can do everything Paulie does, only better," Roach concluded. "I see Amir starting off very fast and very aggressive. Body shots will be the key. And Amir will trade hooks with him. Paulie has talked himself into some big fights, but I think he talked himself into too big a fight this time. I don't see it going long. And if it does, Amir is in great shape. He'll be able to push Paulie hard at a fast pace and knock him out late. Paulie was a world champion. He's got heart. But Amir is just too much. We're going to make a statement in this fight."

In sum; Malignaggi would be in the ring against a younger (twenty-three vs. twenty-nine), taller (five feet ten vs. five feet seven), harder-hitting, and possibly faster opponent. The 5-to-1 odds in Khan's favor (which most observers thought were high) reflected that reality.

When Paulie looked at Amir, he saw bits and pieces of himself the way he was six years ago. Young, fast, talented, charismatic, with hopes for a hall-of-fame career ahead. Malignaggi wanted to slam the door to that future in Khan's face and break his nose.

On fight night, Malignaggi arrived at his dressing room at Madison Square Garden at 8:15. The room was small; twelve-feet square with a gray linoleum-tile floor and white cinderblock walls.

Paulie shadow-boxes in his dressing room before a fight more than most fighters do. Over the next two-and-a-half hours, he was constantly getting off his chair, dancing around, moving his hands.

"Keep that right hand in position when you jab," Sherif Younan instructed. "He comes in a straight line. Circle both ways. Work angles. Walk him into something that will make him think twice."

Referee Steve Smoger came in and gave Paulie his pre-fight instructions. If one were looking for bad omens, Smoger had been the third man in the ring for Cotto-Malignaggi.

Younan wrapped Malignaggi's hands and gloved him up.

For the next half-hour, Paulie hit the pads on and off as Younan offered a stream of encouragement and advice.

"When you're hooking, keep your right hand high . . . You have better footwork than he does . . . Time to shine, champ. Time to shine . . . He's gonna hit the air all night long . . . When frustration sets in, that's when you take him."

Danny Milano put Vaseline on Malignaggi's face.

"I'm gonna fuck him up," Paulie said.

In the end, it was a bad night for Malignaggi. The tip-off that he was in trouble came early in the fight. The first few rounds were entertaining and fast-paced. But Paulie wasn't using his legs defensively the way he'd used them when he was young.

Round three was Malignaggi's best round of the fight. He moved effectively, got some solid punches in, and slowed Khan down a bit. But his face was starting to puff up.

Soon, Khan was landing jabs and righthands at will. Then it was combinations with power in each shot. Even when Paulie made Amir miss, he seldom made him pay. And when the opportunity presented itself (which was often), Khan pushed down hard on the back of Malignaggi's head and neck. That's a foul, but one that referees often overlook.

In round five, Khan started landing hooks to the body. Midway through the stanza, a hard body shot hurt Paulie. Amir followed by pushing down hard on the back of Malignaggi's head, and Paulie took advantage of the moment by touching his knee to the canvas.

"That body shot hurt," he admitted afterward. "I figured, okay, he's pushing my head down, so I'll go down without a knockdown being called and get a few seconds rest. Amir knew it."

From that point on, Khan dominated the fight. By round nine, he was beating Malignaggi up. Paulie had nothing to keep him off. His last line of defense was his toughness and his pride.

It wasn't enough. One minute and twenty-five seconds into round eleven, Steve Smoger stopped the fight. Khan won every round on each judge's scorecard. He didn't want it more than Paulie. He just fought better. The most significant number of the night wasn't Amir's 259-to-127 edge in punches landed. It was that he connected on 40 percent of his punches.

The once-elusive Malignaggi wasn't.

After the fight, Khan told boxing fans what they wanted to hear. He said he'd like to fight Marcos Maidana next and then the winner of Timothy Bradley vs. Devon Alexander.

As for Malignaggi; he isn't as old a fighter as Khan made him look. Let's not forget that, five months ago, Paulie outboxed Juan Diaz. He can still beat a lot of guys. But he'd be a decided underdog against any of the 140-pound elite.

Fighters who rely on speed and reflexes as their edge over opponents peak young. Malignaggi's career as a fighter is on the downward side of the hill. Against Khan, once again, he didn't use his legs the way he used to. But this time, it wasn't by design.

Also, against Khan, Paulie's neck gave him trouble. "My neck was dead," he said afterward. "That's left over from the Hatton fight. It doesn't take much to aggravate it. Amir kept pushing down on my head and neck. After a while, I was afraid to throw a right hand because, if I missed, my head would be hanging out there."

Worse, Paulie seems to be losing the mental edge that drove him as a fighter. He no longer believes in himself the way he once did. He knows he can lose. The hunger isn't quite the same either. He has been a champion. He has proven as much as he's going to prove as a fighter. Boxing is now a job, not a passion.

Khan-Malignaggi was a bad styles match-up for Paulie. But in truth, he didn't fight with the same resolve that he showed against Miguel Cotto.

Against Cotto, Malignaggi was badly beaten up. By the end of the fight, his face looked like it had been distorted by a computer-imaging program. But he never stopped trying to win the fight. By the time it was over, he'd won four rounds. One judge gave him five.

Against Khan, by contrast, there came a point in the middle rounds where it seemed as though Paulie was resigned to his fate and his goal was to survive with honor. It's harder for a fighter to walk through fire when he's older.

Naazim Richardson recently observed, "A fighter takes two things from every fight; punishment and experience."

Right now, Paulie is taking more punishment than experience from his fights. And the punishment is mounting. His hands have been broken multiple times. There's permanent damage to nerves in his face as a consequence of the Cotto fight and a neck problem courtesy of Ricky Hatton. It's a given that he'll have arthritis later in life. How much more punishment to his body does he want to take?

The good times never last long enough for a fighter. Let's hope that Paulie cuts the bad times short. He has fought with honor throughout his career. He won every fight that he was expected to win and some that he wasn't. But the human body is more fragile than we like to think it is. Paulie knows that from personal experience; his own and the experience of others.

On August 16, 2008, a young man named Ronnie Vargas was shot to death. Vargas was a promising young fighter; a three-time New York Golden Gloves champion with an 8-and-0 professional record.

Four days later, Paulie visited the Ortiz Funeral Home in the Bronx (where the family was sitting) and gave his IBF championship belt to Vargas's father so Ronnie could be buried as a champion.

If Paulie has as much respect for himself and his body as he has shown over the years for his fellow fighters and boxing, he'll think seriously about moving on to the next stage of his life.

Every time a fighter steps into the ring, his life is at risk. The powers that be shouldn't increase that risk.

An Appalling End to Foreman-Cotto

QUESTION FOR BOXING REFEREES: A fighter collapses when his knee gives way during the seventh round of a twelve-round fight. When he rises to his feet, he's in obvious pain and can't move properly or put weight on the leg. The fighter collapses several more times. His chief second advises the referee that he wants the fight to be stopped. The fighter wants to continue. The referee should: (a) ignore the chief second, tell the fighter to "suck it up," and allow the fight to continue; (b) stop the fight.

On June 5, 2010, at Yankee Stadium, Yuri Foreman defended his WBA 154-pound championship against Miguel Cotto. Foreman is a Chabad rabbinical student and the first practicing Orthodox Jew to win a world title since Jackie "Kid" Berg in 1932. He's also the first Israeli citizen ever to win a world championship belt.

Foreman's ethnicity was central to the promotion. In that spirit, I'd planned to report on Foreman-Cotto in the form of a column explaining the fight to my eighty-four-year-old Jewish mother.

"Foreman and trainer Joe Grier schmoozed in the corner between rounds. 'You want I should throw the jab?' Yuri asked."

If there was a controversial decision, I could write that the loser was "kvetching about the judges." If Yuri won, co-managers Murray Wilson and Alan Cohen would be "kvelling" with pride. The sanctioning body officials would be labeled "no-goodniks." Somehow, I would have found a way to mention the fact that Top Rank publicist Lee Samuels is a "mensch."

Then reality intervened in the form of what I believe was a gross error in officiating by referee Arthur Mercante that requires serious commentary.

Let's put the matter in context.

Yuri Foreman is a three-time Israeli national amateur champion, who came to the United States to pursue a career in professional boxing. He turned pro in 2002 and compiled a record of 28-and-0. The highlight of his career to date was a November 14, 2009, victory over Daniel Santos that brought him the WBA crown.

Foreman has the body of a throwback fighter. He's well-conditioned but without a chiseled look. The key to his style is to move constantly and use his legs to keep an opponent at long range. Footwork is crucial to everything he does. He's hard to hit and throws a lot of punches that keep opponents off balance. He boxes more than he fights.

In twenty-eight fights, Yuri has scored only eight knockouts; none during the past four years. But that doesn't make him a soft touch. After Manny Pacquiao defeated Miguel Cotto last November to retain his 147-pound title, there was talk of Manny moving up in weight to challenge Foreman in the hope of winning a belt in yet another weight division. Team Pacquiao nixed the fight, saying that Yuri was too tall and they didn't like his style.

"It's a real honor that the greatest pound-for-pound fighter in the world doesn't want to fight me," Foreman said in response. "Aside from winning the world title, this is the greatest compliment I've received in boxing."

Yuri is charming with a self-deprecating sense of humor. Several days after dethroning Santos, he was asked how his life had changed since becoming a world champion.

"When I talk, people listen a lot more now than they did before," he answered. "But my wife [Hungarian-born model and former amateur boxer Leyla Leidecker] still makes me take out the garbage."

In recent years, Foreman has been trained by Joe Grier (a former police officer, who fought professionally in the 1970s). Grier has a reputation as a good trainer and, like his fighter, is a man of dignity and grace.

Also, there's another bit of information about Yuri that should be mentioned. He wears a brace on his right knee when he fights. "It's for an old injury," he says. "When I was fifteen, I fell off a bike."

Foreman is promoted by Top Rank, whose CEO (Bob Arum) has visions and implements them. As long as a fighter performs in the ring, Top Rank can get him to the dance.

In this instance, the dance was Foreman against Miguel Cotto in Yankee Stadium.

Cotto is a star with victories over Shane Mosley, Joshua Clottey, and Zab Judah to his credit. For most of his career, he has won fights by beating opponents down. But lately, Miguel has been the beatee. He suffered brutal punishment in knockout losses to Antonio Margarito and Manny Pacquiao. Even though he's only twenty-nine (the same age as Foreman), many in the boxing community think that his best days as a fighter are behind him.

Most of the people who picked Foreman to win the fight (and there were quite a few) did so based on the belief that Cotto is damaged goods. Also, this was Miguel's first fight at 154 pounds, whereas Yuri had fought at that weight throughout his pro career.

But the case for a Cotto victory was strong. Miguel's weakness is his chin. Yuri, with eight knockouts in twenty-eight fights, seemed ill-equipped to exploit that vulnerability. Yuri was the naturally bigger man, but Cotto was the bigger puncher. There were times when Miguel outboxed Shane Mosley, so the assumption was that he could outbox Foreman. In other words; Foreman-Cotto was a match-up between a fighter who could box and a fighter who could both box and punch.

More significantly, Cotto had fought and beaten Mosley, Clottey, and Judah. He'd knocked out Ricardo Torres, Carlos Quintana, Muhammad Abdullaev, and Randall Bailey. Those opponents were in a different league from the competition that Yuri had fought.

In sum; the consensus was that Foreman-Cotto boiled down to two questions: "What does Foreman have?" and "What does Cotto have left?" Within that framework, the bout had the potential to be a career-defining fight for Yuri and a career-ending fight for Miguel. A win for Foreman would establish him as a star in the boxing firmament. A loss for Cotto would mean that he no longer held that distinction.

Yuri understood the risks involved. "To be a real champion," he said, "you don't fight easy fights. You fight other champions. It's not something that falls from the sky when I get this opportunity. I worked very hard to get what I have, and I will work very hard to keep it."

But before the fight could proceed, there was, in Arum's words, "an oops."

Jonathan Ballan (the lead bond lawyer for the financing of Yankee Stadium) had reserved portions of the stadium for his son's Bar Mitzvah party on the night of June 5th. Ballan's contract also called for photos of the Bar Mitzvah boy to be flashed on the large stadium screen in center field for thirty minutes. That blending of conspicuous spending with a traditional religious rite was incompatible with the fight.

In due course, the Yankees and Ballan amended their contract to allow Foreman-Cotto to move forward. Terms of the agreement were not announced, although the Yankees thanked the Ballan family for its "graciousness, understanding, and good will." It was later reported that Ballan gave up the right to use the scoreboard in exchange for an unspecified number of autographed baseballs, personal meetings for his son with Foreman and Arum, and ringside seats for up to 240 guests.

Then there was another twist.

Team Foreman thought that it had a deal for Emanuel Steward to serve as a training consultant in the weeks leading up to the fight. But in late March, Foreman's co-manager, Murray Wilson, learned that Steward was negotiating with the Cotto camp for a more lucrative position as Miguel's trainer.

That led Wilson to declare, "Manny Steward is uninvited. He was the one who originally called to do this. He's the one who wanted to help Yuri out. Maybe it was more of trying to help Manny out. I liked him and I still like, but it's not too nice to have no balls. All he had to do was pick up the phone and tell me he wanted to train Cotto. I haven't spoke to him [since I learned he was interested in training Cotto], but I have no desire to speak to him because whatever he has to say means nothing."

Later, Murray was more direct. "This is the first time in five years that I haven't rooted for Miguel Cotto," he said. "Miguel is one of my favorite fighters. Miguel, I like. Manny Steward can go fuck himself."

Outdoor fights in mammoth stadiums are part of American boxing lore. The original Yankee Stadium is at the heart of that tradition. Jack Dempsey, Gene Tunney, Rocky Marciano, and Sugar Ray Robinson are among the storied warriors who did battle within its walls.

Joe Louis fought in Yankee Stadium as a black hope against Primo Carnera and Max Baer. By the time he entered the stadium ring to face Max Schmeling on June 22, 1938, in what was arguably the most important prizefight of all time, Louis was America's hope. That night was the first time that many people heard a black man referred to simply as "the American."

Times change. An African-American is now president of the United States. In 1938, the state of Israel didn't exist. Now an Israeli citizen would be defending a world title in the main event.

Arum had promoted the last fight at the original Yankee Stadium (Muhammad Ali vs. Ken Norton in 1976). Promoting the first fight in the new stadium, he said, was "a crowning achievement in my career."

The stadium venue was a key element in pre-fight promotion for Foreman-Cotto. The other hook, of course, was Foreman's Israeli citizenship and status as a rabbinical student.

Yuri is a "feel good" story. Early in his career, he was unable to support himself through boxing. Then Bruce Silverglade (the owner of Gleason's Gym in Brooklyn) introduced him to Wilson and Alan Cohen. Murray and Alan bought Foreman's contract from Gary Gittelsohn for $80,000 and became his co-managers in 2003.

"We've paid Yuri six hundred dollars a week since then," Wilson says. "Yuri's biggest payday before now was $60,000. He got that when he won the title from Santos. Even though Alan and I are entitled to 30 percent of his purses, we've never cut his purse. The Cotto fight will be the first time we've taken our percentage. It's not about the money. We really are doing it for Yuri."

What drew Wilson and Cohen to Foreman?

"Jewish," Murray says. "That's it. I wanted to see a Jewish success story in boxing."

"Are you excited?" Wilson was asked three days before the fight.

"Anxious," he answered. "I'm confident, but I want it to happen already. How many weeks can I have a bad stomach?"

Eric Raskin recently wrote, "You can count on one finger the number of championship-level boxers who are working toward a rabbinical career."

That distinction made Foreman a magnet for publicity in the weeks leading up to the fight. He was the grand marshal in New York's annual Salute to Israel Parade and a guest on *Jimmy Kimmel Live.* The *New York Times* and *Wall Street Journal* ran feature articles about him. The *New York Daily News* referred to Yuri and his wife Leyla as "the Brangelina of boxing."

"The Puerto Rican community has a lot of boxers; so for them, this is old hat," Arum proclaimed. "For the Jewish community, particularly the Orthodox Jewish community, this hasn't happened in a long long time."

Foreman's ring walk, the media was told, would be preceded by the sounding of the shofar (a horn, traditionally that of a ram, used in Jewish religious rites).

"There will be two highlights for me on fight night other than the fight," Arum said. "One will be when they play "Hatikva" (the Israeli national anthem) for the first time ever in the old or new Yankee Stadium. The other will be when Yuri begins his ring walk to the sound of the shofar. That's something that has never been seen or heard in the whole long history of boxing. We are very fortunate to have Israel's number one entertainer, Yoni Dror of Tel Aviv, attending the fight to sound the shofar. Yoni is beyond compare when it comes to sounding the shofar."

Yoni is also Arum's nephew.

On the day of the fight, Foreman observed the Sabbath (from sunset on Friday until sunset on Saturday) in a Manhattan hotel room. He left the hotel at 9:08 PM and drove with a police escort to Yankee Stadium. In his dressing room, he taped an eight-foot-long Israeli flag over the lockers at one end of the room. Then he took a Bible from his gym bag and bowed his head while reading from the Book of Psalms. Five minutes later, he kissed the book and put it back in his gym bag.

"Yuri" is the Russian translation of "George." Former heavyweight champion George Foreman is also a man of faith.

"I think this a great thing he did in reading his Bible in the dressing room," George says. "I would read the Bible in my [hotel] room before a fight; but I cannot remember reading in the dressing room before a match."

Shortly before Foreman left for the ring, Israeli singer Shalva Berti stepped between the ropes and sang "Hatikva." Top Rank's international television feed could be seen and heard on a TV set in Yuri's dressing room. Yuri stood silently as "Hatikva" was sung, shifting his weight from one foot to the other.

Arum had hoped for a crowd of 30,000 to 35,000. Despite the pre-fight publicity, Yankee Stadium didn't catch on as a venue the way Cowboys Stadium had for Pacquiao-Clottey earlier this year. Foreman-

Cotto engendered a good television rating (3.9), but the on-site attendance was only 20,272. Yankees president Randy Levine and chief operating officer Lonn Trost selling a fight isn't the same as having Dallas Cowboys owner Jerry Jones on call every step of the way. And Yankee Stadium didn't have Pacquiao on the card.

The referee for Foreman-Cotto was Arthur Mercante Jr (son of Hall of Fame referee Arthur Mercante, who died earlier this year). Arthur Sr was known throughout the boxing community as a man of integrity and competence. Over the years, his son has developed his own body of work.

The first part of Foreman-Cotto boiled down to boxing basics. Miguel was the aggressor. Yuri sought to stem the tide with lateral movement and enough punches of his own to keep Cotto from rolling over him. Foreman's punches sting. Miguel's were the harder blows. Cotto appeared to be more concerned with finding Yuri than he was with getting hit.

The third round saw the first of what would be several strange acts by Mercante. With 1:42 left in the stanza, Foreman's mouthpiece fell out of his mouth. Arthur saw it and immediately picked it up. There was a lengthy lull in the action, but he didn't call time. Instead, he waited more than a minute before leading Foreman to Cotto's corner. Emanuel Steward protested that he was the wrong guy to rinse the mouthpiece and put it back in; that Yuri wasn't his fighter.

"No! No! You clean it," Mercante ordered.

That was a clear departure from boxing protocol.

Round four was Foreman's best round of the fight. He landed several hard lead righthands after feinting with his jab and won the stanza on each judge's scorecard.

Round five belonged to Cotto. Round six was close.

Halfway through the scheduled twelve rounds, Miguel was ahead 59–55, 59–55, and 58–56 on the scorecards. Yuri had a bloody nose and a cut on his left eyelid. But he was still in the fight.

Then things got crazy.

Forty-five seconds into round seven, as Foreman was moving laterally to his right along the ring perimeter, his right knee gave way and he fell hard to the canvas. He rose in obvious pain, hobbling when he tried to walk.

"Walk it off, champ," Mercante told him. "Suck it up, kid. I'll give you five minutes." Then he asked, "Is it your ankle?"

Given the fact that Yuri was wearing a knee brace, an ankle injury wasn't the most likely possibility.

Foreman said no.

"Is it your knee?"

Yuri nodded.

"Suck it up, kid," Mercante repeated.

Foreman wanted to continue fighting. Less than a minute after he went down, the action resumed. At that point, Yuri was a seriously compromised fighter. Forty-five seconds later, again with no punch being thrown, his knee buckled and he fell once more to the canvas.

"Oh, shit," Mercante muttered. His words sounded as though they were spoken more in anger than out of concern for the fighter. "Suck it up," he said. "Do you want more time? You're a game guy. Do you want to go?"

Foreman appeared to be in no condition to fight, but he was a champion with a champion's heart.

Mercante instructed that the action resume.

With one minute left in round seven, a Cotto left hook knocked out Yuri's mouthpiece. Mercante let the entire round finish without giving the mouthpiece to the corner to put back in.

Mercante's handling of round seven was bad. His conduct of round eight was worse.

Grier readied Foreman for the eighth round in the hope that Yuri could regain his mobility. But it was quickly clear that, not only couldn't he move to avoid punches, he couldn't get power on his own blows. At the 1:30 mark, while trying to move laterally, he staggered and almost fell again.

"I knew then that it was a serious injury and that it wasn't something he could recover from," Grier said afterward. "Yuri had no mobility and he couldn't get leverage on his punches. He was just a target."

At that point, following proper procedure, Grier asked Ernie Morales (the New York State Athletic Commission inspector assigned to Foreman's corner) to tell Mercante that he wanted to stop the fight. Morales stood on the ring apron to get Mercante's attention. Arthur admitted after the fight that he saw and heard the inspector. And he knew that Morales was assigned to Foreman's corner because he'd seen him in Yuri's dressing room when he gave the fighter his pre-fight instructions. But Mercante pointedly ignored the request.

"Yuri was starting to get banged up," Grier recounted later. "He couldn't properly defend himself because he only had one leg. The referee wasn't listening to the inspector. I had to get it stopped. I asked if I could throw the towel in, and the inspector said 'go ahead.'"

With 1:15 left in round eight, Grier threw a white towel into the ring. Both corners came through the ropes to embrace their respective fighters.

Then Mercante did a disservice to boxing. If he had doubts as to where the towel came from, he could have asked Grier if he'd thrown it in. Grier would have answered, "Yes, sir." The responsible thing for Mercante to say in response would have been, "Okay; the fight is over."

But that's not what happened.

Instead, Mercante shouted, "Everybody out of the ring. I don't want the towel. The corner is not throwing in the towel [apparently, he knew it came from the corner]." Then he turned to Foreman and asked, "You all right, champ?"

Obviously, Foreman wasn't all right.

"You're fighting hard. I don't want to see a move like that. Suck it up. Walk it off."

The action resumed. But as Grier said, Foreman was no longer able to properly defend himself. The fight was clearly unwinnable. In fact, it was no longer a professional prizefight. It was a beating.

Foreman's knee gave way and he staggered several more times before the end of the round.

After the eighth stanza, Mercante went to Foreman's corner. "Who threw in the towel?" he demanded.

"I did," Grier told him.

Mercante turned and walked away. He didn't even talk with Foreman. Grier, understanding that he'd been forbidden to stop the fight, reluctantly readied his charge for the ninth round.

Meanwhile, ring announcer Michael Buffer, having been misinformed that the towel had come from an "outside source," announced that incorrect information to the crowd.

Thirty seconds into round nine, Cotto landed a hook to the body. Yuri's knee gave out again and he fell to the canvas. Finally, Mercante stopped it.

In the dressing room after the fight, Foreman was disappointed but accepting of what had happened. "I felt a lot of pain," he said. "It was very sharp and my knee was weak. I didn't want to stop the fight, but I couldn't box like I had to. If the leg was fine, I would stay in my game plan. Without the leg, I couldn't move and I had no leverage on my punches."

Grier thanked Ernie Morales for doing what he could to stop the fight.

"The inspector did the right thing, and so did I," Joe said. "I'd throw the towel in again if I had it to do over. All that happened after that was, Yuri took unnecessary punishment. He was fighting with dignity, but he only had one leg. I wanted it to stop while he was still on his feet; not down on the canvas. I know you're not supposed to throw a towel in. I told the inspector I wanted them to stop the fight. The inspector told the referee. And the referee told them to keep fighting. What else was I supposed to do?"

Arthur Mercante came in the room to congratulate Foreman on his courage.

"You should have stopped it," Yuri's wife said.

"He wasn't going to get hurt," Mercante countered.

"You don't know that."

"Each time he collapsed, he got back up, throwing punches.

"It made no sense," Leyla pressed. "What did you expect was going to happen? Nothing was going to change. There was not going to be a miracle that he could start to move again."

Mercante left the dressing room; but not before pointing to several text messages he'd received on his cell phone telling him that the HBO commentators had praised his work during the fight.

Yuri lay down on a rubdown table, and a doctor put the first of seven stitches in his left eyelid.

Two days later, it was announced that Foreman had torn the meniscus in his right knee and suffered stretched ligaments. As of this writing, he's scheduled to undergo surgery at NYU Medical Center to rebuild his anterior cruciate ligament (ACL). On June 9th, Mitch Abramson of the *New York Daily News* reported that Dr. Gerard Varlotta (who examined Foreman's right knee and will oversee his treatment) declined to speculate on whether Mercante's refusal to stop the fight exacerbated the injury. "I have no opinion on that," Varlotta said. Asked if he believed that it was wise for Foreman to continue fighting on the damaged knee, the doctor responded, "I can't answer that."

During the past week, a number of people have praised Mercante for his handling of the fight. New York State Athletic Commission chairperson Melvina Lathan told Michael Woods of Sweetscience.com, "I think Arthur did a remarkable job. He did what he was supposed to do. He knows the rules. He responded appropriately. All in all, it was a magical evening of boxing."

I have a different opinion. I think that Mercante's handling of the fight was appalling.

People on both sides of the debate are digging in their heels on the issue. I ask that both sides consider the following thoughts carefully.

First, let's start with some facts.

Early in round seven, as previously noted, Foreman's knee gave way and he fell to the canvas. He rose, debilitated and in obvious pain.

New York State is a member of the Association of Boxing Commissions. Section 33 of the *Referee Rules and Guidelines* adopted by the ABC in 2008 states, "The referee must consult with the ringside physician in all accidental injury cases. The referee, in conjunction with the ringside physician, will determine the length of time needed to evaluate the affected boxer and his or her suitability to continue. If the injured boxer is not adversely affected and their chance of winning has not been seriously jeopardized because of the injury, the bout may be allowed to continue."

Foreman's injury "seriously jeopardized" his chance of winning the fight. Mercante is an intelligent man, so presumably he understood that. Also, Arthur failed at that juncture to consult with Dr. Rick Weinstein (an orthopedic surgeon, who was the ringside physician in Yuri's corner) as provided for by Rule 33. Instead, he urged Yuri to "walk it off" and "suck it up," and let the fight continue.

When Foreman's knee buckled and he collapsed again less than a minute later, Mercante followed the same procedure.

The key to Foreman's success as a fighter is his mobility. In rounds one through six of the fight, Cotto had landed an average of eleven punches per round. In round seven, with a disabled fighter in front of him, he landed twenty-nine, including twenty-seven "power" punches.

Joe Grier understood Foreman's fighting heart and wanted to give him every reasonable opportunity to win. But as the next round progressed, it was clear to Grier that Yuri's injury was not something that the fighter could "walk off" and that it would only get worse.

Corner inspectors are the eyes and ears of the commission. They don't have the authority to stop a fight. But they do have the authority to tell the referee that a fighter's corner wants it to be stopped. Midway through round eight, when Yuri staggered and almost fell again, Grier asked inspector Ernie Morales to tell the referee that he wanted to stop the fight.

Morales relayed the request. Mercante refused to honor it.

At that point, with the inspector's permission, Grier threw a white towel into the ring.

I'm hard-pressed to think of another instance when a chief second asked that a fight be stopped (let alone, an instance when a fighter was hobbling around the ring on a severely injured leg) and the referee refused to stop it.

In handling the fight the way he did, Mercante showed disrespect for Grier (a capable trainer who knows his fighter). One can speculate that, had it been a "name" trainer in the corner such as Freddie Roach or Teddy Atlas rather than Grier, Arthur would have stopped the bout.

After the fight, when Mercante was interviewed by Max Kellerman on HBO, he was a bit evasive, as evidenced by the following colloquy:

> Kellerman: "Do you know who threw in the towel?"
> Mercante: "At the moment, I didn't know."
> Kellerman: "Do you know who it is now?"
> Mercante: "I kind of know."

Kind of?

After round eight, Mercante had gone to the corner and demanded, "Who threw in the towel?"

"I did," Grier told him.

Arthur didn't ask, "Why?"

He didn't say, "Tell me what you're thinking."

He turned and walked away.

If that's standard protocol in New York, then New York needs to overhaul its standards.

That left Grier in a quandary. "I wanted to stop it," he said afterward. "But Arthur made it very clear to me that only he could stop it. Mercante didn't want to hear anything from anyone. I didn't know if it was ego, him saying that only he could stop the fight, or if he was affected by the fight being in the stadium. But it was very confusing. Who knows the fighter better than the corner? Yuri was fighting on one leg. I was trying to protect him from getting seriously injured."

After the fight, one of the things that Mercante said in support of his decision was, "There was no need to stop the fight. They were in the middle of a great fight. That's what the fans came to see."

But referees are taught from day one, "You don't worry about the crowd. You're there to ensure a fair fight and protect the fighters. You do what you have to do to fulfill these obligations, whether or not it makes the crowd happy."

Shame on anyone who thought that seeing a one-legged fighter get beaten up was "entertainment."

After the fight, award-winning writer George Kimball speculated as to why Mercante conducted himself the way he did. Kimball wrote, "Mercante Jr may have viewed his assignment as his opportunity to reinvent himself as his own man, with a distinct style incorporating the cult of personality into his strange concept of a referee's duties. He seemed to envision himself less as an honest broker there to enforce the rules than as a co-equal participant, whose high-profile function was at least as important to the proceedings as that of the boxers themselves."

Whether or not that's correct, Mercante projected the image on fight night of a man who was more concerned with exercising his authority than he was with protecting a fighter.

It's not enough for a person in authority to exercise power. Power should be exercised wisely. "Taking charge" is fine as long as a referee does the right thing when he takes charge. And there's more than one way to "take charge." A take-charge referee could have told Foreman in round seven, "You're a courageous fighter and I know you want to keep fighting, but it's over."

The issue here isn't whether or not Mercante had power under the law to allow the fight to continue over the objections of Foreman's corner. It's about common-sense judgment. Just because Arthur wasn't required by law to stop the fight doesn't mean he shouldn't have stopped it.

Arthur also exercised his authority within the law on the night of June 26, 2001, when Beethavean Scottland fought George "Khalid" Jones in a bout that was nationally televised from the flight deck of the U.S.S. *Intrepid*.

Prior to Scottland-Jones, Mercante had been criticized for his performance in three high-profile bouts. On each of those occasions (Razor Ruddock vs. Michael Dokes, Pernell Whitaker vs. Diobelys Hurtado, and Michael Bennett vs. Andrew Hutchinson), he'd allowed a fight to continue after one of the participants appeared to be unable to defend himself. Each time, an ugly knockout resulted.

Ruddock-Dokes, Whitaker-Hurtado, and Bennett-Hutchinson involved split-second judgments. Scottland-Jones was a different matter. Scottland took a beating. On three occasions in three different rounds, there were cries from the crowd that the bout should be stopped. In round ten, Scottland was knocked unconscious. He died six days later.

Over time, Mercante put those incidents behind him. They arose again in the hours after Foreman-Cotto, when Tim Smith of the *New York Daily News* asked about Beethavean Scottland and Arthur told him, "It's my understanding that he was injured more from being banged around in the elevator as they were trying to get him down to the ambulance."

That's nonsense. I was physically present nine years ago when paramedics wheeled the gurney with Scottland on it into the elevator on the U.S.S. *Intrepid*. The elevator was too small to easily accommodate the gurney. But Scottland was not "banged around." And before the gurney was put on the elevator, the medical team had already determined that his vital signs were ominous.

Greg Sirb is a former president of the Association of Boxing Commissions and long-time executive director of the Pennsylvania State Athletic Commission. "I think Arthur was horribly wrong in what he did with Yuri Foreman," Sirb says. "When a towel comes in, the referee should call time and ascertain then and there who threw it. If the corner threw it in, that's it. The fight is over. I would never ever overrule a fighter's chief second if he wants to stop a fight. If the chief second says he wants the fight to be over, there's no decision for the referee to make. Whether the rule is written or not, the fight should be over. The fighter's physical well-being, and sometimes his life, are at stake."

Don Turner has been honored as "trainer of the year" by the Boxing Writers Association of America. He has known Joe Grier for thirty years.

"I didn't see the fight," Turner says, "But I heard about it. First, let me tell you about Joe Grier. Joe Grier was a gutsy fighter; he's a good trainer; he cares about his fighters; and he's a great guy. Second thing; the only problem I have with Joe Grier in this situation is that he was too nice a guy. If it had been me in there with my fighter and the referee told me I couldn't stop the fight, there would have been a bigger fight between me and the referee. All trainers want to win. The trainer does everything he can to keep his fighter in the fight. But the trainer knows better than anyone else when his fighter is in trouble and when a fight should be stopped. When the trainer reaches that conclusion, it's not about asking the fighter, 'How do you feel about me stopping the fight?' At that point, it's a dictatorship between the trainer and the fighter. You don't keep a fight going because the fighter wants to fight. When the trainer says 'that's all,' the fight is over."

"Eddie Futch understood that," Turner continues. "When Eddie Futch stopped Joe Frazier from going out for the last round against Ali in Manila, Joe was very unhappy about it. But Eddie knew his fighter and he knew that Joe couldn't defend himself anymore. It took a lot of courage for Eddie to stop that fight. A lot of people, including Joe, were mad at him because he did what he did. But Joe is talking a lot better than Ali is talking these days, and he owes that to Eddie Futch."

Freddie Roach is one of boxing's most respected trainers. "Arthur was wrong," Roach says. "The corner knows the fighter better than the referee knows the fighter. If the corner wants to stop a fight, the referee should stop it. I was in Puerto Rico not long ago and wanted to stop a fight and the inspector told me, 'You can't stop it.' I told him, 'Watch.' I'd walk into the ring and get my fighter disqualified before I let a fight continue under those circumstances."

Finally, there's Emanuel Steward, who is respected throughout the boxing community as a trainer and HBO commentator. Steward had a unique view of Foreman-Cotto. He was in Miguel's corner as the drama unfolded.

"I usually defend referees," Steward says. "It's a hard job. And to be honest; I don't like to say things that upset officials because they might hold it against me down the road. But I'll talk about this because it was horrible. I don't think I've ever seen a referee do a job that bad."

"First, the referee was out of position all through the fight. No one is talking about that. But if you look at a tape, there were times when he was totally out of position. A lot of those times, he was in the corner blocking my view."

"Then there was the mouthpiece thing. That was crazy. He took too long to stop the action so they could put Foreman's mouthpiece back in. And when he brought the mouthpiece over to me; that wasn't my fighter. And he made me put it in. I knew then that something was strange. I was asking myself, 'What's wrong with this guy?'"

"And when the towel came in; that was awful. There are things we have in boxing to protect fighters from their own courage. There's the referee; the ring doctor; and the fighter's corner. The fighter's corner has always been able to stop a fight. The trainer knows his fighter better than the referee does. We're not stupid. If the trainer wants to stop the fight, you stop the fight. Yuri could have been killed. One punch can do it. And it was obvious to everyone except the referee that Yuri couldn't defend himself. If Joe Grier didn't try to stop the fight, people would be saying today that he was an inexperienced cornerman who froze in the spotlight and didn't properly protect his fighter. Even if Joe Grier didn't want to stop the fight, the referee should have stopped it."

"If it was my fighter and I wanted to stop it, we would have had a real confrontation, in the ring right then and there. The referee could say anything he wanted. I'd have told him, 'I don't care what you say. The fight is over.' I have no idea what the man was thinking. The fighter's life was at risk. A bad call in another sport can cost you a point or maybe lose the game. Boxing is a whole different sport. If a referee doesn't understand that, he has a serious problem."

"The whole thing was weird and scary. This wasn't one bad spur-of-the-moment decision. Everything was wrong. There was a whole long string of mistakes. There was bad refereeing and irrational behavior all night long. I've never seen anything like it before, and I hope I never see anything like it again."

"People have to speak out on this. The trainers, the fighters. I have a voice, and I'm going to use it. What this referee did was scary wrong. I wouldn't want my fighter in the ring with this guy. No! No way! Never! If it means having to pull my fighter out of a fight someday, I might do it."

It's possible that the events of June 5, 2010, will make Foreman a bigger gate attraction than he was before. Or maybe, despite the optimistic prognosis of doctors, he'll be a lesser fighter in the future because of unnecessary damage to his knee that he suffered during the final rounds of the fight.

And maybe someday, a fighter will be killed in the ring because a referee will remember what Arthur Mercante did on the night of June 5th and refuse a request by a fighter's corner to stop a fight. That's the worst thing about Foreman-Cotto. Mercante's conduct of the fight set a horribly dangerous precedent. Arthur is a role model. In all likelihood, there will come a time when another referee overrules a fighter's corner and forces a fight to continue because the fighter wants to keep fighting. And the fighter will die. It would be tragic if that becomes part of Arthur's legacy as a referee.

There are those who say that it was appropriate to allow Foreman-Cotto to continue because Yuri had earned the right to "go out on his shield."

That translates into, "Yuri had no chance to win. But the referee should have allowed him get to beaten up, rip open the cut on his left eyelid, shred whatever remained that was holding his right knee in place, and maybe get knocked unconscious. Then, since there were no shields at ringside, he could have been carried out on a stretcher."

Foreman didn't need that to establish his courage.

A wise man once said, "The last thing you do is ask a fighter who might be hurt if he wants to continue. Because if he's any kind of fighter at all, he'll say yes."

That man was Arthur Mercante Sr.

It's not a hard concept to grasp. If a fighter is hurt and his chief second wants to stop the fight, the referee should stop the fight. People can agree or disagree with me. But that's how I feel, and I feel very strongly about it.

John Duddy enters the ring as "Ireland's John Duddy." But he's quick to say, "The nickname doesn't really matter to me. What I'd like to hear attached to my name someday is, 'And the new . . .'"

John Duddy: A Fighting Heart Isn't Enough

John Duddy sat in the "green room" at The Alamodome in San Antonio on the evening of June 26, 2010. Before the night was done, eight thousand fans would watch him do battle. Hundreds of thousands more would see him on television. Few people have an audience of that magnitude at any time in their life.

The room was comfortably large, but it wasn't really a dressing room. There were no lockers or shower.

Decades of sacrifice, pain, passion, and dreams were about to crystalize into a fistfight. John would step onto a small square of illuminated canvas, where he and Julio Cesar Chavez Jr would try to beat each other senseless.

There's an ebb and flow to a fighter's career. An unexpected loss can send his fortunes plummeting like a one-day 20 percent drop in the Dow Jones average. On occasion, a fighter enters the ring, knowing in advance that he's about to engage in a crossroads fight. Win, and he takes a giant step forward. Lose, and he might never climb back to where he was before.

This was a crossroads fight. It wasn't for a world title (which crossroads fights often are). But after this fight, regardless of the outcome, Duddy's future as a fighter would be vastly different from what it had been before.

"A win would mean great things," John had said three days earlier. "The winner has a good path in front of him."

Duddy's pre-fight dressing room is always quiet. There's no music and little conversation.

John sat silent for long periods of time, sipping occasionally from a bottle of vitamin water. At one point, he lay down on a black leather sofa, put his head on a pillow fashioned from towels, and closed his eyes, focusing on the task ahead.

Trainer Harry Keitt, cornerman Jihad Abdul-Aziz, cutman George Mitchell, and manager Craig Hamilton spoke in hushed tones when they spoke at all.

"I hate this part of it," Hamilton said. "Everything up until now, I could try to control. Now it's out of my hands."

Referee Jon Schorle came in and gave John his pre-fight instructions. One concern in the Duddy camp was that John cuts easily.

"I wish I didn't cut, but I do," Duddy has said. "If it bothered me, I wouldn't be a fighter."

Against Yory Boy Campas and Walid Smichet, John had fought with horrific cuts above both eyes but emerged victorious each time. Team Duddy was afraid that Schorle might pull the trigger prematurely. It was an issue they'd planned to raise during the referee's pre-fight instructions.

Schorle brought the subject up himself. "I've seen you fight many times," he told John. "You cut easily. I'm not going to panic if I see blood. You've fought with bad cuts before and won."

The minutes passed.

John gloved up and hit the pads with Keitt. The trainer offered some last-minute thoughts shortly before they left for the ring.

"Don't chase him. Walk him down and break him down, bit by bit. I want smart pressure. If you get him hurt, jump on him."

This wasn't *American Idol*. It wasn't about being voted off an island. John was about to fight for his career and to position himself to keep living his dream. Regardless of whether he won or lost, he would be punched again and again by a man trained in the art of hurting. It was inevitable that he would suffer physical damage. Some of it would be superficial; some, possibly, everlasting.

Such is the life of a professional fighter.

Duddy is an atypical prizefighter. Boxing runs counter to the grain of who and what he appears to be. There's no wellspring of anger; no history of parental abuse. He never slept on the streets or went hungry as a child.

John turned pro in 2003 at age twenty-four after moving to New York from Ireland. His good looks, charisma, and action style of fighting made him a popular figure in the Irish American community. Women's hearts fluttered when he walked by. Men wanted to shake his hand. And he was winning: 23-and-0 with 18 knockouts.

How good was John?

Better than the guys he was fighting.

Then, on February 23, 2008, Duddy fought Walid Smichet (a free-swinging club fighter) at Madison Square Garden on the undercard of Wladimir Klitschko vs. Sultan Ibragimov. An impressive win would have put him next in line for a title shot against middleweight champion Kelly Pavlik.

It was a bad night for the Irish.

When an opponent throws punches in bunches, John tends to get hit. "Watching Duddy against Smichet was the first time I saw a guy get hit with every punch in a six-punch combination," writer George Kimball noted afterward.

John won, barely. Both of his eyelids were ripped open. Thirty-two stitches were needed to close the wounds. "Boxing is hard enough when you're fighting smart," he acknowledged later. "There's no point in making things even harder by fighting stupid. Just because I can take a punch doesn't mean I have to. There's a time to stand and slug, but it's not as often as I've been doing it."

Meanwhile, a storm was brewing. Duddy had been guided throughout his career by Eddie and Tony McLoughlin; brothers who'd become his promoter and manager respectively. He had a large following in the Irish American community. Fans were buying tickets to his fights in large numbers. But he wasn't being paid accordingly.

New York State Athletic commission records showed that the McLoughlins received approximately $250,000 for the Smichet fight. John had been paid less than 20 percent of that amount. And that was just one example.

In autumn 2008, Duddy sought the advice of Craig Hamilton (who, over the years, had successfully managed several fighters). Hamilton made some inquiries and confronted the McLoughlins with what he believed was conclusive evidence of financial improprieties on their part. That was followed by a lawsuit in federal court, alleging breach of contract and other wrongdoing. Soon, John was a promotional free agent and Hamilton was his manager.

"This is a critical period in terms of John's economic future," Hamilton said when the litigation was over. "He should have made more money before, but the McLoughlins did what they did. From now on, at least he'll be getting all of the money that he's entitled to."

Duddy's first fight with Hamilton was a February 21, 2009, unanimous-decision victory over Matt Vanda at Madison Square Garden on the undercard of Miguel Cotto vs. Michael Jennings. His purse (including a share of ticket sales) was $90,000.

Then John stumbled. On April 24, 2009, he crossed the Hudson River to Newark, New Jersey, to fight journeyman Billy Lyell. Lyell had slightly faster hands than John and got off first for much of the night. In round three, an accidental headbutt opened an ugly slice on Duddy's left eyelid. At the close of round four, John shook Lyell with a left hook up top (the best punch of the fight). Billy won the round, but five and six belonged to Duddy, who finally got his jab untracked, backing Lyell up and splitting Billy's nose open in the process.

When John jabbed effectively, he controlled the fight. But he didn't do it often enough. The decision could have gone either way. Lyell won a split verdict.

After the loss to Lyell, John reunited with Harry Keitt. He'd trained with Keitt for most of his pro career, before leaving at Eddie McLoughlin's suggestion to work with Don Turner and then Pat Burns.

Next, Hamilton sat down with Top Rank (which had expressed interest in promoting John) to chart a course for the future. There was the usual back-and-forth with regard to money. During negotiations, Bob Arum was quick to point out Duddy's deficiencies as a fighter, which led Craig to complain, "Bob negotiates like a guy who's seducing a woman. He pursues her for a year. And when she finally agrees to go to bed with him, he tells her she's fat but he still wants to fuck her."

In the end, there was a meeting of the minds.

On October 10, 2009, Duddy pounded out a lopsided unanimous decision over Michi Munoz at Madison Square Garden on a Top Rank card headlined by Juan Manuel Lopez and Yuriorkis Gamboa. Three months later, he returned to the scene and knocked out Juan Astorga in the first round.

The pieces of the puzzle that Arum and Hamilton were putting together were falling into place.

On March 13, 2010, John journeyed to Dallas for a showcase fight against Michael Medina on the undercard of Manny Pacquiao vs. Joshua Clottey in Cowboys Stadium. He controlled the action throughout the bout en route to a ten-round triumph.

"It didn't feel any different, really," Duddy said of the spectacle at Cowboys Stadium. "It's like when I first fought at Madison Square Garden. It's a beautiful wrapping, but the present inside is what counts."

John's father, Mick Duddy, had come to Dallas for the fight. Mick knows the hard side of boxing, having compiled a 3-and-4 record as a club fighter in the 1980s.

"John is living his dream," Mick said in the euphoria of Dallas. "Where I come from, people can only dream of this sort of thing; being part of this event in this stadium, fighting on the same card as the best pound-for-pound fighter in the world. I'm so proud of John. And more than that, I'm happy for him. But I have to be honest; there's always a wee bit of fear in me. I put it in the back of my mind. But this is boxing. I know that everything could change with one punch. And I don't just mean losing a fight."

Meanwhile, seven days after John Duddy made his professional debut at a small club-fight show in New York, Julio Cesar Chavez Jr entered the ring for the first time in Culiacan, Mexico.

Chavez had (and still has) a hard act to follow. His father was one of Mexico's greatest fighters. Julio Cesar Chavez Sr won 107 times in a 115-bout career and captured championships at 130, 135, and 140 pounds.

Junior has been brought along slowly by Top Rank. He began boxing at 130 pounds and, by the start of 2010, had worked his way up to 160. His record stood at 40-and-0 with 1 draw, but the opposition was suspect at best. Many of his opponents had come from places like Indiana, Missouri, Oklahoma, Kansas, Nebraska, and Minnesota. The number of African-American opponents he'd faced could be counted on Arum's fingers with digits to spare. Yet, because of his name, he'd become the biggest draw in Top Rank's "Latin Fury" pay-per-view series.

"Chavez," Bart Barry writes, "built his following the old-fashioned way. He inherited it."

But in fairness to Julio, he'd turned pro with virtually no amateur experience, so it was logical for him to learn his trade against less-than-stellar opposition. And anyone who's unbeaten in forty-one fights, no matter what the level of opposition, can fight a bit.

Chavez-Duddy was a fight that both camps had been pointing toward. Each fighter had a "name" and was marketable. Each fighter was confident that he could beat the other. Chavez was guaranteed a $500,000 purse. Duddy would receive $125,000 plus an additional $10,000 in training expenses. It was the first time in his career that John was the "opponent" and the "B side" of a promotion. The fight would be for the World Boxing Council's middleweight "silver belt."

In recent years, the WBC has become a parody of itself, creating new titles in exchange for sanctioning fees and looking for other ways to separate fighters from anything of value (such as fight-worn equipment). The other major sanctioning bodies aren't much better. But WBC president Jose Sulaiman seems particularly shameless and self-righteous about it.

The WBC received $18,750 in sanctioning fees for attaching its "silver belt" to Chavez-Duddy. More significantly, perhaps, Sulaiman gained control over the assignment of officials.

The Alamodome was the site of one of the most blatant robberies in boxing history, when Pernell Whitaker thoroughly outclassed Julio Cesar Chavez Sr on September 10, 1993, in a WBC title fight, only to have two of the judges rule the bout a draw.

The Duddy camp wanted a twelve-round fight, believing that the two "championship" rounds would work to John's advantage. The price it paid was bringing the WBC into the mix.

"Fighting Julio Cesar Chavez Jr for the WBC silver belt in Texas isn't a recipe for a fair fight," Hamilton acknowledged. "Texas has had problems in the past when guys come in to fight someone from Texas or a Mexican fighter. There's no question who Jose Sulaiman wants to win. Chavez Jr is practically his grandson. And Julio is a cash cow for Top Rank. I don't care what Arum says. Top Rank wants Chavez to win."

"But there's really no choice," Hamilton continued. "This is the right fight for John. It's a fight he can win, and winning will help him get to where he wants to be. Chavez isn't going to Ireland and we're not going to Mexico, so it makes economic sense to have the fight in Texas. We need a belt for the fight to be twelve rounds, so we're stuck with the WBC. All I can do is lobby for a fair fight and let people know that I won't go quietly if John gets robbed."

Duddy, for his part, said simply, "I'm coming to do my job, like I do for every fight. I don't appoint the referee and judges. I have to take care of my part of the bargain. After that, what happens happens."

Team Duddy was optimistic that what happened would be good. John doesn't have the physical gifts of an elite fighter. And he's prone to defensive lapses. But his footwork is good; his chin is great; he's always in shape. And over the years, he has demonstrated a will of iron.

Chavez was used to brawling with opponents who weren't physically or mentally tough enough to brawl with him. John could brawl.

"I think it will be a tough physical fight," Duddy said. "The two of us are pretty aggressive fighters. I plan to keep the pressure on all night. I can box; I can punch; I can take a punch. And I can do it for twelve rounds. I've been in fights where I had to answer the question, 'Do I want to be a fighter or do I want to quit?' Chavez hasn't had to answer that question. I'll be going into waters where I've been before and Chavez hasn't."

Duddy was a better fighter than anyone Chavez had fought. Also, the two men had one common opponent. Julio fought Matt Vanda twice in 2008. In the first fight between them, Chavez emerged with a split-decision triumph that most observers regarded as a gift. In the second fight, the verdict in his favor was more honest.

Duddy fought Vanda in 2009 and won a 99–91, 99–91, 97–93 decision.

And more important, Chavez had a reputation for coming into fights in less-than-stellar condition and fading late. Indeed, in his most recent outing (against Troy Rowland), he'd been so out of shape that at times he looked like a caricature of himself.

Not coming to a fight in the best shape possible is the first step toward quitting in a fight.

"Julio wasn't putting in the effort that is needed to be a world-class fighter," Bob Arum acknowledged. "You can have all the skills. But if you're not training properly and you struggle to make weight, you're not going to give a first-class performance. Finally, Julio listened. He understood that Duddy is better than all of the other guys he's fought and that he had to raise his game to beat John."

In the past, Julio had trained in Mexico with his uncles, Rodolfo Chavez and Miguel Molleda. For Chavez-Duddy, he trained in Los Angeles with Freddie Roach.

Chavez had visited Roach at the Wild Card Gym in Los Angeles earlier this year. "The day I saw him train Pacquiao was the day I decided I want to be part of this," Julio said later. "If I wanted bigger and better things, I had to make a change. I was used to doing my own thing; and I knew that I couldn't train that way if I want to be great. The fight against Rowland and the first fight against Vanda were the worst times of my life. I had to lose twelve pounds in three days before the Rowland fight. That's when I told myself, 'I can't go on like this. I knew I had to make a change. So why not do it with the best."

Roach had expected to begin work with Chavez in early-May, but Julio was a no-show in Los Angeles. It was unclear whether that was because of visa problems or ambivalence on Chavez's part.

"It got to a point where I was going to give him one more day and then call the whole thing off," Freddie remembers. "You want six to eight weeks preparation time for a situation like this. And when Julio arrived, we only had four weeks. Also, I'd heard all the stories about how he's lazy and he won't do this and he won't do that. I'm not going to yell at a grown man. The way I look at it is; we'll discuss what to do. Then, if you don't want to do it, I don't want to be with you. There was an over-under on how long Julio would last with me. Most people figured that he'd be gone in a week. But he was great. I saw right away that he wanted to learn. He did everything I asked him to do. He told me that he'd done four weeks of conditioning in Mexico before he came to Los Angeles; so by the time I started working with him, he was in as good shape as he's been in for some of his fights. I pushed him. He never complained. We had a great training camp."

Alex Ariza oversees the conditioning program for Roach's elite fighters.

"In an eight-week camp, you start with strength," Ariza says. "The last three weeks, you focus on footwork and speed. Here, we only had four weeks; so we skipped the strength phase and went right to speed. Julio had always been surrounded by people who let him do whatever he wanted to do. But at the Wild Card, he wasn't the one who dictated the terms. The first day, I woke him up at five o'clock in the morning to go running. The next day, he was up at five o'clock on his own, ready to go. He responded well to every challenge we put to him."

Initially, Chavez had doubts regarding parts of his new training regimen. "Alex made me drink at least one gallon a water every day," he recalled shortly before fighting Duddy. "I said to him, 'I won't make weight.' And Freddie told me, 'Don't worry about it. Alex knows what he's doing.'"

As for the overall picture, Chavez noted, "Any time you make a move to the unknown, you get nervous. I wasn't sure what to expect. But I have never been with a trainer as good as Freddie. I had heard great things about him. But until you are with him, you don't know what he's capable of doing. The things they ask me to do are not hard to do. They just ask that it be done at a certain pace. I was not used to working that intense for that long a time. I needed someone to direct me and show me what I needed to do. Before, I didn't have a belief in my conditioning to do all the things I wanted to do in the ring. Now I know I'm in the best physical shape that I've ever been in and I am well prepared. This fight is my biggest challenge. Duddy is a very strong, very good fighter. But I'm very confident. This is the start of the big part of my career."

Roach had a similar view.

"We know what we have in front of us, and we'll be ready for it," the trainer said of Chavez-Duddy. "Julio is in great shape. He knows he can go twelve rounds without getting tired. He isn't quite where I want him to be with the moves we've been working on. But he's improving and he knows what he has to do to win the fight. Julio's jab will be the key if he uses it the way he should. I want him to box and keep Duddy at the end of his jab. If he does that, he can make it an easy fight. If he brawls, it gives Duddy a chance. Julio likes to go inside and go to the body. I'm not going to take that away from him. It's in his DNA. But I want him to get inside in an intelligent way."

The odds were 7-to-2 in favor of Chavez. For the first time in Duddy's career, he was an underdog. Once the bell rings, good looks and charm don't help. Moreover, as previously noted, there was a belief in some circles that the playing field would be tilted in Chavez's favor.

In the months leading up to the fight, Craig Hamilton placed a series of telephone calls to Dickie Cole (administrator of combat sports for the Texas Department of Licensing and Regulation). His primary concern was the appointment of officials. Technically, the State of Texas would designate the referee and judges. But as a matter of course, Cole was expected to adhere to the recommendations of Jose Sulaiman.

Sulaiman was hardly an impartial observer. Twelve days before the fight, he declared, "This is now the time for Julio to prove if he's ready for a title challenge. If Julio wins, he'll fight for either the middleweight or super-welterweight championship, whichever is available. I believe he's going to be a world champion. He has tremendous opportunities and great ability as a boxer. With his new trainer Freddie Roach, we are going to see the real Chavez."

On June 7th, the WBC advised Top Rank (which informed Hamilton) that the officials for Chavez-Duddy would be referee Jon Schorle (who has homes in Texas and California) and judges Glen Rick Crocker of Texas, Julie Lederman of New York, and Jurgen Langos of Germany. In Hamilton's mind, Langos's appointment cast a pall over the proceedings.

"We know that Sulaiman wants Chavez to win the fight," Craig noted. "If he's bringing a judge all the way from Germany to Texas for a fight between an Irishman and a Mexican, that judge is going to know it too. And the judge is going to understand that, if he scores the fight for Chavez, he's likely to get some very lucrative WBC judging assignments in the future. I know the crowd will be rooting for Chavez. I hope that doesn't include the referee and judges."

Duddy was philosophical when apprised of the situation.

"This is the biggest fight of my career so far," John said. "And I'm not going in it to lose. I know what I bring to the fight. If it's good enough, it's good enough. If it's not, it's not. It's not about Texas; it's not about Chavez's father. When the bell rings, it's just him and me. I expect that this will be the toughest fight of my career. And if I have my way, it's going to be the toughest fight of his career as well. One of two things will happen. If he quits, he quits. And if he fights, the better man will win."

It was a good fast-paced action fight that began with Duddy as the aggressor. Chavez was clearly the quicker of the two men and landed when he got off first. Julio didn't jab in the early going as much as Roach wanted him to. But he found a home for his left hook and lead righthand.

By round four, it was a slugfest. Duddy wanted to brawl. Chavez obliged him, landing the harder more effective punches. Then in round six, John landed a hard counter right that buckled Julio's knees and left him looking momentarily like a man who was trying to walk in a canoe that was floating downriver.

After six rounds, two of the judges had the fight scored dead even. More importantly, it was a war of attrition, which was the fight that John wanted. The second half of the bout was supposed to be his. But the first six rounds had taken more out of him than they'd taken out of Chavez. Julio had landed the harder punches. He was better-conditioned than he'd ever been before. And the seven-year age difference between the fighters was showing.

In round seven, Chavez started beating Duddy up. As the fight wore on, John absorbed hellacious punishment. His face turned an ugly shade of purple and began to swell. Time and time again, he was driven to the ropes. Julio landed blow after blow. John took the punishment and fired back.

"Go out and finish this guy," Roach told Chavez several times between rounds.

Chavez pounded Duddy mercilessly. John simply would not fall.

"Fuck," Freddie muttered more than once during the late rounds. "This guy won't quit."

"I thought about stopping it," Harry Keitt said afterward. "But each time John came back to the corner, he was alert and focused. He kept throwing back. He threw punches the whole twelve rounds."

Rounds eleven and twelve were the two extra rounds that Team Duddy had wanted. Now they were a walk through fire with no realistic hope of victory. Chavez was loading up on his punches, confident that John had lost the power to hurt him. But John kept fighting with everything that was in him. He wasn't just trying to survive. He was trying to win.

Chavez didn't want it more. He just fought better.

This writer scored the bout 117–111 for Chavez. That was in line with Julie Lederman (117–111) and Glen Rick Crocker (116–112). Jurgen Langos watched the fight from La-La Land and gave every round to Chavez. That warrants a word on the officiating.

Jon Schorle's conduct of the fight enhanced his reputation as an honest competent referee. His pre-fight instructions were a model of clarity. During the fight, he performed his duties in a manner that ensured a level playing field, while closely monitoring Duddy's physical condition as the bout progressed.

Lederman and Crocker (both capable judges) turned in scorecards that were well within the range of honest competent scoring.

That leaves Langos. His responsibility wasn't to score every round for Julio Cesar Chavez Jr. It was to turn in a scorecard that accurately reflected the fight.

There were seven rounds in Chavez-Duddy that Julio clearly won (three, four, seven, eight, nine, ten, and eleven). John clearly won round six. Rounds one, two, five, and twelve were up for grabs. To score the fight a shutout for Chavez strains credibility. And it was particularly offensive given the courage that Duddy showed in the face of brutal adversity.

The most charitable explanation for Langos's scorecard is that Jurgen was tired after his long trip from Germany and might have had trouble concentrating on the fight. State athletic commissions in the United States should make a point of sparing him the burden of similar trips in the future. It's not enough to have two honest capable judges at a fight. Suppose Chavez-Duddy had been close, with Lederman and Crocker split on the issue of which fighter won. Langos would have cast the deciding vote.

Apologists for the WBC might say that Langos "did no harm" this time.

He could have.

In the dressing room after the fight, Duddy looked like he'd been beaten up by three men in an alley. He was holding an icepack, shifting it from one eye to the other. His face was bruised, battered, and swollen.

John had fought with incredible heart and earned respect for his courage. But he isn't boxing to win moral victories. He went into the sport to make life-changing money and become middleweight champion of the world.

"I'm sorry," he told Hamilton. "I let you down."

"Don't say you're sorry," Craig responded. 'You did everything you could. You're my man."

A commission doctor asked for a post-fight urine sample. When the task was done, John signed a label that would be affixed to the tube and asked, "Do I have to walk in a straight line and touch my nose, or can I have my check now?"

Boxing is a humbling sport.

John's father came into the room.

"I love you, son," Mick Duddy said.

Father and son embraced.

John left the room with a towel wrapped around his waist and went next-door to shower.

"There's no way you can be around this guy and not fall in love with him," Hamilton said. "As a fighter, he gives you everything he has, in the gym and in every fight. As a person, you couldn't find a nicer guy. He has a kind word for everyone. He's appreciative when you do something for him. He takes his responsibilities seriously; personally and professionally. I wish there were more people like him."

Duddy returned, dried himself, and dressed.

"You don't have to go to the press conference," Craig told him.

"I don't mind," John said. "If I can't deal with losing, I shouldn't be in boxing."

There was a quick call to his wife. "I'm all right," John assured her. "I tried my hardest . . . I love you . . . I'll see you tomorrow."

Then he went to the post-fight press conference and told the gathering, "Julio fought a good fight. There was a lot of pressure on him. He performed and answered all the questions I asked of him. I took him into deep water. And yes, he can swim."

It's unclear where Chavez will go from here. His camp and WBC president Jose Sulaiman would love him to become a world champion. Toward that end, the WBC rates Julio #1 at 154 pounds. And he now holds the organization's 160-pound "silver belt." But things get complicated from there.

Sergio Martinez is the WBC middleweight champion. Realistically speaking, Chavez would have little chance against Martinez at this point in their respective careers. Alex Ariza thinks that, with proper conditioning, Julio can return to 154 pounds and fight for the now-vacant WBC super-welterweight throne.

"Julio is an athlete," Ariza says. "He's only twenty-four years old. He understands boxing much better than people give him credit for, and we've barely tapped into his potential. Give Freddie two or three full training camps and give me the eight weeks that Julio is in those camps. A lot of people will be surprised at what we accomplish."

Then Ariza voices the view, "I honestly believe that, if Julio had stayed in Mexico and come into this fight like he came into his earlier fights, John would have knocked him out. John threw a lot more combinations than we expected him to throw. He gave Julio a lot more angles than we thought he would. He was strong. He was in good condition and resilient. His fight plan was perfect for the Chavez of eight weeks ago. And I've never seen a fighter fire back harder when he's hurt than John did. He never went into survival mode. There wasn't a moment in the fight when he wasn't trying to win. He doesn't have the physical gifts that Julio has. That was the difference. But he showed incredible determination and heart. John made a fan out of me. He personifies sportsmanship and everything that's good about boxing."

Duddy wants to keep fighting. "In all walks of life, we have our ups and downs," he said after losing to Chavez. "Boxing is no different. You get up before the count of ten and move on. I hate to lose, but you can't walk around with it."

"You can't overreact to a loss," Hamilton added. "Did this loss hurt? Absolutely. It hurt watching John get beaten up and it hurts in terms of his career. But in any other sport, 29-and-2 is a good record. In boxing, it's good too."

The plan now is for Duddy to have one or two comeback bouts; then maybe a fight against Yuri Foreman at Madison Square Garden. Chavez is still a work in progress. John is pretty much a finished product. He's a solid fighter with a fighting heart. In the ring, that's not always enough. But he's at peace with himself and who he is.

"I love my life," John said the day after his loss to Chavez. "I have a wonderful wife. I'm fortunate to have the family and friends I do. And there's boxing. I wish I'd performed better last night. But I am what I want to be."

Michael Grant has the physical assets to be a champion. But the intangibles aren't there.

Michael Grant: The Reluctant Dragon

On the morning of April 29, 2000, Michael Grant had a 31-and-0 record with 22 knockouts and was regarded by many (including the decision makers at HBO) as the heir apparent to the heavyweight throne. His early opponents looked as though they'd been in a cement mixer when he finished with them. People marveled at his size, strength, stamina, and coordination. Some observers called him the best pure athlete ever to take up boxing and a prototype of the heavyweights who would reign in the new millennium.

That night, Grant was knocked down four times by Lennox Lewis in a bout that ended in the second round. Michael's proponents noted that he'd started boxing late in life and turned pro with only twelve amateur bouts to his credit. "Give him time," they said. "He can still be a great fighter."

But Bobby Miles, who worked with Don Turner in training Grant for the Lewis fight, sounded a cautionary note.

"The problem," Miles said, "is that Michael doesn't really like boxing. It's just not something he likes to do; and he still thinks like an athlete, not a fighter. In most sports, there's a code of sportsmanship and gentlemanly conduct. If you're a fighter, you have to approach each fight like a gladiator in the Roman Coliseum. You have to be mean. You're fighting for survival. Tyson, Duran, guys like that; they understand. All great fighters do. Ray Leonard might have smiled and said nice things, but in the ring he was a mean son-of-a-bitch. Right now, Michael just isn't mean enough."

Thirteen months after losing to Lewis, Grant returned to the ring and was stopped in one round when he broke his ankle in a freak occurrence after being knocked down by Jameel McCline. That was followed by seven consecutive knockout victories. Then, in 2003, Michael was knocked down four times by Dominick Guinn in a bout that was halted in the seventh round.

In the seven years following his loss to Guinn, Grant had eight fights. All of them were wins. None was against a legitimate top-forty fighter. On August 21, 2010, Michael returned to the spotlight to fight Tomasz Adamek at The Prudential Center in Newark. His largest purse since losing to Guinn had been $25,000. For Adamek, he would be paid $75,000. More important, a victory would catapult him back to the bigtime.

Adamek was a 10-to-1 betting favorite. But those odds seemed long, given the fact that Grant is a well-conditioned 6-foot-7-inch 260-pound athlete, who has skills and would outweigh his opponent by 44 pounds.

"Everybody is talking about how he's slick," Michael said several days before the fight. "I don't see no slickness. He's a very simple ABC-type guy. I don't see him getting beyond my jab. And if you're getting past my jab, you're in range of my right hand. Anytime they step one inch past that jab, it's the right hand that's coming."

Still, Grant looked nervous in the dressing room before the fight; similar to the way he'd looked on the night he fought Lennox Lewis. A fighter can go into a fight thinking that (1) he will win; (2) he should win; or (3) he might find a way to pull it off. Michael appeared to be contemplating the third option.

Craig Hamilton co-managed Grant from 1995 through the loss to Guinn. They parted amicably at a time when Craig felt that Michael didn't appreciate what was being done for him on the managerial end. Now Hamilton was in Michael's dressing room to show support as a friend.

"I don't have a good feeling about this fight," Craig said as he left the dressing room and moved toward his seat at ringside. Michael is bigger than Adamek. He's stronger than Adamek. He's by far the better athlete. He might even be faster. And Adamek can be hit; he's not Pernell Whitaker. If Michael uses his physical gifts, Adamek will be in trouble. But Michael won't use his physical gifts because he doesn't have the instincts of a fighter. Adamek is very tough mentally, and Michael isn't."

The Prudential Center was a sea of red and white, the colors of the Polish flag. Virtually all of the 10,972 fans in attendance were rooting for Adamek and cheered his every move.

Grant began the fight in a posture akin to survival mode. Adamek was in front of him and there to be hit. But it was jab . . . jab . . . jab . . .

Worse, it was a stay-away-from-me jab, not a hurting jab. And there was no right hand behind it.

In rounds three and four, it appeared as though Grant might be able to impose his size and strength on Adamek. He shook the smaller man each time he landed solidly. But Tomasz continued to outwork Michael and initiate the action.

More significantly, there are fighters who throw more punches with a broken hand than Grant did with his healthy right hand over the course of twelve rounds. Consciously or subconsciously, he seemed to be telling himself, "If I make this a firefight, Adamek will fire back. If I go all out, Adamek will go all out too. So why don't I play it safe and reduce this to my jab against Tomasz's flurries."

By round eight, Grant had a tired cruiserweight in front of him, and Adamek was cut above the left eye. At that point, it was obvious to everyone in the arena except Michael that he should jump on Tomasz and try to manhandle him. Instead, he kept jabbing.

In the late rounds, it seemed as though Adamek was struggling to hang on physically and Grant was struggling to hold on mentally.

Finally, in round twelve, Michael came out hard. But it was too, little too late.

The judges scored the bout 118–110, 118–111, and 117–111 for Adamek. This observer had it 116–112. The bottom line was that Tomasz wanted it more and dug deeper. Grant was good enough to beat Adamek, but he didn't seem to know it.

"It was a disappointing effort," Hamilton said afterward. "But that's Michael. This fight meant so much to him. He's thirty-eight years old. He needs money. If he'd won, he would have been in line for a half-million-dollar payday in his next fight; maybe more. But he fought the way he always does. It's not a question of courage. Every time in his career that Michael has been knocked down, he's gotten back up. But he lacks confidence, and confidence is crucial to a fighter."

"Michael had a fighter in front of him tonight who was scoring points but not really hurting him," Hamilton continued. "He could have let go with his punches and given so much more than he gave. But his number-one priority is always to make sure he can get to the end of a fight. Pacing yourself is one thing, but a fighter has to open up from time to time. Michael is in survival mode from round one on. Then it's round twelve and he knows he can get to the end of the fight, so he opens up. But it's too late. What can I say? Michael wasn't cut out to be a fighter. The fact that he got as far as he did in boxing is testament to what a great athlete he is. He could have accomplished so much more if he'd had the temperament of a fighter. But he doesn't, and that's that."

Throughout 2010, Manny Pacquiao's fame kept growing.

Manny Pacquiao: The People's Champion

Outside the ring, fully clothed, Manny Pacquiao looks almost delicate and vulnerable. The first reaction that many people have on meeting him is surprise that he's so small. His voice is soft. There's a gentle quality about him.

But in the ring, Pacquiao is a destroyer. He won his first world title in 1998 at 112 pounds and hasn't lost since dropping a twelve-round decision to Erik Morales in 2005. Since then, he has been undefeated in thirteen fights, including knockout victories over Morales (twice), Oscar De La Hoya, Ricky Hatton, and Miguel Cotto. At age thirty-one, he has collected belts against credible competition in eight weight divisions.

Pacquiao's profile exploded following his 2008 stoppage of De La Hoya. Thereafter, *Time Magazine* observed, "His private life, as well as the ins and outs and ups and downs of his training regimen, are tabloid fodder."

But Pacquiao is more than a celebrity curiosity. Earlier this year, the voters in Sarangani province elected him to Congress. He's a unifying force for Filipinos at home and around the world. In its most recent year-end issue, *Time* included Pacquiao on its list of "people who matter" and referenced him as a "living legend" and "savior," both for boxing and the Filipino people.

"Manny Pacquiao is this generation's Muhammad Ali," says his promoter, Bob Arum. "I have never promoted a fighter who has so captivated a country and a people the way that Manny does. He's idolized and followed by every Filipino and his appeal is worldwide. Thanks to Manny Pacquiao, boxing is now retaking its proper place on the world stage."

Numbers vary from day to day. But as of this writing, typing "Manny Pacquiao" into Google's search engine engenders 19,200,000 "results." Floyd Mayweather elicits less than 10 percent of that total.

And the Pacquiao phenomenon keeps growing. At a time when boxing is struggling in the United States, he's becoming a crossover star. Earlier this month, 16,500,000 viewers saw him on *60 Minutes.*

"Manny Pacquiao," Jim Lampley notes, "is having a lovefest with the world while beating the crap out of people."

The lovefest continued in Dallas on November 13, 2010, when Pacquiao squared off against former welterweight champion Antonio Margarito.

Pacquiao-Margarito was seen by many as a morality play. Margarito is regarded as a man of questionable sportsmanship as a consequence of illegal inserts that were found in his handwraps prior to a 2009 fight against Shane Mosley. His trainer at the time, Javier Capetillo, took responsibility for the incident, saying that he'd grabbed the wrong knucklepads "by mistake" and that Antonio was unaware of the problem.

Capetillo, appropriately, has been banned from practicing his trade in the United States. Margarito's license to box was revoked by the California State Athletic Commission, which refused to reinstate him earlier this year.

Arum, who promotes Margarito, defends his fighter, saying, "What really irritates me is that there is not one fact to indicate that Margarito knew there was anything wrong with the handwraps. You cannot gloss over that by saying, 'He must have known.' What do you mean, he must have known? What kind of legal standard is that?"

Arum is correct in that the California commission never made a serious effort to prove that Margarito was complicit with regard to the illegal handwraps. The CSAC could have asked the district attorney's office to conduct a criminal investigation that would have included DNA testing and interviews with both Margarito and Capetillo conducted by trained law enforcement personnel. But that request was never made.

No one except Capetillo (and possibly Margarito) knows how and when illegal handwraps first found their way into Antonio's arsenal. But just as a mugger who has been caught in the act by police swears that this is the first time he has ever attempted such a dastardly deed, there are those who assume that Margarito used the same inserts without being caught in previous fights.

Pacquiao has been on the receiving end of ugly innuendo regarding the alleged use of performance-enhancing drugs, so he understood what

Margarito was going through. Still, Manny was of the view that it was "impossible" that Antonio did not know.

Pacquiao's trainer, Freddie Roach, went further, saying, "I think that Margarito's gloves were loaded in some of his earlier fights and I also think that they were loaded in the gym. You'd want to practice with the inserts, so you know how they feel and what they do to your hands. Rashad Holloway and Craig McEwan both sparred with Margarito before the Mosley fight. They told me that he was one of the hardest punchers they'd ever faced. But Victor Ortiz and Ernie Zavala sparred with him and told me he punched like a girl."

Knowledgeable people differ in good faith as to whether Margarito should have been given the opportunity to fight Pacquiao. Some think that the decision by the Texas Department of Licensing and Regulation to license him without a hearing was a thumb in the eye to boxing. Virtually everyone agrees that the situation was further exacerbated when Antonio and his trainer, Robert Garcia, were seen on HBO's *24/7* series making fun of the incident by taping "cinderblocks" to Margarito's hands.

"When you're caught doing something, you don't make fun of it," Roach told Lem Satterfield of Fanhouse.com. "Boxing is our sport. He put plaster of Paris on his hands and he's making jokes about it? I think Margarito is an asshole."

Be that as it may; Margarito was fighting in Dallas for a purse of $3,000,000 plus an upside based on pay-per-view buys. A win would give him everything he'd had before and more; with the exception of his good name.

Pacquiao-Margarito was contracted for a catchweight of 150 pounds. That enabled the WBC to put it's 154-pound belt on the table (for a sanctioning fee, of course) and allowed the promotion to talk about the possibility of an unprecedented eighth world title for Pacquiao. Trainer Naazim Richardson (the man who discovered the inserts in Margarito's knucklepads prior to the Mosley fight) put the matter in perspective when he said, "Forget the belts. What matters is that, fight after fight, Pacquiao puts his ass on the line."

Then the plot thickened. There were dire reports out of Pacquiao's training camp in the Philippines, which began with four weeks in Baguio followed by a week in Manila.

"Manny is having the worst training camp of his career," Roach said. "His focus is not 100 percent. He told me after three days of training, 'I miss my job.' I said, 'This is your job.' He said, 'No, I miss congress.' Stuff like that scares me. He hasn't been consistent. There have been too many distractions. Manila was the worst because they all wanted him. He even missed a day of training; he had to meet the president. I said, 'Who gives a fuck about the president? We have a fight coming up.'"

Roach has a well-deserved reputation for candor. When he talks, people tend to believe him.

In late-October, Team Pacquiao journeyed to Los Angeles for two weeks of final preparation. Then it descended on Dallas.

There's no entourage like a boxing entourage, and Pacquiao's was substantial. Manny had chartered an American Airlines 757 that brought 180 people from the Philippines to the United States. "Air Pacquiao" cost him $120,000 plus food, lodging, and fight tickets for many of the travelers. Peter Nelson (who is collaborating with Roach on the trainer's autobiography) heralded their arrival.

"When Pacquiao fights in Cowboys Stadium," Nelson wrote, "his countrymen will colonize Arlington, Texas, forming a populace replete with advisors, cooks, priests, security, political chiefs-of-staff, a five-piece band, mentors, apprentices, past exiles for crimes now forgiven, future ones for crimes yet committed, and, of course, his mother. Where he goes, his people follow. They have nowhere else to be but living on his largesse. Manny Pacquiao has become the 7,108th island of the Philippines."

At the final pre-fight press conference on November 10th in Dallas, Roach proclaimed himself satisfied with Pacquiao's physical and mental condition. "Manny catches up quickly," Freddie said. "In the past, he spoiled us. Usually, he's ready to fight after five weeks of training camp. This time, there were some distractions and he wasn't always there mentally like I wanted him to be, so it took the full eight weeks. But when we got to Los Angeles, everything was fine."

Meanwhile, an ugly diversion had intruded upon the proceedings.

Roach suffers from Parkinsonism, believed to have been caused by blows to the head sustained during his boxing career. On Tuesday of fight week, a video that showed Margarito, stablemate Brandon Rios, and Robert Garcia making fun of Freddie's symptoms surfaced on the Internet. Margarito was seen holding his shaking arms in front of him and moaning, "Oh, Freddie Roach." Garcia pointed to Rios (whose head was tilted to the side and shaking while he pretended to have trouble speaking) and said, "Hey, that's Freddie Roach."

Margarito, Garcia, and Rios should have apologized at the Wednesday press conference. Instead, they tried to justify their conduct, saying that they were simply mocking Roach's inadequacies as a fighter.

Roach has a thick skin, but the video bothered him. "I got a lot of calls that there was a video out there making fun of me," he said at the press conference. "I don't have a computer with me, so my assistant brought it over. I had trouble sleeping last night. I wanted to fight these guys. I know I'm too old and I can't beat them up, but I hate these guys. I can't do anything about what they did, but you know what? It's okay. They'll pay for it."

Finally, on Thursday morning, Garcia called Roach and apologized. Then, at the undercard press conference that same day, Rios said he was sorry. Margarito appeared after Rios (claiming without much credibility that the video had been unfairly edited) and declared, "I will never make fun of Freddy Roach or anyone with that disease." But unlike Rios, Antonio did use the word "apologize."

"I was in a bad mood for a while about the videos," Roach said afterward. "They didn't just make fun of me. They made fun of a whole society of people. But Robert apologized, and I felt like it was a sincere apology. I think they realize that they went a bit too far. I'm a forgiving person and I accept their apology. This isn't *The Freddie Roach Story.* Let's just get on with the fight."

Ah, yes; the fight. Pacquiao was a 4-to-1 favorite. And in the days leading up to the encounter, Roach explained why:

- "Margarito is tough; he'll come to win. But I've watched tons of film on him. He's always the same, completely predictable. He winds up on all of his punches, so you can see them coming a mile away. He likes to exchange and he's hittable. When Manny can hit somebody, I usually don't worry that much about the fight."

- "Margarito will come out attacking. We'll feint a lot because he chases the feint; give him a lot of movement, side to side; never let him set his feet. We'll see a competitive first four rounds. Then Manny will start breaking him down. He won't be able to handle Manny's speed. He'll begin feeling Manny's power. Manny will beat him up badly. This will not be a difficult fight for us. I don't see any issues."

- "I'm not worried about Margarito. He's made to order for us. I don't see sound fundamentals. He has poor footwork. He doesn't cut the ring off. He follows his opponent around. And he's too slow to beat Manny. You can watch Manny on TV and say, 'Oh he's fast.' But you don't know how fast until you get in the ring with him. And there's no sparring partner in the world that can prepare you to fight Manny because no one else in the world can fight like him. And another thing; when people fight Manny, they aren't prepared for his speed but they also aren't prepared for his power. I'll be disappointed if Manny doesn't knock him out."

Most observers agreed that, if Margarito had an edge, it was his size. He was five inches taller than Pacquiao and most likely would outweigh Manny on fight night by at least fifteen pounds.

"Size doesn't win fights," Roach countered. "Skill does. And Manny is the most skilled fighter in the world."

"Stop thinking of Pacquiao as a small fighter," Naazim Richardson added. "All of us once weighed ten pounds."

But size in boxing translates into power and the ability to take a punch. That's why the sport has weight divisions. At some point, big becomes too big to handle.

"Boxing history is rife with great fighters who went one weight class too high," Bart Barry wrote. "Margarito's relentlessness would not be enough if he were Pacquiao's size. But he is much bigger. Margarito will lope forward, hands low and wide, smiling as Pacquiao hits him fifty times every round. He will not be discouraged. He will be the largest man Pacquiao has faced. He will be a man who fights with a special kind of resentment. He will be outclassed but not outwilled."

Margarito's battle plan was pressure, pressure, and more pressure. Wear Pacquiao down. Suffocate him with punches. He would be more concerned with doing damage to Pacquiao's physical well-being than protecting his own.

"He's a great fighter," Margarito said of Pacquiao. "We all know that he's fast and lands punches from all angles. But I think it's impossible that he'll have the power of a super-welterweight. He might hit me with five to one at first, but I'm too strong for him. I will gradually break him down and knock him out."

And there was another issue. In truth, Pacquiao would be coming into the fight in less than optimum physical condition.

Like Muhammad Ali before him, Pacquiao feeds off distractions. They keep his mind fresh in the gym and provide an escape from the emotional pressures of boxing. But there came a time when distractions took Ali away from the gym more than they should have and his lack of focus on boxing became a problem. He stopped pushing himself to the extent necessary to maintain his previous level of ring excellence. A sad decline followed.

Sixteen days before Pacquiao-Margarito, Top Rank matchmaker Bruce Trampler watched Pacquiao train at the Wild Card Gym in Los Angeles and reported, "I've never seen Manny look this bad. He was flat and listless. He was faking timeouts. 'My headgear is loose' and stuff like that. He's not where he should be, and Freddie says that he needs two weeks more than he has to get him ready. Manny just doesn't seem to be as motivated this time as he has in the past. It seems like training is a job for him now instead of a game that he enjoys playing."

"I also watched Margarito train," Trampler continued. "He looks very motivated. He's in tremendous shape. He came into camp ten pounds lighter than he usually does. When Manny fought De La Hoya and Hatton, they were dead meat. Cotto was on a downward slide when Manny beat him. Margarito might be as good now as he was before the fall from grace. He's slow and his punches are long and slow, which is to Manny's advantage. But he'll throw so many punches that he'll land some big ones; especially since Manny is so offensive-minded and might not be in good enough shape to move for twelve rounds."

One day later, Pacquiao traveled to Las Vegas to attend a rally on behalf of Nevada senator Harry Reid, who was locked in a tight re-election battle against Sharron Angle. There are 50,000 Filipino-American voters in Nevada.

That diversion was troubling to Alex Ariza (Pacquiao's strength and conditioning coach). Three days before the fight, Ariza put the matter in perspective.

"The best shape I ever saw Manny in was for the Cotto fight," Ariza noted. "He was a relentless juggernaut in training for that one. He never had a bad sparring session. He was hurting everyone he hit. He was 100 percent ready for Cotto and he was close to 100 percent for Hatton. The Clottey fight, I'd say he was at 90 percent. This time it's less. He's in shape, but he's not in Manny Pacquiao shape."

"Manny did very little physical work between the Clottey fight and the start of training camp for this one," Ariza elaborated. "I wanted to start right in on strength and conditioning, but he wasn't ready. And once we started, he was cutting corners. There was excuse after excuse. He missed sessions for Congress; he missed sessions for physical ailments. He had plantar fasciitis on his left foot and that became an excuse for not doing sprint work that we normally would have done. Then he had an excuse for not doing the swimming that he was supposed to do instead of the sprint work. Manny controlled the tempo of his own training this time. He took breaks when he wanted to take breaks and rested when he wanted to rest. Margarito won't let him do that. Strength and conditioning work is hard; it's supposed to be hard. Manny stopped doing some of the things that were hard. Then he stopped the strength and conditioning work altogether two weeks earlier than he should have if he was going to have maximum endurance."

Why did Pacquiao make those choices?

"I'd say a number of factors played into it," Ariza answered. "The fear factor that he had in the past doesn't seem to be there. Being in Congress requires more time than any of his previous outside activities did. And being in Congress has taken away some of his mental focus. Manny is passionate about being in Congress, and that has shifted some of his passion away from boxing. At this point, there's nothing he can do to improve his condition. From now on, it's all psychological, so we have to do everything we can to reassure Manny and make him feel that he's at 100 percent. But when the fight is over, I'll sit him down and tell him, 'Never again.' I think, deep down inside, Manny knows that he could have done more to get ready for this fight. And there's a price you pay on the night of a fight when you've done less than you should. I don't know what that price will be. Will he tire more easily? Will he take ten more punches than he should? Twenty punches? It's a good feeling for a fighter to know that he's going into the ring in the best shape possible and fully prepared. And it's an uneasy feeling to go in with something less."

An hour after Ariza spoke those words, Pacquiao finished a workout in Longhorn Exhibit Hall E (a huge room in the Gaylord Texan Hotel that had been converted into a makeshift gym). Wearing red trunks and a blue sweatshirt, Manny watched as Freddie Roach worked with Amir Khan and Julio Cesar Chavez Jr; two of the trainer's other fighters.

By 7:45 PM, a hundred invited guests had gathered at the far end of the room. There were tables and chairs for thirty of them. The rest were standing. Pacquiao donned a straw hat and walked over to a group of musicians that included three guitarists, a keyboard player, and drummer (known collectively as "The Manny Pacquiao Band"). Two back-up vocalists joined them. For the next seventy-five minutes, Manny sang.

"I bless the day that I was born for you . . . Two hearts that beat as one . . . I can't resist your touch . . ."

"At this point, it's all about keeping Manny happy," Rob Peters (the point man in Pacquiao's security detail) explained. "He loves doing this; it relaxes him. Right now, he's having fun, singing love songs. And Margarito is on a treadmill somewhere, killing himself to make weight."

"I'm not worried about Manny's concentration at this stage of the game," Roach added. "Singing puts his mind in a good place. It makes him happy, and he's a much better fighter when he's happy. Besides, Manny won't get tired singing. If he does, I'll have more than his singing to worry about."

On Friday afternoon, the fighters weighed in at Cowboys Stadium. There was the usual pageantry. Michael Buffer warmed up the crowd. WBC president Jose Sulaiman presented Dallas Cowboys owner Jerry Jones with a statue of an Olmec warrior in recognition of Jones's designation by the WBC as its "Man of the Year."

Two days earlier, at the final pre-fight press conference, Sulaiman had presented Bob Arum with an identical statue as "one of the two greatest promoters of the past three hundred years."

Jones looked at the statue as though Sulaiman had taken a wad of chewing gum out of his mouth and handed it to him.

Then the fighters got on the scales. Margarito was at the maximum weight allowed; 150 pounds.

Pacquiao disrobed. His body wasn't quite as defined as it had been for recent fights . . . 144.6 pounds.

On the night of the fight, Freddie Roach arrived at dressing room F300 at Cowboys Stadium at 5:45 PM. Peter Nelson and training assistant Billy Keane were with him. A commission inspector was also present.

Roach is a man of little formality. Asked once what his full name was, he answered, "Fred Steven Roach."

Is his middle name spelled with a "v" or "ph"?

"I don't know. I'll have to look it up on my birth certificate."

Roach didn't seek fame. It found him. He was schooled as a fighter and then as a trainer by the legendary Eddie Futch. Looking back on the experience, Freddie recalls, "The hardest thing in the world for a fighter is when he realizes that he won't be a champion. I know because I had to face that."

Futch told Roach that he was taking too many punches and had to retire. In recent years, Freddie has had that same conversation with Oscar De La Hoya, Bernard Hopkins, and James Toney.

How did it go?

"Oscar told me that I was a loser, although he didn't say it to my face. He said it to the media. Bernard told me, 'You just lost your check.' And James told me to go fuck myself."

Roach lives for boxing. He could retire now and be financially comfortable for the rest of his life. But he loves the sport and likes helping young men achieve their dreams. The fact that he was never a champion drives him and has made him a better trainer.

Emanuel Steward says, "There are very few guys I'd trust my fighters to these days, but Freddie is one of them. He's old school. He understands basics and teaches his fighters basics before he goes on to anything else. He's a great strategist. He's creative. He's honest with his fighters. He doesn't bullshit them to keep his job. And he knows what he's doing during a fight. When a fighter comes back to the corner after a bad round, the trainer has to do more than shout at him to win it for his kids. He has to explain to the fighter what he did wrong and how to correct the problem. When Freddie's fighter comes back to the corner between rounds, he gives him something useful to work with."

How good is Roach? Paulie Malignaggi says that, when he watched a tape of the HBO telecast of his fight against Amir Khan, he listened to Roach's corner instructions.

"After the third or fourth round," Malignaggi recounts, "Freddie told Amir, 'I need you to feint. If you feint, he's going to drop down and then you do this.' I'm saying to myself, 'Wow. That is my reaction to a feint. I never focused on it before, but that is how I respond.' Freddie knew me better than I knew myself."

When it's crunch time during a fight, Roach has ice in his veins. But he never takes himself too seriously. Pacquiao's rise to glory has given him a certain celebrity status of his own. Freddie has been the subject of numerous high-profile media stories, leading to quite a bit of attention from the opposite sex.

Two days before Pacquiao-Margarito, a young blonde was chatting Roach up in the hotel.

"You don't want to hang out with me," Freddie told her. "I eat at Denny's."

One gets the feeling that Eddie Futch is looking down on Roach and smiling. One also gets the feeling that history will treat Freddie kindly. Like Futch, he ennobles the sport of boxing.

When a fighter's hands are wrapped, the man doing the wrapping runs long strips of tape between each finger (other than the thumb) on each hand. Most trainers apply the tape flat; six strips in all. Roach likes to roll each strip vertically so they resemble sticks of incense. He calls the strips "ligaments."

Sitting in Pacquiao's dressing room, Roach began rolling the strips while conversing with Nelson and Keane.

"Manny loves to watch himself on television," Freddie said. "Between rounds in Vegas, he watches himself on those big video screens. The first time it happened, I tapped him on the cheek to get his attention and he told me, 'I'm listening.' In Cowboys Stadium, he can't see the screen because it's above the ring, so I won't have to compete for his attention."

"Sometimes, when we're getting ready to fight a guy who I know does something dirty, I'll try to teach Manny the same tactic for retaliation. Manny will say to me, 'Coach; I can't do that.' But there's one trick I taught him that he likes. If the other guy goes wide with a hook to the body, you jam an elbow into the inside of his forearm before he lands. It's legal, but it hurts like hell. [Guillermo] Rigondeaux did it to me once, and I had a bruise on the inside of my forearm for a month."

Pacquiao is Roach's signature fighter. There's remarkable chemistry between them. Emanuel Steward observes, "It's rare that you have a great boxer and a great trainer and the chemistry between them is this good. That's one of the reasons they've done so well together."

Roach began working with Pacquiao in 2001. At the time, Manny had awesome physical gifts but was largely a one-dimensional fighter. Jab, jab, straight lefthand. Roach improved his charge's footwork, balance, and defensive skills; added a right hook to his arsenal; and brought consistency to his technique.

"Building a fighter from scratch is good in that the fighter doesn't have any bad habits," Freddie says. "But he doesn't have any good habits either. Trust me; Manny had some good habits when I started with him."

Cutman Miguel Diaz entered the dressing room. He was wearing black pants. Pacquiao won't wear black for a fight and he doesn't like anyone in his corner to wear black either.

"Don't worry about it," Roach told Diaz. "You're wearing a red jacket. Manny won't notice."

At 7:20, by prearrangement, an observer from Margarito's camp entered. Because of the Margarito handwrap scandal, it had been agreed that each side would have a representative in the opposing fighter's dressing room for the entire pre-fight proceedings and each trainer would fashion his fighter's knucklepads in front of the observer and a commission inspector.

Billy Keane left for Margarito's dressing room.

Roach began folding gauze into knucklepads.

At 8:05, Buboy Fernandez (Pacquiao's assistant trainer and longtime friend) arrived; a sure sign that Manny was in the building.

Buboy arranged Pacquiao's trunks, robe, and shoes (a color-coordinated white with gold trim) on a rubdown table.

Diaz's red corner jacket was adorned with advertising logos from a previous fight.

"Buboy," Miguel queried. "Is the advertising on this jacket okay, or will it be a problem?"

"No problem for me," Buboy answered. "They're not paying me for the advertising. They're paying Manny."

At 8:10, Pacquiao entered with thirty-six people in tow. The group included adviser Michael Koncz, Geng Gacal (Manny's longtime lawyer), and Wakee Salud (a close friend).

Word came that Margarito had weighed in on "the unofficial HBO scale" at 170 pounds. With a five-pound deduction for the clothes he was wearing, that translated into 165 pounds. Manny was at least seventeen pounds lighter.

The dressing room was cleared of non-essential personnel.

Pacquiao put on his trunks and did some stretching exercises.

"I'm going over to watch Margarito wrap," Roach told him. "If you need anything, ask Miguel. Is that okay?

Pacquiao nodded.

With Diaz assisting him, Manny started to wrap his own hands. Margarito's representative objected to virtually everything, including the tape provided by the commission and the knucklepads approved by the commission. The inspector overruled the objections.

Margarito's co-manager, Sergio Diaz, entered and lodged more objections. They too were overruled.

Roach returned. Diaz finished wrapping.

At 9:30, there was a problem. Billy Keane telephoned Alex Ariza to report that Margarito was about to take Ephedrine (an appetite suppressant and stimulant) nasally.

"When you stack Ephedrine with caffeine and aspirin," Ariza noted, "you get speed."

Keane said that three cups of coffee had been delivered to Margarito's dressing room.

"It won't show up in his urine unless we test him before the fight," Ariza told Roach. "An ECA stack burns out quickly. A post-fight test will be too late."

Michael Koncz left the dressing room to file a complaint with the commission.

William Kuntz (executive director of the Texas Department of Licensing and Regulation) and Dickie Cole (administrator of combat sports) arrived for an impromptu hearing.

"I want a drug test right now," Roach demanded.

"You focus on what you have to do," Ariza told Pacquiao. "Let the rest of them handle this bullshit.

Pacquiao started doing stretching exercises and shadow boxing.

Robert Garcia entered and complained that no one from the Margarito camp had been present when Roach rolled the ligaments earlier in the evening. He wanted Pacquiao to rewrap.

"It's pieces of tape," Roach countered. "Your guy looked at them and didn't have a problem."

Tempers flared. People from both camps started shouting. Pacquiao looked at Peter Nelson and winked.

Kuntz and Cole announced that they wouldn't administer a pre-fight urine test even though Ephedrine is a controlled drug and its use would be against commission regulations.

Garcia's complaint was overruled.

Keane reported that Margarito had agreed not to use the Ephedrine.

Pacquiao finished warming up.

Once a fighter steps into the ring and the bell for round one sounds, nothing that he has accomplished before matters.

It was a hard-fought battle before an exuberant noisy crowd. The first two rounds were cautiously contested. Margarito was a bit less aggressive than expected. Pacquiao's fast hands kept Antonio at bay.

In round three, Margarito began stalking in more determined fashion. Pacquiao circled, darting in and out, alternating between getting off first and landing sharp counter blows.

In round four, the landscape tilted lopsidedly in Manny's favor.

"Sports are about angles," Roach says. "In any sport, if you can obtain the angle, you put yourself in a better position to win. The basic formula in boxing is that, if you don't stand in front of a guy, you're not going to get hit as much. You put the other guy in a position where he has to move his feet to hit you. If you do that properly—and it's a very quick aggressive move to do it right—when the other guy moves his feet to hit you, he'll turn into your punch. Manny can make that move. Not everybody can."

In the fourth round, Pacquiao raked Margarito with hard lightning-fast punches. One minute into the stanza, he landed a left uppercut as Margarito turned into the blow. Seconds later, Antonio's face was grotesquely swollen and discolored beneath his right eye and blood was dripping from a cut that would require six stitches to close.

Now Margarito was on his back foot, giving ground. Round five was more of the same. But at the start of round six, Manny looked a bit tired. Take away the swelling beneath Antonio's right eye and Margarito might have seemed the fresher of the two men. With thirty seconds left in the round, he backed Pacquiao into the ropes and dug a vicious left hook to the liver. Manny doubled over in pain and spent the next twenty seconds in retreat.

"I was a little worried in the sixth round," Roach admitted afterward.

"He hurt me," Pacquiao would acknowledge.

At that point, Margarito was behind in the fight but very much in it. He'd entered the battle in top physical condition, and the energy level between the combatants seemed to be shifting on some primitive level.

Margarito began round seven by going to the body. Pacquiao, as he'd done before, circled and darted in and out. One of the things that makes him effective is his ability to score while his opponent is punching. The combatants resembled a grizzly bear swatting with his paw at a swarm of killer bees.

Over the next few rounds, Pacquiao landed the more numerous blows, firing back and landing multiple punches each time he was hit. As the bout progressed, he began to take on the look of a man smashing a boulder to pebbles with a sledgehammer.

By round ten, Margarito's right eye was useless and his left eye was closing, which meant that he was fighting with half an eye. The right side of his face was disfigured to the point of mutilation. Referee Laurence Cole stopped the action, raised his left hand to cover Margarito's right eye, and asked the fighter how many fingers he was holding up. Margarito answered. The action resumed. But Antonio was now defenseless against Pacquiao's onslaught.

With twenty seconds left in round ten, as Margarito was plodding hopelessly forward, Pacquiao landed a sharp right hook to the jaw. Antonio's legs buckled and Manny followed with a barrage of punches that left his opponent lurching back to his corner at the bell. He'd been blasted with sixty-four punches during the round; fifty-seven of them, power punches.

The ring doctor examined Margarito briefly from outside the ropes. He couldn't look into Antonio's right eye with a pen-light because the eye was swollen shut.

Round eleven was target practice. On three occasions, Pacquiao stopped his assault and looked toward Cole; in effect, asking him to stop the fight. "Boxing is not for killing," Manny said afterward. But Cole ignored the gesture and the carnage continued; although Pacquiao fought the rest of the bout with what seemed to be a blend of caution and compassion. His concern brought back memories of Bob Fitzsimmons, who said of the brutal beating that he administered to Nonpareil Jack Dempsey in 1891, "I was as kind to him as was possible under the circumstances."

This writer gave Margarito the sixth round. The judges turned in similar cards, scoring the bout 120–108, 119–109, and 118–110 in Pacquiao's favor. Overall, he outlanded Margarito 474 to 229 with a 153-to-32 advantage over the last nine minutes.

After the fight, Pacquiao went to Margarito's dressing room, where Antonio's cuts were being stitched up. They embraced and exchanged words of mutual respect. Then Manny hugged Antonio's wife and left.

Margarito's right orbital bone wasn't just broken. It was splintered. Surgery to repair the damage couldn't be performed until Tuesday, when the swelling had subsided.

Roach was critical of Robert Garcia for allowing the fight to continue. "There's no doubt at all in my mind that he should have stopped it after the eighth round," Freddie said. "Margarito had no chance to win by then and his face was a mess. After round ten, I thought, 'They have to stop it now. If the corner doesn't stop it, someone else will.' But they didn't. Margarito might never fight again after this. For sure, he won't be the same fighter."

Roach weighed his next words carefully before speaking: "Those guys shouldn't have made fun of my physical condition. After what happened tonight, Antonio might have some of the same problems."

Too many people in boxing today who are responsible for stopping a fight don't.

Doctors, cornermen, and referees sometimes forget that fighters have a life beyond the ring. They're not just fighters. They're husbands, fathers, sons. In some instances, they're irrevocably damaged because of punishment they take in the ring.

The cut beneath Margarito's right eye wasn't a major problem. What was happening beneath the cut was. The area swelled up so quickly and in such grotesque fashion that one could assume there was a fracture. That could lead to further splintering of the bone (which happened) and problems with the muscles and nerves around the eye.

Also, there came a time when Margarito had no chance of winning the fight and was no longer able to defend himself. He was still on his feet, but couldn't see the punches coming or stop Pacquiao from landing at will. The only issue was how much more damage (some of it permanent) he would suffer.

After each of the late rounds in Dallas, an HBO cameraman jumped in the ring for a close-up look at Margarito's mutilated features. The ring doctor didn't. In the future, perhaps that process could be reversed.

Meanwhile, Pacquiao's future appears bright. It takes a while to properly assign the word "great" to a fighter. But it can now be said that Manny is great. As David Greisman wrote recently, "He can do it with four hundred punches and he can do it with one. He can do it with power and he can do it with speed. He has stood in with more powerful punchers and taken their hardest shots. He has broken down men who said he could not hurt them."

Pacquiao is so dynamic in the ring that, at times, he seems like a video-game action hero. But what he does is real. He would have been competitive with the best in any era.

Boxing grinds the dreams of most fighters to dust, but Pacquiao's dreams are flourishing. In recent years, his self-belief has grown, both as a fighter and as a person. Ronnie Nathanielsz, who has followed Manny since the formative stages of his career, observes, "What drove him initially was personal. He was fighting to earn a living. After he grew in stature, country and people came first."

Now Pacquiao is a symbol of hope and a true "people's champion." He enjoys that status.

When asked about his purpose in life, Manny answers, "It is to love and to serve. My concern is not only for myself but for what I can give to the people of my country."

Unlike many politicians, he means it. He is what he appears to be and sees the struggle of every Filipino in his own torturous journey.

"I feel what they are feeling because I have been there," Pacquiao says. "I slept in the streets. I ate once a day. Sometimes I just drank water, no food. That was my life before. So hard. I understand the needs of people who need help. My heart hurts when I see people in the street, sleeping. I remember my past when I was young."

Through his work in the ring, Pacquiao has lifted the spirits of his people. Through his work in Congress, he hopes for more tangible gains. He appears to harbor dreams of being elected president of the Philippines. Would that be any more remarkable than what he has accomplished so far?

No sport other than boxing has given rise to an athlete who moved passions, lifted spirits, and impacted on an entire nation in the manner of Joe Louis and Muhammad Ali. Now Manny Pacquiao is having a similar effect in the Philippines and beyond.

We're witnessing a great fighter, who is also a good person. Enjoy the show while it lasts. Manny Pacquiao belongs to the Philippines and to the world. But he also belongs to boxing.

Sergio Martinez vs. Paul Williams showcased boxing at its best.

Martinez-Williams II: The Punch

Boxing is a hunger sport.

All fighters start at the bottom. A rare few make it to the top.

Sergio Martinez was born into poverty. Sports were his way out of the Argentinean ghetto. He was a talented soccer player and cyclist (his first two chosen sports). But his skills in those disciplines were short of world-class. At age twenty, he decided that boxing offered the most promising opportunity to lift himself to a higher socio-economic level. That's late in life to begin learning the sweet science. "But I started at the right time for me," Martinez says. "Too many fighters are pushed into boxing. When I began, I could make the decision to box as an adult."

Martinez turned pro in 1997 and fought 24 of his first 25 fights in Buenos Aires. In 2002, he moved to Spain, where he met Gabriel Sarmiento (his current trainer). Sampson Lewkowicz became his co-manager in 2007 and brought him to the United States. He now lives in Oxnard, California, and is promoted by Lou DiBella.

Martinez is thirty-five years old with 25 knockouts and a 46–2–2 record. His first loss was a seventh-round knockout at the hands of Antonio Margarito ten years ago.

"The loss to Margarito doesn't bother me as much as people think it might," Sergio says. "I had very little experience at the time and ran out of gas. I was much more bothered when I beat Richard Williams [for the IBO 154-pound title in 2003]. After that fight, I looked in the mirror and I couldn't recognize my face. I thought then about giving up boxing. But I didn't know whether it was something I had done wrong in the fight that I could correct or that I just wasn't good enough. So I fought Williams again ten months later and won much more easily. I knew then that I should stay in boxing."

Martinez's only other loss occurred last year in an action-packed fight against Paul Williams. Pierre Benoist turned in a ridiculous 119–110 pro-Williams card. Julie Lederman scored the bout even. Lynne Carter cast the deciding vote 115–113 in Williams's favor.

Four months later, Martinez rebounded with a 116–111, 115–111, 115–112 triumph over Kelly Pavlik to capture the WBC and WBO middleweight titles.

Martinez's ring skills and personal grace transcend the language barrier. There's dignity in his bearing and an elegance about him. He has charismatic good looks. One can imagine him formally attired, dancing the Argentinean tango (although he says that the dance is not in his repertoire). His face has the features of a man who has come through hard times. But there's warmth in his smile. He has maintained his humanity.

"I want to be remembered first as a good person and a man of integrity," Sergio says. "After that, if people remember me as a good fighter, that would be nice."

He has other priorities as well. Given his sports history, would Martinez rather win the Tour de France or be the undisputed middleweight champion of the world?

"Middleweight champion," he answers.

Next question. Would he rather be the undisputed middleweight champion of the world or score the winning goal for Argentina in the World Cup?

Sergio smiles: "Every Argentinean dreams to be Maradona."

Martinez is a good fighter in the wrong era. There was a time when the middleweight champion of the world was in high demand. Now the public has no idea who the real champions are, and there are few legitimate world championship fights. Instead, boxers compete for belts pursuant to rules made by sanctioning body officials who run their organizations for personal aggrandizement and their own financial gain.

Martinez is a legitimate world champion. He earned the title by beating Kelly Pavlik. But once Pavlik chose to not exercise a rematch clause, Sergio found himself without a dance partner.

A second fight against Paul Williams was the natural next step. But Williams's support team (trainer George Peterson, manager Al Haymon, and promoter Dan Goossen) seemed reluctant to take the bout. HBO leaned on them. Then it leaned on the Martinez camp insofar as contract terms were concerned.

Ultimately, at the request of Team Williams, the fight was contracted for 158 pounds (two pounds below the division limit). Martinez was middleweight champion, but the challenger would be announced last in the ring (a prerogative normally reserved for the champion). The $3,000,000 HBO license fee would be split evenly between the two camps. But Goossen would control the promotion of the fight and keep whatever profit was left from the live gate and sponsorships after expenses. Control of the promotion also gave Team Williams the inside track on the appointment of officials.

The fight shaped up as a good one. Williams is one of the few elite American fighters in boxing today. He's twenty-nine years old, six feet two inches tall, and would be entering the ring with a 39-and-1 record. The most notable victories on his ledger were his earlier triumph against Martinez and unanimous-decision wins over Antonio Margarito and Winky Wright. The sole blemish (a loss by decision to Carlos Quintana) was avenged on a first-round knockout four months later.

Williams is an action fighter. Like Martinez, he relishes combat and brings enthusiasm to his craft. The consensus opinion leading up to the bout was that Martinez-Williams embodied everything that boxing should be. A boxer who can punch against a puncher who can box. Two elite fighters with engaging personalities and exciting styles squaring off in a bout with no clear betting favorite.

Each fighter treated the other with respect. Before their first encounter, Williams had told the media, " It's gonna be a pig roast, and I'll stick the apple in his mouth." This time, there was no trash-talking, although both men expressed confidence.

"Martinez is a good fighter, but I've fought him before and I have more time now to prepare for his style," Williams said. "I'm going to do what I do best and put a real beating on him. You'll see even more action and more punches than before, but it won't be that close."

"I will fight him and I will box him," Martinez countered. "I learned things from our first fight that will help me this time. The weight, who is announced first; that sort of thing doesn't bother me. This fight will be hard like the last one. But the last one took more out of Williams than it took out of me. I think I will knock him out."

On November 20th, Martinez arrived in dressing room #119 at

Boardwalk Hall in Atlantic City shortly before 8:30 PM. He'd been assigned to the same room the night he dethroned Kelly Pavlik and had requested those quarters again.

Usually, a fighter who's readying to fight during the second half of an HBO telecast has a twenty-minute window during which he must be prepared to leave for the ring. The time of departure depends on how long the first fight lasts. But tonight's *World Championship Boxing* show would begin with a tape of the November 13th bout between Manny Pacquiao and Antonio Margarito. Thus, Martinez knew that he would walk at 11:05 PM.

Sergio removed his "Team Maravilla" warm-up jacket, opened a bottle of water, and took several sips.

Gabriel Sarmiento set up a laptop computer with two small Sony speakers on a table near the door. Spanish-language music—rock alternating with rap—filtered through the air.

"The day of a fight is a holiday for me," Martinez has said. "I enjoy every moment of it." He seemed relaxed and happy to be where he was. He sent some text messages; then began stretching his legs, whistling from time to time.

Dr. Dominic Coletta of the New Jersey Board of Athletic Control administered a brief physical examination.

Over the next half hour, Martinez walked back and forth across the room to the beat of the music, sat on a folding cushioned chair, sipped from the bottle of water, texted some more, stretched occasionally, and engaged in casual conversation with Sarmiento, Sampson Lewkowicz, co-manager Ricardo Sanchez Atocha, and cornerman Cecilio Flores. At one point, he nibbled on nuts and toasted bread chips that he'd brought in a small plastic bag.

At 9:20, referee Earl Morton came into the room with Aaron Davis (executive director of the New Jersey State Athletic Control Board) to give Martinez his pre-fight instructions. Lewkowicz translated into Spanish.

When Morton was done, Sampson asked, "In the first fight, when Williams was hurt, he was hugging like a love story. What will be done about that?"

"There is no holding in my ring," Morton assured him. "When I say break, I expect both fighters to break clean."

Then things got complicated. Sarmiento likes to wear a Los Angeles Dodgers baseball cap in the corner when he works Sergio's fights.

Davis informed Team Maravilla that no one would be allowed to wear a hat in the corner.

"But Gabriel wears this charming hat, "Lewkowicz explained. "It should not be a problem."

Davis said it was a problem.

Sampson translated into Spanish.

Sarmiento started screaming.

Davis listened for a while; then decided that discretion would be the better part of valor. "Look," he told Lewkowicz, "I'm not the hat police. I've got more important things to worry about."

Sampson translated.

Sarmiento kept screaming.

"I said I'm not the hat police," Davis repeated. "Tell him to read between the lines. It's not allowed, but it won't be a problem."

Again, Sampson translated.

Sarmiento calmed down.

Davis breathed a sigh of relief and left the dressing room.

Pacquiao-Margarito came on the television monitor. Sergio watched for about a minute, then told Lewkowicz, "It was an execution. But the one who should have been executed was Roberto Garcia. As a boxer, you never want the fight to be stopped, but the corner has a responsibility."

Chuck Williams (the WBC on-site supervisor for the fight) entered. Williams is a genial man who takes his responsibilities to the WBC and WBC president Jose Sulaiman seriously.

"Who's carrying the belt into the ring?" Williams asked.

Cecilio Flores identified the belt carriers for both the WBC and *Ring Magazine* belts.

"The WBC requests that you only bring the WBC belt into the ring," Williams told him. "Jose Sulaiman will be watching in Mexico. I hope you won't make him unhappy."

The request did not sit well with Team Maravilla. Undaunted, Williams pressed on.

"After the fight, I'll give the winner a WBC T-shirt that I want him to put on in the ring before the post-fight television interview. I'll also place the WBC belt over the winner's shoulder and across his chest so it's fully visible for the camera."

After Williams left the dressing room, Martinez resumed texting. At ten o'clock, Ricardo Sanchez Atocha started wrapping his hands. When the taping was done, Sergio shadow-boxed in the center of the room for three minutes. Then he lay on a rubdown table while Cecilio Flores stretched and massaged his legs. Upper-body work followed.

At 10:30, Martinez put on his trunks, moved to the center of the room, and began shadow-boxing in earnest. Sarmiento took a four-by-six-inch notepad from his pocket and moved to Sergio's side. The trainer had scripted his instructions for the fight, breaking them down into five points.

"The mistakes of the last fight will not be repeated," Sarmiento began. "Trabajo de amague y golpe con la mano adelantada haciendo pasos laterales hacia nuestra derecha sin entrar lejos de su distancia o fuera de ella."

Martinez continued shadow-boxing. Periodically, he answered, "Entiendo [I understand] . . . Okay . . . Si."

The reading lasted for three minutes.

"What I tell him is very important," Sarmiento explained afterward. "That is why I write everything down, so there is nothing that I forget."

Ricardo Sanchez Atocha greased Martinez down.

Sarmiento gloved Sergio up and worked the pads with him. Padwork alternated with shadow-boxing. At 11:02, the warm-up ended.

If Martinez won, he would be poised for stardom. If he lost, his championship would be gone and the big paydays he dreamed of would slide beyond his reach. In a matter of minutes, his economic future and physical well-being would be on the line.

When the moment of reckoning came, Williams entered the ring wearing fluorescent lime-green trunks with black trim. Martinez followed, dressed in black with red trim. Both the WBC and Ring belts were held high as Sergio stepped onto the canvas. Sarmiento was wearing his Los Angeles Dodgers baseball cap.

Martinez-Williams II picked up where their first encounter left off; with evenly fought, fast-paced, dramatic action. Williams came out hard at the opening bell and Martinez engaged him. Sergio was outlanded 23-to-18, but came on strong at the end of the stanza.

Round two was more of the same. Both fighters were throwing bombs.

"Paul Williams is an excellent fighter," Martinez had said before the fight. "But I have learned from our first fight and found the errors in what he does."

One of the things Martinez had learned was that Williams gives away his height. He doesn't "fight tall." Also, Paul's defense is in his nonstop offense. He doesn't give opponents time to punch. But he doesn't protect himself particularly well when he's punching. He's a confident fighter; perhaps too confident. At the highest levels of boxing, a fighter needs more than nonstop aggression to defend himself.

One minute into round two, Martinez and Williams each launched a lefthand with everything he could put on it. Both punches had knockout power. But Williams is flawed in the delivery of his straight left. He cocks his arm before he punches. He punches a bit wide. And he's inclined to raise his chin and extend it forward as his punch nears its target. He does it all quickly, but a fast well-timed counter can beat him to the punch.

Martinez delivered his blow—an overhand left—more quickly. His fist landed flush against Williams's jaw. Sergio cannot hit a man any harder than he hit Williams. Paul plummeted face-first to the canvas. He was unconscious before he hit the floor.

The moment that Williams hit the canvas, Martinez raised his arm in triumph. The fight was over, and everyone in the arena knew it (except Williams, who didn't know much of anything at that point).

It was a classic, highlight-reel, one-punch knockout.

After the bout, Williams called the blow a "lucky" punch. But when a fighter aims for another man's jaw, throws a perfectly leveraged punch, lands flush, and knocks his opponent out, it's not "luck." As James Corbett noted a century ago, "There is nothing haphazard about it when two trained athletes meet in the ring. Each knows what the other is trying to do to him, and it is his business to take care of himself. It is folly to talk about chance blows."

The knockout sent shockwaves through the boxing industry. It gave Lou DiBella, who has been struggling as of late, new life. Dan Goossen will have to work a lot harder to make money on Williams's next fight. But no one should write Paul off. He's a very good, very exciting fighter.

Al Haymon (William's manager) lost some of his leverage. Haymon's high-profile fighters haven't performed particularly well lately. Chris Arreola fizzled out against Vitali Klitschko and Tomasz Adamek. Andre Dirrell withdrew from Showtime's "Super Six" tournament under a cloud of suspicion. Antonio Tarver is forty-two years old with his only victory in the past thirty-two months coming against Nagy Aguilera. Jermain Taylor has been sidelined since losing four of five fights (including three brutal knockout losses). Danny Jacobs was starched by Dmitry Pirog. Sakio Bika is coming off consecutive losses. Andre Berto is undefeated but has yet to prove himself. That leaves some good young (but untested) fighters on Haymon's roster. And then there's Floyd Mayweather Jr, whose possibilities for 2011 run the gamut from fighting Manny Pacquiao for $40,000,000 to spending time in prison.

Martinez's victory also brought Sampson Lewkowicz into the spotlight. Boxing insiders first took note of Lewkowicz in 2001, when he brought an unknown fighter named Manny Pacquiao to the United States. In addition to Martinez, Sampson currently advises four fighters who hold world championship belts: Chris John, Krzysztof Wlodarczyk, Celestino Caballero, and Donnie Nietes. Other fighters in his stable include Lucas Matthysse, Michael Katsidis, Victor Cayo, Gabriel Campillo, and Hugo Ruiz.

Lewkowicz will turn sixty in January. "I love boxing," he says. "I work twenty-four-seven and never get tired because I love what I do. When I grow up, I want to be like Al Haymon."

But the most important consequence of Martinez-Williams II is that it gives boxing a new star.

Prior to November 20th, neither Martinez or Williams had been able to develop a significant fan base. At the September 23rd kick-off press conference in New York, Dan Goossen told the media that 50 percent of the people polled in Times Square that morning were "familiar with" Paul Williams and knew that the fight was going to take place. That was a stretch. In truth, although the fighters were battling for boxing's number three pound-for-pound ranking and the middleweight championship of the world, public support for the bout was lukewarm. On fight night,

Boardwalk Hall (which accommodates 12,500 for boxing) was configured for 6,800 and there were a lot of empty seats.

With one punch, the storyline of the fight changed from "Martinez-Williams" to "Martinez."

"Latecomers to boxing aren't supposed to be this good," Michael Rosenthal wrote afterward. "He's a natural if there ever was one."

Bart Barry added, "If there is a downside to having as boxing's middleweight champion of the world a Latino who both looks and fights better than Oscar De La Hoya, it doesn't spring to mind."

Stardom came late to Martinez. Even the best fighters have only a short time on center stage. He has come to this peak in his career at age thirty-five, so there is little room for error in his quest to make big money. Sergio will do what he has to do. He will go in tough. He will go down to 154 pounds if the price is right. He will fight as many times a year as need be.

How good is he?

"I watch Martinez fight and I see Pacquiao," says Freddie Roach. "There are a lot of similarities in what they do. Speed, quickness, the way they feint, their use of angles. Martinez is a very good fighter."

Sergio Martinez is like a rose that grew out of asphalt. He is a reminder of what boxing can be.

"I could not dream to be in this place where I am today," Martinez says. "I am very happy."

Each year, I look forward to writing a historical retrospective about one of boxing's legendary champions. In 2010, it was Rocky Marciano.

Rocky Marciano Revisited

Six decades ago, Rocky Marciano was on the verge of a celebrated reign at a time when the heavyweight championship of the world was the most exalted title in sports.

Marciano's image has grown hazy with the passage of time. In part, that's because there's very little good writing to explain what he stood for and how exciting he was in the ring.

Rocky Marciano: The Rock of His Times by Russell Sullivan (University of Illinois Press, 2002) is widely regarded as the definitive Marciano biography, and deservedly so. It's well-written, meticulously researched, and unquestionably the best work on its subject.

A. J. Liebling fashioned six essays about Marciano for *The New Yorker* that captured Marciano in his prime. And long after Marciano's death, William Nack wrote a penetrating article for *Sports Illustrated* that shed light on some of the less desirable facets of the man.

Beyond that, the scholarship is thin. Still, reading the public record and talking with people who knew Marciano, one comes to understand what he accomplished and represented at a time when boxing was second only to baseball as America's most popular professional spectator sport.

I

Rocco Marchegiano was born in Brockton, Massachusetts, on September 1, 1923. Both of his parents emigrated from Italy to the United States in the second decade of the twentieth century. Pierino Marchegiano was a slightly built man; five-feet-eight-inches tall, 130 pounds. Pasqualena Marchegiano was a large woman who outweighed her husband by seventy pounds.

Brockton was a working-class town twenty miles south of Boston. Pierino worked in a shoe factory. The Marchegiano's first child died in infancy. Rocco was the second, followed by three daughters and two more sons. The Marchegianos lived in a two-bedroom apartment with no running hot water or central heat. They were poor and the Great Depression made them poorer.

Rocco dropped out of high school at age seventeen; well short of earning his degree. "I was never good in school," he acknowledged later. "I just didn't care for the books." Over the next three years, he drifted from menial job to menial job; delivering coal, digging ditches, and working in the same shoe factory as his father. He washed dishes, did landscape work, delivered beer, and put in a stint as a short-order cook. On March 4, 1943, he was drafted into the United States Army.

Marchegiano was stationed in Europe for two years during World War II; then in Tacoma, Washington. His first exposure to organized boxing came in 1945, when he entered several Army tournaments. He was discharged from the service in December 1946 and took a job with the Brockton Gas Company, shoveling coal and stoking furnaces for a dollar an hour.

On March 17, 1947, in need of money, Marchegiano fought in the opening bout of a professional fight card in Holyoke, Massachusetts. It wasn't until late in his career that the fight became part of his public record. He fought it under the name of "Rocky Mack" in order to maintain his amateur standing.

The opponent, also making his pro debut, was a local fighter named Lee Epperson, who had a good amateur pedigree. For the first two rounds, Epperson outboxed his opponent, who took punch after punch and kept throwing wild haymakers that missed the more experienced fighter by an embarrassingly wide margin. In round three, a right uppercut landed and knocked Epperson out.

Marchegiano had been promised fifty dollars for the fight. The promoter gave him thirty-five.

One month later, a dream that Marchegiano had nursed since childhood came to an end. Growing up, he had started at center and linebacker in football for Brockton High School. But his true love was baseball. For four years, he'd played catcher for a local American Legion team. He was good.

But not good enough. In April 1947, the Chicago Cubs invited Marchegiano to a tryout. However, he failed to impress and the team decided against offering him a minor league contract. It was then that he turned to boxing.

"If I go into the ring, I might amount to something," he told his fiancée Barbara Cousins. "If I don't, what will I do the rest of my life? Dig ditches?"

Years later, he elaborated on that theme, saying, "My father never made any money and he never had any fun. He was only existing. I saw what the factory did to my father and I didn't want it to happen to me."

During the next year, Marchegiano kept his job with the Brockton Gas Company and had about thirty amateur fights. He was an unskilled boxer and blocked too many punches with his face. But he absorbed everything that opponents threw and moved inexorably forward, swinging wildly until his own sledgehammer blows landed. He lost four times, but won several regional Golden Gloves and Amateur Athletic Union titles.

In June 1948, Marchegiano traveled to New York for a meeting that would change his life. He wanted to resume his professional ring career and had been told that a New York–based manager could do more for him than one in New England. Armed with that advice, he sought out Al Weill.

"Weill was very much disliked by decent people," Jerry Izenberg (the dean of American sportswriters) recalls. "He was manipulative, rude, and arrogant, but also well-connected."

"Crude" and "abrasive" were also often affixed to Weill's name. But he was a brilliant judge of talent who, before putting two fighters in the ring, knew how entertaining their encounter was likely to be and, regardless of their records, who would win. He understood the business of boxing and had alliances with facilitators at every level. He was, in Liebling's words, "one of the most realistic fellows in a milieu where illusions are few."

Weill was also a dictator at heart and insisted on complete control over his fighters. "He gave them the proposition when he met them," syndicated columnist Jimmy Cannon wrote. "They would fight with their bodies, and he would think for them with his mind. They could not argue. He would not tolerate any opinions from them."

Later, Weill would say of his relationship with Marchegiano, "I declared myself right away. I said, 'You got your job and I got mine. You got all you can do to stay in condition and train for fights. I handle everything else.'"

Indeed, when Rocco Marchegiano wanted to marry Barbara Cousins, Weill told him, "Wives hurt fighters. When it's right for you to marry, I'll tell you." That put the impending marriage on hold for two years.

Weill had previously guided Lew Ambers, Joey Archibald, and Marty Servo to world titles. In each instance, the trainer who prepared them for battle was Charley Goldman.

A former fighter who'd retired in 1914, Goldman was often described as "gnomelike" and stood just over five feet tall. A fount of Runyanesque wisdom ("never buy anything on the street; especially diamonds"), he was a strict proponent of clean living, proper diet, and hard work in the gym.

Goldman was widely regarded as an honorable man and as popular in boxing circles as Weill was disliked. The only complaint with regard to his character concerned his frugal (some said "miserly") ways. Once, when asked what he did on dates, Charley answered, "I usually take them to the fights. I get free passes."

The history of boxing turned a page in June 1948 when Marchegiano appeared in Al Weill's office. Weill telephoned Goldman and told him to set up a sparring session so they could gauge Rocco's potential. Later that day, Marchegiano stepped into the ring at a CYO gym on 17th Street in Manhattan with a heavyweight from Florida named Wade Chancey.

Marchegiano didn't look like a professional fighter. He was short for a heavyweight; five feet ten inches tall. His hands were huge, but he had stubby arms that would make it difficult for him to develop an effective jab.

A. J. Liebling later likened what Weill and Goldman saw to "the understander in the nine-man pyramid of a troupe of Arab acrobats. He has big calves," Liebling wrote. "Forearms, wrists, and a neck so thick that it minimizes the span of his shoulders. He is neither tall nor heavy for a heavyweight, but gives the impression of bigness when you are close to him. His face, like his body, is craggy. Big jaw, big nose askew from punching, high cheekbones; and almost always when he is outside the ring, a pleasant asymmetrical grin."

Marchegiano was also two months shy of his twenty-fifth birthday; old for a novice fighter.

"Al and I often looked over green kids who thought they could become fighters," Goldman reminisced years later. "I'll eat my derby hat if I ever saw anyone cruder than Rocky. He was so awkward that we stood there and laughed. He didn't stand right. He didn't throw a punch right. He didn't block right. He didn't do anything right. Then he hit Chancey with a roundhouse right which nearly put a hole in the guy's head, and I told Weill that maybe I could do something with him."

"Charley Goldman," Michael Silver later wrote, "found a block of marble and sculpted it into The Pieta."

Marchegiano entered the ring as a professional for the second time on July 12, 1948. The site was Providence, Rhode Island; twenty-five miles from Brockton. The opponent was Harry Belzarian. Marciano won on a first-round knockout. His purse was forty dollars.

Years later, Belzarian recalled, "The first time he knocked me down, he broke my tooth. Then he knocked me down again. Then I don't remember anything."

Soon after, at Weill's suggestion, Marchegiano changed his name to Rocky Marciano. But Weill wasn't sold yet on his new fighter. He was using him to test other prospects.

On August 23, 1948, in his fifth professional fight, Marciano fought a 15–0–1 heavyweight named Eddie Ross. Rocky was the "opponent" that night. Prior to fighting Ross, Marciano had traveled from Brockton to New York to train occasionally with Goldman, but the trainer hadn't attended his fights.

Marciano knocked Ross out at 1:03 of the first round. Seven days later, when Marciano fought Jimmy Weeks in Providence, Goldman was in his corner.

Marciano fought eleven times during the last six months of 1948, scoring eight first-round knockouts and two in the second stanza One opponent made it into the third round.

Rather than work with the fighter at Stillman's Gym (which was a hub of boxing commerce in New York), Goldman continued to sculpt his creation at the CYO gym on 17th Street.

Marciano had poor balance, minimal defense, and little understanding of how to throw a jab or hook. Goldman taught him how to stand properly for balance and maximum leverage on his punches. Turning Marciano's lack of height into an advantage, he taught him to fight from a crouch, which made him harder to hit and forced opponents to lower their hands to hit him. He taught him the rudiments of defense and schooled him to go to the body.

"You got to realize," Goldman said later, "when I took him over, he didn't know what a body punch was. In the first ten fights I handled him, he didn't throw a single one. Some of those early fights when he didn't know how to fight; he won them all, but I was afraid he'd get killed."

But Marciano had a great equalizer; his right hand. Goldman gave him just enough moves and enough of a jab to get inside and use it.

"I got a guy who's short, stoop-shouldered, and balding with two left feet," the trainer said. "They all look better than he does as far as the moves are concerned. But they don't look so good on the canvas. God, how he can punch."

Marciano began 1949 with four consecutive knockouts. Then circumstances changed. The International Boxing Club was the dominant promotional power in boxing. It controlled the sport at Madison Square Garden and other major arenas. It had contracts for regularly scheduled fights on the emerging medium of television. And it had links to organized crime; most notably through Frankie Carbo.

"Carbo," Russell Sullivan explains, "established a well-organized centralized system of control over boxing. The system featured scores of managers who operated as front men for Carbo. Once a promising fighter arrived on the scene, one of Carbo's managers would muscle in on his ownership. If a fighter or manager refused to play ball, he would be frozen out of quality fights; if he were lucky. Fear and violence were the linchpins of Carbo's system and the bedrock of his power. Directly or indirectly, he controlled scores of judges, officials, managers, promoters, and fighters. His power became such that no big match was made or title awarded without his acquiescence."

Teddy Brenner, who worked for Al Weill in the late 1940s and subsequently became president of Madison Square Garden Boxing, later acknowledged, "Carbo had his fingers on the throat of boxing. If he did not own a certain fighter, he owned the manager. Weill was a boxing politician who held hands with the mob. When Weill was Marciano's manager, he was controlled by Carbo."

In May 1949, Weill became the matchmaker for the International Boxing Club. That meant Marciano could fight against carefully chosen opponents when and where Weill wanted. It also meant that, technically, Weill could no longer manage Marciano, since many state athletic commissions had a conflict-of-interest rule that precluded a matchmaker from managing a fighter. Hence, Weill's stepson, Marty Weill (who had a job-lot commission business in Ohio and knew next-to-nothing about boxing) became Marciano's manager of record.

Marciano wasn't the first fighter to be moved by people of influence. Nor will he be the last. But as 1949 progressed, there was the smell of something more.

On October 10th, the Brockton Blockbuster stepped into the ring in Providence to fight a journeyman named Ted Lowry. Marciano was 20-and-0 with 19 knockouts. Lowry was tough as nails. In 115 fights, he'd been stopped only once. But his record was 58 wins against 48 losses with 9 draws, and he'd lost seven fights in a row.

Lowry hurt Marciano badly in the first, second, and fourth rounds. Each time, he let Marciano off the hook. Many observers including the referee (who warned Lowry for non-aggression late in the fight) thought that he could have done more to win. Even then, the overwhelming majority of people who saw the fight thought that Lowry was the better man over the course of ten rounds. The judges ruled otherwise.

On December 2, 1949, Marciano fought in New York for the first time on the undercard of a heavyweight match-up between Roland LaStarza and Cesar Brion. He won, knocking out an overmatched Pat Richards in the second round.

Four weeks later, he was back at the Garden to take on Carmine Vingo, a twenty-year-old New Yorker with 16 wins in 17 fights. It was a knockdown drag-out brawl with Marciano badly staggered on several occasions and Vingo knocked down three times. The final knockdown, in round six, left Vingo unconscious and in a coma that lasted for several days. He survived but never fought again.

Marciano fought thirteen times in 1949 and ended the year with a 25-and-0 record. On March 24, 1950, he returned to Madison Square Garden to face another New Yorker, Roland LaStarza.

LaStarza was undefeated in 37 bouts. It was Marciano's first "big fight" and his inaugural appearance on television. After ten rounds, the visitor from Brockton was awarded a ten-round split decision. Afterward, Jesse Abramson of the *New York Herald Tribune* wrote, "It was a gift, almost universally condemned around ringside as a miscarriage of justice."

After the LaStarza fight, Marciano returned to New England to further build his record and improve his skills. During the next fifteen months, he had nine bouts against mediocre opponents and ran his record to 35-and-0. On July 12, 1951, he returned to the spotlight against Rex Layne at Madison Square Garden.

Layne was twenty-three years old and had lost only once in 37 fights. More significantly, he'd beaten Bob Satterfield and Jersey Joe Walcott. For the first time in his career, Marciano entered the ring as an underdog. He annihilated Layne, knocking him out in the sixth round. Afterward, Layne recalled, "I was on my face. I heard the count from one to ten. I kept telling myself that I had to get up, but I couldn't move. I couldn't make myself move. It was the strangest feeling."

The fistic community was becoming more interested in Marciano. But there were a lot of critics. Sullivan notes, "This was an era in which boxing men were concerned with style. The great champions of the day—Joe Louis, Willie Pep, and especially the great Sugar Ray Robinson—were supreme stylists; boxers who not only won but also won pretty. Rocky Marciano won ugly. To purists, he degraded the art and science of boxing. Nearly everyone in fight circles felt that Marciano's clumsiness would hinder his climb up the heavyweight ladder. They theorized that he would lose, and perhaps lose badly, if he met an accomplished craftsman such as Ezzard Charles or Jersey Joe Walcott."

Charley Goldman didn't argue with the critics. Instead, he explained, "The great thing about this kid is he's got leverage. He had leverage from the start. And when you teach a fellow like that, you have to go slow because you might change the way he stands or the way he moves and spoil his hitting. Everything new you show him, you have to ask, 'Does it feel natural? Can you hit from there?' We'll teach him the tricks he doesn't know. We've got to polish him up, but then it's up to him. Either he has it or he hasn't."

Bottom line: Whatever way gets results is the right way. Goldman and Marciano were getting results.

Marciano was small for a heavyweight, but he beat men down. He moved forward with a will of iron, arms pounding, throwing punches from every angle, anxious to make contact with any part of his opponent's body to see which of them could give and take more pain. He had to get close to be effective and he was willing to take the punches to do it. He applied nonstop pressure, banging and banging from the opening bell until the end of a fight.

A fighter who comes forward all the time no matter what his opponent throws at him is hard to beat. And every punch that Marciano threw was a knockout punch. "Whenever he hit you, wherever he hit you, he hurt you," Keene Simmons (an eighth-round knockout victim) said.

Boxing is entertainment. Regardless of what the purists thought, more and more fans were coming to appreciate Marciano's wild brawling hit-and-get-hit style. He went for broke with virtually every punch. He could be losing. Round after round, his opponent might outbox him. Then—BOOM!

When an opponent was hurt, Marciano finished him off.

And there was another factor that contributed to Marciano's appeal. He wasn't marketed as a great white hope, but he didn't have to be. The issue was in the back of the public's collective mind.

Writing about the period after Marciano's knockout victory over Rex Layne, Sullivan notes, "The fact that Marciano was white facilitated construction of his positive image in the mainstream press. A slew of articles appeared in such general-interest magazines as *Life, Look,* and the *Saturday Evening Post,* helping kick-start an all-American boy image that would make him the symbol of his age. The general tone of the coverage Marciano received was far more 'up close and personal' than that of his black challengers. Part of this was due to Marciano's friendly engaging manner, which encouraged such an approach. It was also due to the fact that white sportswriters wanted to get up close and personal with the white fighter."

Then came the inevitable confrontation: Rocky Marciano vs. Joe Louis at Madison Square Garden on October 26, 1951.

Louis had reigned as heavyweight champion longer than any man ever; from 1937 through his retirement in 1949. He came back a year later and lost a fifteen-round decision to Ezzard Charles, but scored eight consecutive triumphs thereafter.

Louis-Marciano made sense for both men. Louis, because he needed the money; Marciano, because the Brown Bomber represented both a paycheck and a stepping-stone.

The former champion was three inches taller (six-feet-one) and twenty-five pounds heavier (212) than Marciano. Louis been the betting favorite every time he stepped into the ring as a professional, and this time was no different. The odds were 7-to-5; largely because of Joe's advantage in height, weight, reach, and technical skills and because he was Joe Louis. But those were the shortest odds ever in his favor.

More significantly; Louis was thirty-seven years old. Putting matters in perspective; his last fight prior to his earlier retirement had been an eleventh-round knockout of Jersey Joe Walcott on June 25, 1948. Marciano had engaged in one professional fight (under the name "Rocky Mack") up until that time.

Marciano was on edge in the days leading up to the fight. In response to a reporter's inquiry as to whether he thought he'd win, he snapped, "That was a fucking dumb question. If I didn't think I was gonna win, why the hell would I be fighting?"

Asked if he might choke, he answered, "When I was discharged from the army, I started fighting because I hated the jobs I had before I went into the service. I'm afraid of having to go back and doing some of those same things if I lose to Louis. I'm not going to choke."

The fight was scheduled for ten rounds.

"I remember standing in the ring and thinking how big Louis was," Marciano reminisced years later. "I had never remembered Louis being such a big guy. The top of my head seemed to just about reach the bottom of his chin."

Seconds before the bell for round one rang, Charley Goldman told his fighter, "Make it a short fight. At my age, I can't be running up and down them steps all night."

In round one, Marciano staggered Louis with an overhand right. Then Louis took over with his jab. But by round five, Joe was tiring. Marciano's constant aggression was wearing him down. A punch under the heart in round five made the former champion gasp. His legs deserted him. His power was gone.

Marciano knocked him out in the eighth round.

"I saw the righthand coming, but I couldn't do anything about it,"

Louis said in his dressing room after the fight. "I was awfully tired. I'm too old, I guess. What's the use of crying. The better man won."

Beating Joe Louis gave Marciano widespread recognition. It was Joe Louis. And the fight had been on national television (not just on the east coast as was the case with Marciano-LaStarza).

There were still critics. Harry LeDuc of the *Detroit News* opined, "Marciano's ring ability is without relation to the science of boxing. The execution was a success, but the executioner lacked finesse." Arthur Daley of the *New York Times* wrote, "Louis losing is more important than Marciano winning."

In response, Goldman countered, "They call him crude because he misses a lot of punches. But it's his style. Most fighters Rocky's age are as good as they'll ever be. Rocky only has about three year's real experience, so he's still learning."

And Joe Louis paid tribute to his conqueror, saying, "He was tough, real tough. He's a good fighter; better than most people realize."

After beating Louis, Marciano took a step backward. In a February 13, 1952, bout against Lee Savold in Philadelphia; he looked wild and amateurish. Meanwhile, Savold fought like he didn't want to. After six rounds, the pacifist's corner stopped the contest.

The poor showing led to Marciano being sent back to Providence for fights against Gino Buonvino and Bernie Reynolds, who he disposed of in two and three rounds respectively. Then he returned to New York and looked good, knocking out Harry Matthews (who had won fifty fights in a row) in two rounds at Yankee Stadium.

Charley Goldman now considered his charge ready to fight for the heavyweight championship of the world. That meant facing Jersey Joe Walcott.

Walcott claimed to be thirty-eight years old. There was a school of thought that he was older. He'd gotten his first shot at the brass ring on December 5, 1947, when he challenged an aging Joe Louis for the heavyweight crown. Most observers felt that Walcott won. So did Louis, who'd been knocked down twice and started to leave the ring before the result was announced, only to learn that he was the beneficiary of a dubious split decision. Six months later, they fought again. Trailing on two of the three judges' scorecards, Louis knocked Walcott out in the eleventh round. Then the Brown Bomber announced his retirement from boxing.

On June 22, 1949, Walcott got a third crack at the heavyweight title when he fought Ezzard Charles for the vacant throne and lost a fifteen-round decision. With no opposition of note on the horizon, Charles battled Walcott again on March 7, 1951 and beat him again.

Walcott was now 0-and-4 in title fights. But on July 18, 1951, Charles pushed his luck against Walcott one fight too many. Walcott knocked him out in the seventh round to become what *Life* magazine called "the oldest and most implausible heavyweight champion of the world."

Jersey Joe had one title defense; a fifteen-round decision victory in a rematch against Charles. Then he signed to fight Marciano.

Prior to the fight, Walcott belittled his challenger. "Marciano is an amateur," the champion proclaimed. "He wouldn't have qualified for Joe Louis's bum of the month tour. I guess he can punch, but he's got two left feet. He can't box a little bit. I've never seen anybody easier to hit. If I can't beat this bum, take my name off the record books."

One side issue of note attended the fight. Al Weill had become so obvious about still controlling Marciano through his stepson that the New York State Athletic Commission ordered him to relinquish his job as matchmaker for the International Boxing Club or forfeit his financial interest in the fighter. On September 1, 1952 (twenty-two days before Walcott-Marciano) Weill gave up his role with the IBC.

On September 23, 1952, Rocky Marciano stepped into the ring at Municipal Stadium in Philadelphia to do battle for the heavyweight championship of the world. He was an 8-to-5 favorite; largely because the public didn't think much of Walcott. Forty thousand fans were in attendance. Another 140,000 watched the bout on closed-circuit television, which was available in thirty-one cities nationwide.

In round one, Walcott dropped Marciano with a left hook to the jaw. It was the first time in his professional career that Marciano had been on the canvas. He rose at the count of four and came forward as he'd always done, throwing bombs. An accidental headbutt in round six opened cuts on both men, but Marciano appeared to be in command. Then, in round seven, he began having trouble seeing. An astringent of some sort had found its way into his eyes and was obscuring his vision.

After the seventh and eighth rounds, cutman Freddie Brown took a sponge and doused Marciano's eyes with water. In round nine, his vision began to clear.

"The lead had changed hands three times," A. J. Liebling wrote. "You don't see many fights like that. In the tenth, which was the hardest-fought round of all, Marciano stayed on top. But somehow, the calculations had gone awry. The old fellow looked further from collapse now than he had six rounds earlier."

Sullivan picks up the action: "Halfway through the eleventh, his best round of the fight, Walcott hit Marciano with a ferocious right under the heart that bent the challenger over and made him visibly wince. Some felt that only the bell saved the sagging challenger from being knocked out. It was more of the same in the twelfth, with Walcott pounding Marciano and in complete command."

Walcott was now well ahead on the judges' scorecards and dominating the fight. Marciano needed a knockout to win.

Thirty seconds into the thirteenth round, Marciano backed Walcott into the ropes.

Both men threw perfectly leveraged righthands at the same time.

Marciano's landed. It was a perfect punch; the most devastating in boxing lore.

"Walcott froze, paralyzed," Sullivan recounts. "His eyes glazed over, his legs turned to jelly, and he began a slow-motion collapse."

The blow, Liebling observed, "traveled at most twelve inches, straight across his chest to the champion's jaw. It was about as hard as anybody ever hit anybody. Walcott flowed down like flour out of a chute. He didn't seem to have a bone in his body."

"I don't remember anything," the dethroned champion said in his dressing room after the fight. "I don't know if it was a right or a left. I wasn't tired; I felt good; I was setting my own pace. Then—BANG! It hit me. I still don't know what hit me. I couldn't even try to get up."

Rocky Marciano was the heavyweight champion of the world.

II

History's most celebrated heavyweight champions reflected the eras in which they reigned. Jack Dempsey personified the Roaring '20s. Joe

Louis was perfectly juxtaposed with the trials of The Great Depression and World War II. Muhammad Ali was inextricably intertwined with the turmoil of the 1960s.

Rocky Marciano mirrored the simple optimism of the 1950s. The Great Depression was over. World War II had been won. The economy was booming and America's suburbs were growing. All things seemed possible.

Boxing was second only to baseball as America's most popular professional sport. The National Football League and National Basketball Association had yet to make significant inroads with the American public. Television, which was still in its infancy, was becoming a significant cultural factor. And the sweet science was ideal for small-screen sports programming. All the action took place in an enclosure that was roughly twenty feet square.

Meanwhile, baseball's old guard was changing. Joe DiMaggio was gone. Mickey Mantle and Willie Mays had yet to establish themselves. Among the gods of sports, only Ted Williams and Stan Musial rivaled Marciano in status. Williams who was baseball's most honored player, called the heavyweight championship "the most coveted prize in sports."

To some fans, Marciano symbolized the restoration of boxing's white monarchy after the reigns of Joe Louis, Ezzard Charles, and Jersey Joe Walcott. More significantly, he was embedded in the consciousness of Italian-Americans in the same way that Joe Louis lived in the hearts of his people.

Italian-Americans had few heroes on a national scale. Fiorello LaGuardia had been elected mayor of New York in 1933, but his brethren were largely excluded from the high councils of political power. It wasn't until Lyndon Johnson designated Anthony Celebrezze as Secretary of Health, Education, and Welfare in the mid-1960s that an Italian-American served in the president's cabinet.

Angelo Bertelli starred on the gridiron for Notre Dame. Hank Lusetti excelled in basketball for Stanford. And of course, there was Joe DiMaggio. But the sport that was most open to Italian-Americans was boxing.

There had been an Italian heavyweight champion before Marciano. But Primo Carnera, who wore the crown for less than a year in the mid-1930s, was mob-controlled; many of his fights were fixed; and there came a time when the public knew it.

Marciano was for real. And to the Italian-American community, he was "one of us."

Joe DiMaggio had a passport to a higher level of society. DiMaggio was the essence of style and grace, but DiMaggio was aloof. He gave the impression of being above it all and on a level that other Italian-Americans could never reach. DiMaggio married Marilyn Monroe. Marilyn Monroe would not have married Rocky Marciano.

The morning after Marciano beat Jersey Joe Walcott, he made a promise to himself. "When you're the heavyweight champion of the world, you represent boxing," he said later. "I made up my mind that I would never do anything to disgrace the title."

Thereafter, Marciano spoke on many occasions about what being champion meant to him: "When I fought Joe Louis, I thought it was the biggest thing of my life. But a bigger thing came along the night I fought Walcott for the title. That made the difference; the title . . . Being champion is a thrill. I haven't been champion for long, but it does something to a guy. It makes you surer of yourself, gives you more confidence. It's got everything any guy would want . . . Being champion is everything. You lose the title and you lose people's respect and admiration and, of course, you lose money. It would hurt a lot to find a guy who could lick me . . . What could be better than walking down any street in any city and knowing you're the heavyweight champion of the world?"

Marciano seemed to be a man without artifice who the average person could identify with and understand. People liked him. Even Roland LaStarza, who lost to him twice, said, "The man was a nice guy."

And as Sullivan notes, "This was an era when sportswriters sought to lionize the athletes they covered. Marciano wasn't placed under a microscope, nor was he subjected to the type of prying coverage that might have unearthed his flaws. Instead, he benefited from the journalistic canons of the day and acquired an image that was more super-human than human."

"Marciano," Sullivan elaborates, "had various character flaws, but sportswriters tended to gloss over them, adhering to the credo of accentuating the positive and eliminating the negative. Much of his image was grounded in fact. He really was good to his parents. He was extremely loyal. He respected authority. He was as patriotic as the next man. From outward appearances, he appeared to take his faith seriously. He didn't drink or smoke. Clearly, no one worked harder. Modest, friendly, and likable; Marciano was all of those things. What he did not have enough of, the image-makers embellished. What he did not have at all, they made up. And what he had that did not fit the ideal, they omitted."

Arthur Daley called Marciano "a righteous and truly wonderful guy." Jimmy Cannon referenced him as "a kind and decent man." Shirley Povich of the *Washington Post* labeled the champion "the All-American boy of the heavyweights."

Ed Fitzgerald wrote in *Sport* magazine, "Rocky is a neighborhood kid who married a neighborhood girl and thinks the old hometown is the greatest place in the world. His social activities are confined largely to entertaining friends and relatives at home or making the rounds of their houses and the Ward Two Club and the Seville Council, Knights of Columbus. The priests and nuns of St. Colman's parish where he worships call on him again and again to serve as a model for their lectures to the neighborhood kids."

"Rocky Marciano," Sullivan concludes, "didn't just embody the American Way of Life. He was the American Dream. He was nothing but the eldest son of a poor Italian-American shoemaker. But this was America. And America gave a young boy like Rocco Marchegiano the chance to gain a better life."

Shortly after Dwight Eisenhower was sworn into office, he invited Marciano to a White House luncheon attended by a select group of sports luminaries. Joe DiMaggio, Ben Hogan, and Ty Cobb were among the invitees.

"So you're the heavyweight champion of the world," the president said when he and Marciano were introduced.

"Yes, sir."

"Somehow I thought you'd be bigger."

"No, sir," Marciano responded.

On May 15, 1953, the new champion defended his title for the first time in a rematch against Jersey Joe Walcott. At that point in the long history of boxing, no man had ever lost and then regained the heavyweight crown. The bout was contested in Chicago. Marciano was a 3-to-1 favorite.

Marciano knocked Walcott down in the first round.

"It wasn't a crashing knockdown, the kind that leaves the recipient limp," A. J. Liebling wrote. "This appeared to be a sit-down-and-think-it-over knockdown, such as you might see in any barroom. Jersey Joe must have begun the process of ratiocination right away, but the conclusion at which he was arriving was not instantly apparent. Like a drowning man, he may have been reviewing his whole life, with a long pause on what had happened to him in Philadelphia. The dramatic significance of the fleeting seconds was lost upon the crowd because everybody present, with the possible exception of Mr. Walcott, took it for granted that he would get up within ten seconds."

Walcott chose not to rise from the canvas until ten-and-a-half seconds had elapsed.

"The bum quit," former heavyweight champion James Braddock said afterward.

"He sat there like an old man resting in the park on the grass," Jessie Abramson wrote.

"He should have gotten up," Marciano said. "I would have."

But there was an alternative explanation for Walcott's conduct. As Liebling later wrote, "Marciano is so good in his particular way that there should be a law against allowing him to fight return fights. He takes it out of them."

After a man fought Marciano, it was said, he was never the same.

On September 24, 1953, at the Polo Grounds in New York, Marciano put his championship on the line for the second time. The opponent was Roland LaStarza. Many thought there was unfinished business between them; that Marciano had, in fact, lost their first fight.

The champion added fuel to that fire, saying, "I still bump into people who think I lost. Why, I don't know. Beating LaStarza is the only thing I have to do before I'll be able to fully appreciate being world's champion. Until I do that, I won't be satisfied."

Marciano was a 6-to-1 favorite. LaStarza built up an early lead on points. Marciano fought clumsily and outside the rules. In the second round, he was warned by referee Ruby Goldstein for headbutting. In round three, he hit on the break and after the bell. Rounds six and seven were punctuated by low blows. Then, in round seven, Marciano landed a brutal body shot above the belt and the tide turned.

An ugly beatdown followed. "By the ninth round," Sullivan recounts, "LaStarza's face was lopsided and he was spitting blood. Each Marciano punch would spray droplets of LaStarza's blood onto press row."

The referee stopped the carnage in the eleventh round.

"He's definitely a better fighter than when I fought him before," LaStarza said afterward. "Five thousand percent better."

Charley Goldman seconded that notion, saying, "Rocky has improved in each fight. He now does by instinct what he used to do by memory."

Still, there was considerable room for progress. Marciano remained crude and awkward. He was frequently outboxed for large segments of a fight. "His footwork," Whitney Martin of the Associated Press wrote, "consists of moving forward in a direct line to a point where he is within cannonading range."

Budd Schulberg called Marciano "the master of no defense, who moves in swinging punches like all the club fighters of all time." Jimmy Cannon opined that he had "the style of an avalanche."

Also, Marciano's penchant for fouling might have been an unintended accompaniment to his wild brawling style; but it violated the rules.

On the other side of the coin; Marciano had incredible stamina. He was rarely hurt. He punched with awesome power. And as a fight wore on, he seemed to grow stronger.

"He keeps swinging that pick with all his might," Red Smith wrote. "Chopping at the hard pavement without apparent effect, until all of a sudden the asphalt crumbles and there is only the soft earth underneath."

"It's not like football," Freddie Brown said philosophically. "Rocky never gives you the ball."

"Rocky is not in there to outpoint anybody with an exhibition of boxing skill," Ed Fitzgerald observed. "He is a primitive fighter who stalks his prey until he can belt him with that frightening right-hand crusher. He is one of the easiest fighters in the ring to hit. You can, as with an enraged grizzly bear, slow him down and make him shake his head if you hit him hard enough to wound him. But you can't make him back up.

Slowly, relentlessly, ruthlessly, he moves in on you. Sooner or later, he clubs you down."

Donald Turner journeyed to New York in the early-1960s as a fighter and later became a trainer. The list of fighters that he has worked with is headed by Larry Holmes and Evander Holyfield. "My first professional trainer was Charley Goldman," Turner recalls. "We used to sit and talk about Rocky Marciano all the time."

"Marciano," Turner expounds, "had as much determination as any fighter ever. There was no quit in him at all. He knew what his limitations were and he made up for them by working as hard as any fighter who ever lived. Once a boxer starts cheating in training, he can't be great. Marciano never cheated in training. Out of the thousand or so days that he was champion, I'll bet he was in the gym and working hard for all but a hundred-and-fifty of them. If there was a problem in training camp, it was that they had trouble getting sparring partners because Marciano hit them so hard. He wouldn't even take a phone call during the ten days before a fight. That's how focused his mind was. In terms of trying his hardest and working as hard as he could, Marciano did everything the way it was supposed to be done. Then the fight would start and his strategy was, 'I'm coming. I'm throwing. I'm going to hit you with everything I can, anytime I can, anywhere I can.' He'd wear you down. Fight after fight, he'd be getting outboxed and maybe beaten up. Then, all of a sudden, the other guy was stretched out on the canvas."

"Marciano wasn't a good technical fighter," adds Emanuel Steward. "But he was a smart fighter in a crude sort of way. The more I watched films of his fights, the more I realized how he maximized the limited skills that he had. He'd crouch down low; so once he got inside, it was hard to get a clean shot at him. You had to drop your hands to hit him, which meant he could come over the top with that overhand right. And there was another move, where he'd come in like he was going to clinch and you'd relax a bit and he'd hit you with a short left hook to the chin."

"He wasn't that big," Steward continues. "He wasn't that coordinated. He wasn't that fast. His balance was poor. He had short arms. He cut easily. But he was always in incredible condition. He was incredibly strong physically. He'd punch, take whatever punches you threw at him, and punch some more."

Bob Girard handed Marciano his fourth amateur defeat (the last time that Marciano lost a fight). "I beat him because it was three rounds," Girard said years later. "There were a hundred guys who might have stayed three rounds with him. But no man in the world was going to beat Rocky in fifteen rounds. Every time he hit you, you saw a flash of light. You either grabbed him or you moved back. Because if he hit you twice, you were gone."

"He hits you with something that looks like a little tap to the crowd," cornerman Freddie Brown noted. "But the guy who gets hit shakes right down to his legs."

"He must be good," Charley Goldman concluded. "He always beats the other guy."

On July 17, 1954, Marciano returned to the ring to fight Ezzard Charles.

Charles was one of the great light-heavyweights of all time. He'd succeeded Joe Louis as heavyweight champion by beating Jersey Joe Walcott for the vacant title in 1949. Two years later, Walcott returned the favor. Ezzard was only thirty-two years old, but his body bore the wear and tear of ninety-four professional fights.

There were 47,000 fans in Yankee Stadium. Marciano was a 7-to-2 favorite. Charles controlled the early stages of the fight, bloodying the champion's nose in the first round and opening an ugly gash on Marciano's left eyelid in the fourth stanza. The cut bled throughout the night despite Freddie Brown's efforts. Afterward, Brown admitted, "With a cut like that, you got to be nervous."

In round five, Marciano got his rhythm going and landed some good shots, including one after the bell.

"In the sixth round," Liebling reported, "Charles began to go slack like every other fighter after Marciano's punches have begun to tell. They have a cumulative effect that asserts itself."

Charles regained the advantage in rounds seven and eight. "He fought savagely," Liebling wrote. "The bounce and snap had left him for good now, but his determination was unbelievable. His face, rather narrow with a high curved nose, changed in shape to a squatty rectangle as we watched. It was as though he had run into a nest of wild bees."

Rounds nine through fifteen belonged to the champion. Sullivan recounts, "Marciano's punches were not only rocking Charles, but were also beginning to make a definite impact on the challenger's appearance. His right eye gradually closed and his lower lip became split and swollen. More strikingly, a lump the size of an egg suddenly appeared on the left side of Charles's jaw."

The challenger was now also having trouble breathing because, in the eighth or ninth round, Marciano had hit him in the Adam's apple.

Marciano won a unanimous decision. "Rocky numbs you all over," Charles said afterward. "Wherever he hits you, he hurts you."

The fight was good enough to warrant a rematch. They met again at Yankee Stadium on September 17, 1954. This time, Marciano was a 6-to-1 favorite. He dominated the early stages of the bout and put Charles on the canvas in round two. After that, the challenger fought with extreme caution. Marciano's most effective blows were after the bell and low.

In round six, everything changed. Marciano came out of a clinch with a gash on his left nostril that split his nose and cut to the bone. Charles would say that the wound came from a punch. Marciano claimed that it had been caused by an elbow. Films of the fight are inconclusive as to the cause.

Either way, blood was spurting.

"I knew something was wrong," Marciano said afterward, "because the blood was running like from a faucet."

Nothing Freddie Brown did in the corner after the round could stop the blood from flowing. "He looked like he's got two noses, both bleeding," the cutman said afterward. "I never saw a cut like that before."

Marciano continued to press the action and land the more punishing blows. But time was short. The damage to his nose could easily force stoppage of the fight. He was in greater danger of losing than ever before in his ring career.

In round eight, he knocked Charles out.

"Rocky was great when he had to be great," Al Weill said.

Eight months later, Marciano journeyed to San Francisco to fight England's Don Cockell.

Cockell looked like the Pillsbury Doughboy. In reality, he was a fat light-heavyweight who'd been knocked out five times by opponents far less imposing than Marciano.

The British public was intrigued by the fight. Liebling described the challenger as "a fat man whose gift for public suffering has enlisted the sympathy of a sentimental people." Sullivan puts the matter in perspective, noting that the bout "was widely cast as a test run for Marciano's nose."

Only 15,000 fans were in attendance at Kezar Stadium. Cockell played the role of a human punching bag with valor. Marciano looked clumsy and amateurish. "That was a very bad fight," he admitted afterward. "I wasn't sharp and I knew it."

Marciano also fouled repeatedly, headbutting and hitting Cockell below the belt and after the bell several times. More flagrantly, he hit the challenger when the Brit was on one knee after being knocked down in the ninth and final round.

"On my wife and baby," Marciano pledged when the fight was over, "I don't do one of those things knowing I do it."

"He was a bit deaf when it came to hearing a bell," Cockell said.

Meanwhile, Marciano wasn't making the money he wanted to make. Three decades earlier, Tex Rickard and Jack Dempsey had ushered in an era of million-dollar gates. Dempsey had been paid accordingly. But Marciano's biggest purse had been $250,000 (for his first fight against Ezzard Charles). For the Cockell bout, the amount was $115,000. None of his championship encounters had captured the public imagination.

That changed on September 21, 1955, when Marciano fought Archie Moore.

Moore was a great light-heavyweight, who'd been denied an opportunity to fight for the title until December 17, 1952, when, at age thirty-nine, he was given a shot at Joey Maxim. He made the most of it, beating Maxim and successfully defending his crown four times. Then, on May 2, 1955, he stepped up in weight and decisioned Nino Valdes, who was the top-ranked heavyweight contender at the time.

That set the stage for Marciano vs. Moore. They met at Yankee Stadium on September 21, 1955; three months shy of Moore's forty-second birthday. The challenger weighed 188 pounds; only four ounces less than the champion.

Largely because of Moore's loquacious personality, a crowd of 61,574 was on hand. Former heavyweight champions Jack Dempsey, Gene

Tunney, Joe Louis, James Braddock, and Max Baer were at ringside. Four hundred thousand paying customers watched via closed-circuit in 133 venues across the country. Marciano was an 18-to-5 favorite. His purse would be $470,997 ($3,770,000 in today's dollars).

Marciano began the action wild as always. In round two, his wildness almost cost him the fight. A perfectly timed righthand counter put him on the canvas for only the second time in his career. He rose quickly, but was on shaky legs. "I was dazed," he admitted afterward.

Then, instead of letting Moore go for the kill, referee Harry Kessler erroneously began a mandatory eight-count, forgetting that the rule was not in effect for title fights. That gave Marciano extra time to recover. Years later, Moore would say of Kessler and that moment, "He knows I hate him. I hate him to this day."

Marciano survived the second round. Then, inexorably, he wore Moore down.

"Rocky didn't know enough boxing to know what a feint was," Moore said afterward. "He never tried to outguess you. He just kept trying to knock your brains out. If he missed you with one punch, he just threw another. I felt like someone was beating all over my body with a blackjack or hitting me with rocks. I had the braggadocio and the skill and the guts, but that wasn't enough. Marciano beat me down."

Marciano put Moore on the canvas twice in the sixth round and hit him after the bell for good measure. "That was unintentional," the challenger said afterward. "And I hit him back unintentionally."

In round eight, Moore was knocked down for the third time but was saved by the bell. In the ninth round, he was counted out.

"The biggest fight in years was one of the best in years," Red Smith wrote.

"A lot of colored guys think Marciano couldn't fight," Moore told Donald Turner several years later. "But that's not a fact. It's a prejudice."

After Marciano-Moore, the public's appreciation of the champion grew. Then, to the surprise of the boxing world, on April 27, 1956, he announced his retirement from boxing.

Marciano was only thirty-two years old and had fought as a pro for less than eight years. But he'd trained long and hard for each of his fights and taken incredible punishment.

"I am retiring because of my wife and baby," Marciano said in his retirement statement. "I am comfortably fixed and I am not afraid of the future."

Naturally, there was skepticism. But Marciano had an answer for the skeptics. "I'm going to profit by other people's mistakes," he said. "If Joe Louis couldn't make a successful comeback, I'm not going to attempt it."

Marciano's retirement coincided with the explosion of other spectator sports in the United States. In 1950, when he fought on television for the first time, there were 3,100,000 TV sets in America. By the time he faced Archie Moore, there were 32,000,000 sets and the medium was becoming adept at conveying the magic of sports.

After leaving the ring, Marciano made some television appearances and had a few product endorsements. He was constantly getting involved in business deals; a bowling alley, a restaurant, a sausage company, a spaghetti restaurant chain. Some were profitable. Most lost money.

In 1959, after Ingemar Johansson dethroned Floyd Patterson, there was talk of a comeback fight against the new heavyweight king. But Marciano nixed those rumors, saying, "I don't want to be remembered as a beaten champion."

Throughout his career, Marciano had managed to steer clear of any visible mob involvement. That was important to rebutting the underside of the Italian-American stereotype and keeping him clean in the public eye. It's likely that Frankie Carbo had a piece of Marciano by virtue of their mutual tie to Al Weill. But that was never part of the public record.

One of Marciano's friends, Ed Napoli, said after the fighter's death that Rocky had been offered a lucrative inducement to throw the Cockell fight, in which the Brit was a 10-to-1 underdog. According to Napoli, Marciano told the mobster who made the offer, "You disgust me. I'm ashamed that you're Italian. Get out of here and don't come back."

But after Marciano retired, he became openly friendly with several mob figures, including Carbo.

"He saw Carbo as having class," Sullivan writes. "Someone who knew how to dress, how to live, how to move, how to command respect, and how to treat other Italians. Moreover, Marciano liked the aura of danger and excitement that surrounded Carbo."

William Nack elaborates on that theme, writing, "As celebrated a folk hero as he was to the workaday Italian-American, Marciano found himself to be an even more-respected figure among members of the underworld; a life-sized icon whose company and favor were sought by hoodlums wherever he went. Over the years, Marciano kissed the cheeks of many of the major crime family bosses. [But] in spite of the social contact he had with hoodlums, he feared the violence and notoriety of the underworld and made it a point not to get involved in their businesses."

The exception to that rule, according to Nack, came when Marciano loaned $100,000 to Pete DiGravio (a loan shark linked to the Cleveland mob). From Rocky's point of view, he was merely investing in a business. He wasn't involved in the street end of things.

Still, the association with the mob was there.

Frank Saccone (Marciano's longtime accountant) later recalled, "We'd go to these elaborate restaurants and sit with fifteen, twenty underworld characters. I was a naïve accountant from Brockton. I thought they were just friends of Rocky's. Rocky finally told me who they were. They couldn't do enough for him. They'd say to him, 'I got a beautiful tailor. Let me take you down there and get you some suits.' They'd buy him six suits, three dozen shirts. He loved it and they loved him."

In a similar vein, Richie Paterniti (a friend of Marciano's during the retirement years) told Nack, "Wherever we went, there were mob guys. They loved him because he represented what mob guys really want to be. He was Italian and he beat up every guy he faced. He exuded power, an air of authority. They all wanted to be with him. They kissed his ass."

Nack further recounts, "When Vito Genovese was dying, he put out the word that he wanted Marciano to visit him in prison. Rocky went to Leavenworth to show Genovese films of his fights."

The picture that Nack paints of Marciano in retirement isn't pretty.

Before Marciano turned pro, he was dating Barbara Cousins, six years his junior and the daughter of a Brockton policeman. The press charitably referred to her as tall, blonde, and statuesque. They were married on December 30, 1950, over the objection of Weill, who feared that wedlock would interfere with Marciano's training and, more importantly, his control over the fighter. On December 6, 1952, Mary Anne Marciano was born. Thereafter, Barbara suffered five miscarriages.

Marciano was not a "family man" where his wife and daughter were concerned. As a fighter, he was away from home more often than his profession demanded of him. Subsequent to his leaving the ring, he and Barbara moved to Florida, but he was rarely there. The marriage had become an empty shell.

"There were women for Marciano everywhere he went after his retirement," Nack writes. "That a woman be waiting for him was as requisite for his appearance as the folded $100 bills."

Dominic Santarelli (a longtime social acquaintance and fringe underworld figure) later recalled, "If Rocky ever went to some place and there was not a girl waiting for him, he'd never come back. He never had an affair. I don't think he had sex with the same girl twice. Any girls he had sex with, you couldn't bring her to dinner no more. That's it. Get rid of her. He never wanted to see her again."

"Rock was insane about girls, all the time," Richie Paterniti remembered. "That's all he wanted to do. Rock had orgies and parties. We had girls every single day and night. I had a suitcase that I took all over, filled with vibrators and electric massagers and all kinds of creams and oils."

"He couldn't stand married life," Saccone told Nack. "He had no relationship with his wife."

In 1968, the Marcianos adopted an infant boy, Rocco Kevin, who bore a definite resemblance to his father. By then, Barbara had developed a serious drinking problem, smoked heavily, and was grossly overweight. She died of lung cancer in 1974.

Meanwhile, in retirement, Marciano became obsessed with money beyond the bounds of rational behavior.

Fighters fight for money. That's a given. After Marciano defeated Rex Layne in 1951, Al Weill observed, "Rocky is a poor Italian boy from a poor Italian family and he appreciates the buck more than almost anybody. He's only got two halfway decent purses so far, and it was like a tiger tasting blood."

Marciano himself said in 1955, "When you're the heavyweight champion, the money is the big thing you're going for because that's why you became a fighter in the first place. They're going to criticize you if you blow all your dough on fast living, and they're going to criticize you if you hold onto it. I'd rather keep the money and let them knock me that way."

Well and good.

But as he grew older, Marciano carried things too far. He had a pathological aversion to paying out. When he ate in restaurants (which was often), he did so only with friends or business associates who picked up the check or in places where he wouldn't be billed.

Fellow hall-of-fame fighter Willie Pep later recalled being at nightclub with Marciano. The people at the next table bought them several rounds of drinks, so Pep bought a round in return.

Marciano took Pep into the men's room and chewed him out. "Don't do that."

Pep protested, "Rocky; they've been buying us drinks all night."

"And they're going to keep buying," Marciano instructed. "You don't pay for anything when you're out with me. It makes me look bad if I don't buy a round."

Don Elbaum, who was friendly with Marciano during the retirement years, recalls, "I was in Cleveland one time when Rocky flew in as the guest of honor for a dinner. He arrived at the airport with no suitcase and wearing shorts. His explanation was that he'd run to catch the plane and they hadn't been able to load his luggage. So the organizers of the dinner had to buy him a suit to wear that night. I heard he did that a lot."

"Rocky also had a thing about paying for telephone calls," Elbaum continues. "He used slugs or a trip-wire that returned his money after he made a call from a pay phone. One time, I was in New York, staying at a hotel across the street from the old Madison Square Garden. I was going out for lunch when Rocky stopped me in the lobby and asked, 'Don; do you mind if I use your room to lie down for an hour? I'm really tired' I said it would be an honor and gave him the key. The next day, when I checked out, there was a twenty-five-dollar charge on my room bill for long-distance telephone calls. Twenty five dollars back then was a lot of money."

Marciano structured his life in retirement so that he paid for virtually nothing. There were free rooms, free meals, free transportation. "The whole object of his daily existence," Nack writes, "the reason for the network that moved and sustained him from place to place, was to get him from one sunset to the next without spending a dime."

One night, Marciano went to see Jimmy Durante perform in Las Vegas. Durante took to the stage and announced, "Ladies and gentlemen;

in our audience tonight we have the undefeated heavyweight champion of the world—and America's guest—Rocky Marciano."

Marciano was not amused. Yet he constantly hustled for more. He was always traveling. And he was obsessed with cash.

There were times when Marciano would take half of what he was promised for a speaking engagement if the tender came by cash rather than check. Part of his motivation was tax evasion. He never declared income unless there was a paper trail. When IRS inquiries came, Frank Saccone managed to have them transferred to the IRS office in Brockton.

"They loved Rocky there," Saccone later recalled. "It wasn't difficult to get rid of cases. He was a great charmer."

Marciano also had an irrational mistrust of banks. He hid large sums of money in curtain rods, light fixtures, toilets, and cities unknown. As much as two million dollars by some estimates. After his death, as a matter of record, none of it was found.

On August 31, 1969, one day shy of what would have been his forty-sixth birthday, Marciano boarded a small plane with the pilot and one other passenger for a flight from Chicago to a speaking engagement in Des Moines, Iowa. It was a free flight, courtesy of the pilot, which would enable Marciano to cash in his original plane ticket.

The plane crashed in a field near Newton, Iowa, killing all three men onboard.

Evaluating Marciano as a fighter through the prism of history elicits a wide range of responses. Some experts consider him great. Top Rank's Hall of Fame matchmaker Bruce Trampler takes a contrary view.

"Look at a tape of Marciano," Trampler says. "Then ask yourself what you'd do if he was offered to you now as an opponent for a halfway-decent heavyweight. I'd take him in a minute for one of our guys. Sure, he didn't duck anyone. There was no one for him to duck. I think he's the most overrated fighter of all time."

The great fighters who Marciano beat were getting on in years when he fought them. Joe Louis was thirty-seven. Jersey Joe Walcott was thirty-eight. Ezzard Charles was only two years older than Marciano, but had the wear and tear of close to a hundred fights on him. Archie Moore was forty-one and had answered the bell for round one almost two hundred times.

Add to that the fact that, too often, Marciano's rough brawling style bordered on dirty.

And he would be too small to compete in the heavyweight division today.

That said; all a fighter can be is the best of his era. And Marciano could beat any fighter of his time. His uninterrupted reign as heavyweight champion of the world lasted for forty-three months. Over the past eighty years, only Joe Louis, Muhammad Ali, and Larry Holmes exceeded that standard.

Getting hit and losing rounds never discouraged Marciano. No one ever broke his will. He was as tough in the thirteenth round as he was in the first. Time and again, he dug deep within himself and found what was necessary to win. As much as any fighter ever, he got the maximum out of what he had. In the ring, his character always stood up under pressure.

As for Marciano outside the ring; Jerry Izenberg sums up with the thought, "To be a fighter—any fighter, let alone the kind of fighter that Marciano was—you have to be a little nuts. He was a strange person but not a bad person. In a lot of ways, he was a very decent guy."

One area where Marciano's decency was on display involved the issue of race. During his career, segregation was law in much of the land. Indeed, when Marciano entered the ring for his first professional fight, Jackie Robinson had yet to play in an official major league baseball game.

Yet "throughout his career," Sullivan notes, "Marciano avoided playing on racial issues. He never made a snide comment about the color of his opponent's skin, nor did he ever subtly try to raise the specter of a race conflict."

The key to Marciano's legacy, of course, is that he retired as an active fighter while he was the undefeated heavyweight champion of the world and stayed retired.

In other sports, magic numbers come and go. In baseball . . . 60 . . . 714 . . . 2,130 . . . 4,191 . . . are all gone. It's the way of the world. Standards for immortality change.

But a half-century after Rocky Marciano's retirement from boxing, his record of accomplishment still stands. He entered the ring forty-nine times as a professional fighter and emerged victorious forty-nine times.

Boxing's magic numbers remain "49" and "0."

Round 2

Curiosities

Harold Lederman has become a cult figure in the world of boxing.

At the Fights with Harold Lederman

I've known Harold Lederman for twenty-five years. We've spent hundreds of hours together at media events, social occasions, and fights. But it occurred to me recently that I'd never spent a night at the fights from beginning to end with Harold. On September 1, 2010, at Oceana Hall in Brooklyn, I added that experience to my journey through life.

Harold began judging professional fights in 1967. He has been HBO's "unofficial ringside judge" since 1986. One can make a compelling case that he should be enshrined in the International Boxing Hall of Fame as a ring judge, television commentator, and boxing's quintessential fan.

Harold loves it when he walks through a hotel lobby and total strangers stop to talk boxing with him.

He loves boxing people. "There's something special about them," he says. "Even the bad ones are fun to be around."

He's a pharmacist by trade and works for Duane Reade. His assignments for HBO take him out of town for up to five days at a time. So when Harold is in the store, it's often for a thirteen-hour shift. He'll leave home at six o'clock in the morning and be out until ten at night.

"I work hard," he says. "Wherever I lived, I was always one of the hardest-working guys in the neighborhood."

Harold wears an HBO Boxing watch that employees were given to commemorate an anniversary. He doesn't remember which anniversary, but says it was "a long time ago." By his own description, he's "not a jewelry kind of guy." He has a wedding ring "somewhere at home; I forget where."

He's unfailingly cheerful. Asked to recall the last time he got angry, Harold says, "Who knows? There's not enough time in life to get angry."

His voice is unmistakably his own, as is his distinctive high-pitched laugh.

I told Jim Lampley, Larry Merchant, and Emanuel Steward that I was going to the fights at Oceana Hall with Harold. Over the years, they've watched a few fights with Harold at their side.

"Harold is the mayor at ringside at every fight he goes to," Lampley told me. "Whether it's in the United States or on foreign soil, Harold knows everybody and everybody knows Harold. He's a global ambassador for boxing, and his enthusiasm for life is wonderful. Harold is ebullient about everything. He's ebullient about going to a used bookstore. He's ebullient about what he ate for breakfast. He's ebullient about bumping into Livingston Bramble on the elevator. That's the glory of Harold."

"It's unusual for someone who has been part of boxing for as long as Harold to maintain a wide-eyed enthusiasm for the sport," Merchant offered. "Harold has a wide-eyed enthusiasm for boxing that's beyond compare. When we do a show at an arena away from the hotel we're staying in, HBO arranges for a car to take us to the arena. Harold never goes with us. That's because, without fail, he's at the arena hours ahead of us, watching every preliminary fight, saying hello to every judge, and shaking hands with virtually every fan in the arena."

"Harold is the greatest boxing fan on the face of the earth," Steward added. "The joy that he has for even the most ordinary fights is like nothing I've ever known. There has never been anyone like Harold before, and there will never be anyone like Harold again. If you opened him up, boxing would pour out of his veins."

Oceana Hall is in the Brighton Beach section of Brooklyn. Even at club shows, Harold arrives before the first fight and stays until the last one is over. The first fight was scheduled for 7:15 PM. He drove by my apartment on Riverside Drive in Manhattan and picked me up at six o'clock. It took an hour to reach the venue. Harold talked boxing the entire way.

"Eileen and I have been married for forty-seven years," he reminisced. "The night before we got married, we went to the fights at Madison Square Garden. Gaspar Ortega beat an Italian kid from the Bronx named Billy Bello in the main event. Our honeymoon was in Miami, and we went to the fights there too. Tony Mammarelli was in the main event at that one."

"When I started at HBO, I worked with Barry Tompkins, Larry Merchant, and Ray Leonard. Ray was one of my heroes. I kept pinching myself, saying, 'I can't believe it. I'm on television with Ray Leonard.' I knew how to score a fight, but TV was a whole new ballgame for me. Those guys took me under their wing. They were wonderful to me."

"I used to go to a hundred fight shows a year. Don Elbaum was promoting in Atlantic City; Russell Peltz was promoting in Philadelphia. How could I not go to their shows? It was a three-hour drive each way. I'd go to the fights, get home at two o'clock in the morning, sleep for four hours, get back up, and go to work. Every one of those shows was worth it. But I'm older now; I just turned seventy, I don't run to Philadelphia and Atlantic City the way I used to. Now, including the HBO shows, I go to maybe fifty shows a year."

We reached Brighton Beach Avenue at seven o'clock and parked on the street two blocks from Oceana Hall. Dmitriy Salita was headlining the card.

Salita is a rarity in boxing; an Orthodox Jew with a 30–1–1 record. His sole loss was a first-round stoppage at the hands of Amir Khan in England last December. This show would be his comeback fight and also the debut of boxing on The Jewish Channel.

Oceana Hall is an unusual club-fight venue, with gilded columns and a decorative hardwood floor. It can hold eleven hundred people for wedding receptions and bar mitzvahs. For boxing, the number is eight hundred.

Harold is a celebrity at club fights. Like Madonna, he's identifiable on a first-name basis. When we walked in, everyone wanted to say hello to Harold, and Harold wanted to say hello to everyone. Making his way to his seat, he schmoozed with promoter Brian O'Shea, ring announcer David Diamante, a half dozen people from the New York State Athletic Commission, and at least as many fans.

Then the fights started. These were club fights. Six four-round bouts and one six-rounder with the main event scheduled for eight. Adding their records together, the first twelve fighters to enter the ring had a total of 9 wins, 19 losses, and 3 draws. But for Harold, each bout was a unique work of performance art.

The participants in the first fight were introduced. Junior-welterweights. A fighter from Connecticut, who was 2-and-0 with two knockouts, against a fighter from Baltimore, who was 0-and-1.

"I hate to say this," Harold said seconds before the opening bell. "But the guy from Baltimore looks like he doesn't want to fight."

Once the bell rang, it was also clear that the guy from Baltimore didn't know how to fight. He had no idea where to hold his hands or how to position his feet and was knocked out with the first solid punch of the night.

Fight number two was a different story. Thomas Baldwin (1–0) against Felix Rangel (0–4–1). Harold offered expert commentary as the action unfolded.

"You can't miss Rangel with a right hand. I guess that's why he's 0-4-and-1. But he's hanging in there . . . Look at that! Rangel is fighting back. He's here to win . . . This is a very good fight."

In the final round, the contest became a nonstop slugfest. Baldwin was in big trouble but survived till the bell. Harold stood with the rest of the crowd and applauded when it was over. He doesn't formally score bouts when he's not officially working. "But I keep a scorecard in my mind," he told me. "And I've got this one dead even."

The bout was declared a draw.

"I love it when a guy wins a fight that he's not supposed to win," Harold said. "A draw isn't as good as a win; but for Rangel, it's pretty good."

Now the crowd had been drawn into the action. Salita, who was born in Ukraine, has a sizeable following within the Orthodox Jewish Community. Brighton Beach has a heavy Russian population. This was a blue-collar multi-ethnic crowd, loud and appreciative.

"These are boxing fans," Harold noted. "And they know boxing. I love crowds like this."

Fight number three matched Benjamin Morales (1–0) against Rafael Vasquez (pro debut). It was another good action fight. Early on, Vasquez was teeing off and landing righthands at will. A lot of them. But Morales hung tough. He had never lost as a pro and didn't want to lose now. He showed enormous heart.

Heart wasn't enough. All three judges (plus Oceana Hall's "unofficial ringside judge") scored the fight 39–37 for Vasquez. As Morales left the ring, he was crying.

"I feel bad for him," Harold said. "He tried as hard as he could. He was just outgunned."

As evening progressed, former fighters like Dana Rosenblatt and Junior Jones came by to say hello. So did trainer Tommy Gallagher and ring judge Glenn Feldman. Harold had a word (strike that; Harold had several paragraphs) for each of them.

"I got a funny story to tell you . . . Do you remember when you fought . . . I was just thinking about that fight we went to together in . . ."

Paulie Malignaggi gave Harold a hug and told me, "This guy knows boxing. A lot of TV commentators aren't really into it. It's just a job to them. Harold is the best fan there is in boxing and he knows the sport. When a fighter gets on network television, a lot of people ask, 'Where did he come from?' I guarantee you, Harold has been following that fighter since he turned pro."

"And by the way," Paulie added; "Harold talks more than I do."

Harold talked nonstop throughout the fights. A unanimous four-round shut-out decision for Jonathan Cuba (2–2) over Hector Rivera (2–5–1). A twenty-second knockout for Frank Galarza (pro debut) over Nicholas Morris (0–1). The twenty seconds included the ten-count.

Harold watched every minute of every fight and noticed everything. Cuts, swelling, loose tape on a fighter's glove, an untied shoelace.

"Do you ever get bored at the fights?" I asked.

"Never."

The sixth fight of the evening saw DeCarlo Perez (0–0–1) take on Filiberto Nieto (1–6). Nieto was a human punching bag. Perez didn't punch very hard, but the punches added up. Early in round four, Nieto turned away from the action and walked to the ropes. Referee Sparkle Lee started counting.

"For God's sake," Harold muttered. "When a guy turns away, stop the fight. What's she counting for?"

The ring doctor stepped in and stopped the action.

"I don't like to see guys get hurt when there's no reason for it," Harold told me.

Moments later, Sparkle Lee walked by.

"Hey, Sparkle," Harold shouted. "When a guy turns away, stop the fight. He turned away because he was getting beaten up and didn't want to fight anymore."

There was a break in the action before the seventh fight. Harold went to a concession stand near the front doors and bought a Dmitriy Salita T-shirt for his wife.

"Eileen likes T-shirts," he told me. "I don't know what she does with them. But whenever I come home from the fights with a T-shirt for her, it makes her happy."

Mike Ruiz (9–4) won a unanimous decision over Josh Beeman (4–7–2). Then it was time for the main event: Dmitriy Salita vs. Franklin Gonzalez.

Gonzalez had a 13-and-5 record. But he'd lost three of his last four fights, with the lone victory coming against an adversary who was 1-and-5. In truth, he was as safe as a main-event opponent could be and still pass muster with the New York State Athletic Commission.

There was a standing ovation as Salita entered the ring. Each man had weighed in at 149 pounds. Gonzalez looked soft around the middle.

The fight started. Gonzalez, a southpaw of modest ability, plodded forward. Dmitriy moved laterally and backward, popping his jab. He looked tentative and rusty.

"If Dmitriy doesn't stop backing up," Harold noted, "this fight is going to be a stinker."

In round two, Gonzalez got brave and started winging punches. The punches landed. Round three was more of the same. An ugly welt appeared beneath Dmitriy's left eye.

"Dmitriy is fighting the wrong fight," Harold observed. "When he punches, the other guy doesn't. He should be backing this guy up with his jab."

Then, in round four, Gonzalez stopped punching. Giving him the benefit of the doubt, he was showing the effects of not having spent much time in the gym. From that point on, Dmitriy continued to fight a safety-first fight and Gonzalez hardly fought at all.

"Gonzalez isn't punching," Harold offered. "He's just standing there, not throwing anything, waiting to get hit and letting Dmitriy steal rounds."

It was an easy fight to score. Each judge and virtually everyone else in the arena had it 78–74 for Salita.

"I'm happy Dmitriy won," Harold said. "I like him; he's a good kid. But the other guy just stopped fighting. He could have made it a much better fight than it was."

At the end of the evening, Harold didn't just leave the arena. He stopped to shake hands with everyone who approached him. Then we got in the car to go home.

"I love club shows from the bottom of my heart," Harold told me as we drove through the Battery Tunnel into Manhattan. "You see good fights; you see bad fights. You see good shows; you see bad shows. But I'm always happy when I'm at the fights. I had a great time tonight."

True crossover superstars in boxing are few and far between.

Who Will Be Boxing's Next Crossover Superstar ?

Over the past fifty years, five boxers have become crossover superstars in the United States. In chronological, order, they are—drumroll, please!

Muhammad Ali, Sugar Ray Leonard, Mike Tyson, George Foreman, and Oscar De La Hoya.

There have been other great fighters.

Evander Holyfield, Roy Jones, Marvin Hagler, Roberto Duran, and Larry Holmes (to name a few) made huge amounts of money. In some instances, they lay legitimate claim to boxing's pound-for-pound throne. But they weren't besieged by non-sports fans or surrounded by hordes of people when they walked down the street.

Ring prowess, in and of itself, isn't enough for a fighter to "cross over." Being a crossover superstar means that non-sports fans are drawn to you and all heads turn when you enter a room.

Or phrased differently; my mother knows your name and face.

Muhammad Ali won a gold medal as Cassius Clay at the 1960 Rome Olympics and upset Sonny Liston to claim the heavyweight championship of the world. Then everything changed. Once upon a time, he'd been regarded as telegenic, charismatic, and charming. Now, suddenly, he was telegenic, charismatic, and exceedingly threatening to the American establishment.

Clay adopted the teachings of a black separatist religion known as the Nation of Islam and changed his name to Muhammad Ali. Then he refused induction into the United States Army at the height of the war in Vietnam. That put him on the front page of every newspaper in America. He was exiled from boxing; written off as road kill after comeback losses at the hands of Joe Frazier and Ken Norton; and ultimately defeated George Foreman in Zaire to reclaim the heavyweight throne.

By virtue of his conduct in and out of the ring and the sheer force of his personality, Ali became a crossover superstar.

Like Ali, Ray Leonard won an Olympic gold medal (in Montreal in 1976). Like Ali, he beat the best as a pro. But equally important, Leonard understood that he had to create his own identity to achieve crossover superstar status. He did that as boxing's "All-American Boy."

Leonard had star power; a face and persona that the American public could embrace. There were gaps between his public image and the reality of his life. But Ray played his on-stage role well. The public liked Sugar Ray Leonard.

Mike Tyson made his mark in boxing as an exciting talented fighter. He "crossed over" when he became a train wreck.

Tyson was a perfect storm that touched down in the area where sports and America's tabloid culture coincide.

"My intentions were not to fascinate the world with my personality," Tyson said as his career drew to a close. "I just wanted the boxing world to bear witness to my existence. I didn't know that I was going to be some big worldwide motherfucker; when I walk the streets of Paris, the whole block shuts down."

George Foreman was unpopular in his first incarnation as heavyweight champion. Despite winning a gold medal at the 1968 Mexico City Olympics, he turned people off with a rude surly persona. He was Sonny Liston redux at a time when "bad boys" weren't commercially viable.

In 1987, after a ten-year self-imposed exile, Foreman returned to boxing. He was thirty-eight years old and weighed 267 pounds (fifty more than he'd weighed when he knocked out Joe Frazier to win the heavyweight crown).

The "new" George Foreman was good-natured, even jolly.

He joked about eating hamburgers.

"All I know about boxing is that it hurts," he said.

Appearing on *The Tonight Show* in 1990, Foreman was quizzed about his next opponent.

"Is Adilson Rodrigues a good fighter?" Johnny Carson asked.

"I hope not," George answered.

Foreman was the anti-Tyson and one of the great public-relations experts in sports history. On November 5, 1994, seven years into his comeback, he knocked out Michael Moorer to regain the heavyweight championship of the world.

Score one for aging fat people everywhere. Soon, Foreman was boxing's king of endorsements; from Meineke Mufflers to his own Lean Mean Grilling Machine.

As Foreman's star reached its zenith, Oscar De La Hoya was beginning his own climb up the ladder.

De La Hoya followed the Sugar Ray Leonard blueprint (Olympic gold medal and All-American Boy image) with a Hispanic-American twist.

Like Ali, Leonard, Tyson, and Foreman, "Oscar" benefited from free broadcast television exposure early in his career. But he received his biggest boost from HBO's marketing machine when the network made him the face of HBO-PPV. That put him on the edge of the new media.

All of which brings us to the question: "Who will be boxing's next crossover superstar in the American market?"

Manny Pacquiao and Floyd Mayweather Jr are the leading contenders. Each is a marvelously gifted fighter. Pacquiao has a winning personality and engenders good will wherever he goes. Mayweather has a flair for self-promotion and enjoys the spotlight, whether he's playing good guy or bad.

But each currently falls short of crossover superstar status. Pacquiao has crossed over (and then some) in his native Philippines. But many people in America don't know his name, and many more don't know his face.

Mayweather talks a lot about how famous he is. But the truth is that he could walk through Times Square tomorrow with little recognition and less fuss.

I've got an idea. Why don't Pacquiao and Mayweather fight each other? With all the publicity that Mayweather-Pacquiao would engender, the winner would stand a good chance of becoming boxing's next crossover superstar.

At age eighty-four, my mother still goes where the action is.

My 84-Year-Old Mother Meets . . .

Three years ago, I brought my mother to a press conference at Madison Square Garden to meet Don King. Then I posted an article on Secondsout.com entitled (appropriately enough) "My 81-Year-Old Mother Meets Don King."

Neither my mother nor I expected what followed. There were emails from octogenarians asking for dates. Publicists offered to take us to lunch, so I could write about my mother meeting their fighters. There was even a request for an interview from the NYU student newspaper.

Why the NYU student newspaper?

My article had referenced the fact that my mother was taking a course in global politics at the school's midtown campus.

My mother is now eighty-four. Each day, she's out and about. She goes to concerts, theater, movies, and museums. She plays bridge, has an active social life, and still takes a course at NYU.

"New York," she says, "is like a Disneyland for old people."

My mother has an adventurous spirit. She thought it would be fun to meet some hardcore, in-the-trenches, boxing people. So earlier this month, I set up a lunch at Portobello's.

Portobello's is a pizza place in lower Manhattan. The chicken parmesan is good. But Venice has canals, and Portobello's has pizza. The grandma's pizza (cheese, pesto, and tomato sauce) is my favorite.

Anthony Catanzaro (who runs Portobello's) is a boxing guy. He began in the sport as a mentor to Paulie Malignaggi. Now he has a managerial stake in junior-welterweight prospect Christian Martinez and advises several other fighters.

The guest list for the Eleanor Hauser luncheon included (drum roll, please):

Harold Lederman: HBO's unofficial ringside judge and possibly the nicest man in boxing.

Craig Hamilton: The foremost boxing memorabilia dealer in the United States and one of the sport's best managers.

Vinny Maddalone: New York's most popular active heavyweight.

Paulie Malignaggi: Quiet, subdued . . . Just kidding. Paulie is Paulie. He'll also be in the record books forever as a 140-pound world champion.

David Diamante: The ring announcer with the stentorian voice, David now owns Diamante's Brooklyn Cigar Lounge. In the past, he has worked inter alia as a rock drummer, fry cook, bike messenger, and emcee for Scores East (an upscale adult club in New York).

Don Elbaum: The greatest living American and a quintessential boxing guy. "Let me tell you about my mother," Elbaum said when I invited him to the lunch. "My mother had an idealized image of me. After I'd been married for ten years and had two sons, she still thought I was a virgin."

Seven hardcore, in-the-trenches, boxing people.

Dick Schaap once wrote, "I hate the sport of boxing. I think it's barbaric, and I don't think it should be allowed. But I love the people who are in it."

Schaap would have loved this gathering. Think King Arthur and his Knights of the Round Table. Or at the very least, Dorothy Parker at the Algonquin.

The first thing that my mother saw when we arrived at Portobello's was a sign on the sidewalk outside the restaurant that read, "Welcome Mrs. Hauser." We went inside and the festivities began.

Anthony Catanzaro knows how to throw a party. And he's a gracious host. The food kept coming.

Boxing people being what we are, we kept eating.

"My mother was a fantastic cook," Harold reminisced. "Her name was Fannie Lederman. One time, I invited a friend named Woody Weinstein home for dinner. My mother made a huge brisket and put a platter of meat on the table in front of Woody. He started to take a piece so he could pass the platter around. And she told him, 'No. That's your portion.'"

Paulie and Vinny were coming off announcing gigs. Four nights earlier, Paulie had been the color commentator for a fight card in Philadelphia that was televised by Comcast. Two nights after that, Vinny was behind the microphone for the pay-per-view telecast of David Tua versus Monte Barrett in Atlantic City.

"I was a little nervous," Vinny said. "When you're commentating, you have to think before you speak. But the hardest thing for me was; I'd sparred fifty rounds with Monte, getting him ready for the fight. I could root for him, but I couldn't let my bias show."

"Another thing that's hard," Paulie added; "if a fight is boring, you have to keep your own excitement level up. You don't want to lie to the viewers, but you have find a way to break the monotony and keep them involved."

Why had they become fighters, my mother wanted to know.

"I watched *Raging Bull* and all the *Rocky* movies," Vinny told her. "Then, when I was in college, I entered a toughman contest. It seemed like a good idea at the time. After that, things just happened. I have no regrets."

"Boxing gave me the opportunity to be somebody," Paulie explained. "And I've made a pretty good living from it. The first fight you have as an amateur is the turning point. After that, either you know you want to be a fighter real bad or you know you never want to do it again. After my first fight, I knew I wanted to be a fighter. The business is corrupt and run by morons. I hate the business. But I love being a fighter."

Vinny is nearing the end of his ring career and thinking ahead to life after boxing. Toward that end, he's now part-owner of the Ringside Bar & Grill; a restaurant in Whitestone, New York. It seats fifty with room for thirty more at the bar.

"I'm there every Friday and Saturday from three in the afternoon till four in the morning," he told us. "The food is good; paninis and salads, nothing fancy."

Paulie's ring future is uncertain. Earlier in the day, it had been announced that he'd parted ways with his longtime promoter, Lou DiBella.

Craig voiced the view that Lou had done a good job of promoting Paulie. Paulie voiced the view that he could have been marketed more aggressively.

"The next time you fight, we'll go out and paint graffiti about you on a bunch of buildings," David Diamante suggested helpfully.

David's most visible signature trait is his hair, which he hasn't cut in twenty-two years. Neatly braided, it extends to his waist.

"Is it hard to wash?" my mother queried.

"Washing it is easy," David told her. "Drying it is hard."

Harold asked my mother if she'd ever gone to a fight.

"No; and I don't want to. I don't like to see people get hit; not even on television."

"When boxing is bad, it's the worst," David offered. "But at its best, it's a beautiful sport."

Eventually, the conversation worked its way around to, "It's hard for me to believe that my son became a boxing writer."

"Life makes plans for us," Anthony (in full philosophical mode) noted. "And they're not always the plans we make for life."

At the end of the lunch, Anthony asked my mother to sign a boxing glove. It's now hanging inside Portobello's on the west wall next to gloves signed by Sergio Martinez, Mark Breland, and Winky Wright.

Then David offered to take my mother home on his motorcycle. She opted for more conventional vehicular transportation with Harold.

"I like meeting new people," my mother told me as we left Portobello's. "It was an adventure."

And what did she think of the people she'd just met?

"They couldn't have been nicer. Paulie is adorable; a little cocky but as cute as can be. Vinny is a lovely fellow. David has an elegance about him."

"What about his hair?

"It looks good on him. It's a style; he wears it well."

And the others?

"Craig is very smart. Anthony was a wonderful host."

And Harold?

"Boy; does he love boxing."

Perspicacious readers might note that there has been no mention so far of Don Elbaum's actual attendance at the gathering.

That's because Elbaum was a no-show.

Shortly after I arrived home, the telephone rang.

"Jesus; I'm sorry," the greatest living American said. "I was running all over the place. Please, please, please apologize to your mother for me."

"I'll be happy to. But I should tell you; the title of the article I'm writing now is "My 84-Year-Old Mother Is Stood Up By Don Elbaum"

"Wait! I have excuses."

"Okay; let's hear them."

"My computer crashed, so I lost track of the date. Is that good enough?"

"No."

"Okay; let me try again. I was kidnapped by terrorists and held for ransom."

"Don, that's absurd. No one would pay two cents for you."

"I know. When they found that out, they let me go for free."

"Next."

"It makes me nervous to be around beautiful women. Your mother should like that one."

"Keep going."

"I just bought a used car and it's not registered yet. I was afraid that, if I drove into New York, I'd be arrested. How many excuses is that?"

"Four."

"All right. I'm running out of excuses, so I'll tell you the truth. Do you want to know the truth?"

"Absolutely."

"This is truth, the whole truth, and nothing but the truth, so help me God. I spent the afternoon trying to get laid by a roundcard girl I met last week in Philadelphia."

AND A POSTSCRIPT ON DON ELBAUM

Don Elbaum telephoned recently to spread a message: Boxing fans should no longer be depressed about the demise of Pacquiao-Mayweather. A new mega-fight is on the horizon.

Elbaum is an adviser to Joey Abell; a twenty-eight-year-old heavyweight from Coon Rapids, Minnesota. Joey has a (somewhat padded) 25-and-4 record, with 24 of his victories coming by way of knockout.

Elbaum swears that Abell is "the hardest punching heavyweight since John L. Sullivan." He further proclaims, "When it comes to pure punching power, I'd rank Joey, Earnie Shavers, and Mike Tyson one-two-three in that order."

Note to readers: When pressed, Elbaum acknowledges, "To be completely honest, Earnie Shavers at his peak might have punched as hard as Joey."

2008 was a bad year for Abell. On April 26, 2008, he was knocked out in four rounds by Andrew Greely, who has lost 16 of his last 17 fights (the sole win coming against Abell). On September 5th, Joey lost a six-round decision to forty-four-year-old Al Cole (who was coming off a forty-two-month layoff and three consecutive losses). Then, on November 28th, he was disqualified in a bout against Jason Nicholson, who has triumphed twice in his most recent 27 outings.

But Elbaum is quick to note that Abell rebounded in 2009 with five wins over "the toughest guys I could find; and they were hard to find because most guys are afraid to fight Joey."

Bottom line: Abell is now tentatively slated to face off against forty-one-year-old Frans Botha in Uganda for the coveted WBF heavyweight championship.

"What's the WBF?" you might ask.

"It used to be the World Boxing Foundation," Elbaum answers. "But the people who ran it couldn't get along with each other, so they split into two groups; the WBF and the WBF."

Huh?

"The World Boxing Foundation and the World Boxing Federation," Elbaum explains. "But maybe the World Boxing Federation came first; I'm not sure. The president of the one I'm talking about is Australian. You can look up which is which on the Internet."

"Anyway," Elbaum continues, "Botha was supposed to fight Evander Holyfield in Uganda for the heavyweight title of one of the WBFs. Joey was going to be on the undercard. But the money wasn't there when Evander wanted it, so Evander pulled out and they moved Joey into the championship fight. They don't have a heavyweight champion yet; so if Joey beats Botha, he'll be the first. I think Botha is already heavyweight champion of the other WBF. So unless Botha has been stripped, if he beats Joey, as far as WBF heavyweight champions are concerned, Botha will be both."

"The promoter is an African-Swedish person," Elbaum adds. "I'm not sure what his last name is. I just call him Eddie. He's a great guy. We're expecting 80,000 people at Nelson Mandela Stadium in Uganda for the fight. You gotta come."

Botha-Abell was originally scheduled for February 27th. That enabled me to tell Elbaum, "February 27th is my birthday, and I'm not spending it in Uganda."

"Your birthday?" Elbaum countered. "That's fantastic. Then you really gotta come. I guarantee you; we'll have 80,000 Ugandans sing "Happy Birthday" for you and we'll bake you the biggest cake ever. It will be in the *Guinness Book of Records.*"

It wasn't to be. Elbaum later called to report, "The fight is still on, but we have to move it to a new date because the money hasn't arrived yet. Eddie sent it by wire transfer eight days ago. He's at the bank now trying to find out what happened to it. Could you move your birthday back a couple of weeks?"

That's why he's Don Elbaum and we're not.

One of the sad things about boxing today is that the satire below had the ring of truth. Then again, most satire does.

Flights of Fantasy

The World Boxing Council announced this week that it is withdrawing recognition of 160-pound champion Sergio Martinez and 147-pound champion Andre Berto because of the conduct of their promoter, Lou DiBella.

"This is like the problem we had with Chris Arreola, who we removed from the rankings and refused to let fight for our title for six months because he used bad language after he lost to Vitali Klitschko," WBC president Jose Sulaiman declared. "I like Lou DiBella. He is my friend. But Lou DiBella swears all the time. He insults people by saying things like 'boxing is a miserable fucking business' and 'the people who run boxing are assholes.' For the good of boxing, this must stop."

Sulaiman said that the sanctions would extend to all of DiBella's fighters. This means that Kermit Cintron, Randall Bailey, and Allan Green will be among those removed immediately from the WBC rankings.

"But I am a fair man," Sulaiman said. "Each of these fighters may apply for immediate reinstatement to the WBC rankings. All that is necessary for each of them to do is to send a request for reinstatement to the WBC together with a check in the amount of one thousand dollars to cover the administrative fee. And because I bend over backwards to help boxers, Martinez and Berto may apply for immediate reinstatement if they send me the trunks that they wore on the night that they won the WBC championship."

When advised that his son, Mauricio, took Sergio's trunks on the night that Martinez defeated Kelly Pavlik, Sulaiman responded, "I am sure that Mauricio did this for the good of boxing."

After being told of Sulaiman's announcement, DiBella declared, "This is one more example of why boxing is a miserable fucking business and further proof that it's run by assholes."

* * *

Oscar De La Hoya is planning to fight again. After a period of reflection following his 2008 knockout loss at the hands of Manny Pacquiao, boxing's Golden Boy will enter the ring on November 20, 2010, one week after the proposed bout between Pacquiao and Antonio Margarito.

"I couldn't live with myself if I ended my career sitting on the stool against Pacquiao," De La Hoya told Secondsout.com. "I want to go out with a big bang. I want to show everybody around the world that boxing is alive and well. I want them to say, 'Look at this big event.' So I am returning to the ring at the MGM Grand on November 20th to fight Freddie Roach. Freddie Roach is a formidable opponent. I ask myself, 'Can I win a fight against an opponent with his incredible ring savvy?' But I promise you that I will be up to the task."

"This fight is personal for me," Oscar continued. "Freddie Roach said some things that have really upset me. And he really got my blood boiling when he trained Manny Pacquiao to beat me. When the bell rings, I'm going to punish Freddie Roach. I don't know who will train me. But I know for certain that he will be the best trainer I ever had and that I will train harder than I've ever trained before and it will be the best training camp of my life."

Golden Boy CEO Richard Schaefer seconded De La Hoya's thoughts and added, "We have no doubt that this fight will be one of the biggest boxing events of all time."

The MGM Grand Sports Book says that Roach has opened as a 7-to-5 favorite.

* * *

Floyd Mayweather Jr adviser Leonard Ellerbe issued a statement today denying that Mayweather's 2008 wrestling match against Big Show had been fixed.

"Here are the facts," Ellerbe's statement read. "Floyd and myself speak to each other on a regular basis. The truth is that there was never any agreement to prearrange the outcome of the fight between Floyd and Big Show. Floyd would never demean his status as an elite athlete by doing anything like that. I know that Bob Arum is telling people that the fight was scripted. Either Bob Arum or myself is not telling the truth, but history tells us who is lying."

Shortly thereafter, Richard Schaefer issued a statement of his own, declaring, "I agree with Leonard entirely with regard to the very exciting athletic competition between Floyd and Big Show. I stand firmly behind Leonard's remarks."

Meanwhile, Oscar De La Hoya has sought to explain his June 10th interview with Univision in which he stated, "We are very very close to finalizing the contracts [for Mayweather-Pacquiao]."

"The interview with Univision was in Spanish," De La Hoya noted. "And I've spoken so much English lately that my Spanish has gotten rusty. I meant to say, 'No sé nada sobre ningunas negociaciones,' which means, "I know nothing about any negotiations.'"

Also regarding Mayweather-Pacquiao, Richard Schaefer today denied Don King's claim that he doesn't relate properly to Floyd Mayweather Jr because he can't speak ghetto-ese.

"I speak six languages Schaefer declared. "German, Swiss German, French, English, Spanish, and Ghetto-ese. "I will prove it to you. Yo! Motherfucker! Give me some bling."

* * *

WBC president Jose Sulaiman announced today that the WBC has decided to sanction the 2011 Super Bowl.

"This was a very wise decision that has been made by our board of governors," Sulaiman told delegates at the annual WBC convention. "The Super Bowl is the biggest event in football and the WBC is the biggest name in boxing. The next Super Bowl will be paid—excuse me, I meant to say played—in Cowboys Stadium on February 6, 2011. Now, we will put the WBC and the Super Bowl together, and a coveted green belt will be given to each member of the winning team."

"This will be for the good of boxing and for the good of football," Sulaiman added. "For this reason, we have decided to cut the sanctioning fee that we will ask of the NFL from our normal 3 percent to a flat fee of three million pesos. It is my dream that, someday, the baseball World

Series, the Masters tournament in golf, the Indianapolis 500 automobile race, and all other great sporting events will take place under the supervision of the WBC. Perhaps someday at the Olympics, each winner will be given a green belt instead of a gold medal. I know that the Olympic athletes would like that."

* * *

Fresh off his victories against Harry Yorgey, Joel Julio, and Joachim Alcine, Alfredo Angulo has signed to fight an Everlast heavy-bag on HBO's *Boxing After Dark*.

"This will be another great night for HBO Sports," senior vice president for sports programming Kery Davis said. "To my knowledge, no one has been able to stop the heavy bag short of the distance, so it's a real test for Alfredo."

Angulo's promoter, Gary Shaw, seconded Davis and added, "Alfredo has looked great in the gym against the heavy bag. But HBO expert analyst Max Kellerman warned, "The heavy bag takes a good punch and moves around better than some of the opponents that Angulo has fought recently on HBO. I think it's a toss-up fight."

* * *

WBC president Jose Sulaiman announced today that Julio Cesar Chavez Jr will fight Mexican legend Erik Morales in February for the WBC heavyweight championship at a catchweight of 161 pounds.

"The WBC Board of Governors has decided to return Vitali Klitschko to his status as heavyweight champion emeritus," Sulaiman told a news conference in Mexico City. "To be the WBC heavyweight champion emeritus is one of the greatest honors in boxing. This means that the WBC heavyweight championship is now vacant. The WBC championship committee in its wisdom has decided that Chavez and Morales should fight for the coveted green belt. For the first time in history, whoever wins, the heavyweight champion of the world will be from Mexico."

During a question-and-answer session following the announcement, a reporter questioned why Chavez and Morales were fighting for the

WBC heavyweight championship, given the fact that Chavez has never fought above 160 pounds and Morales has fought above 135 pounds only twice in his life.

In response, Sulaiman declared, "Manny Pacquiao and Antonio Margarito fought for the WBC 154-pound championship and neither man was allowed to weigh-in above 150 pounds. Sergio Martinez and Paul Williams fought for the WBC 160-pound championship and neither man was allowed to weigh-in above 158 pounds. This is the same principle, and I am a man of principle."

★ ★ ★

David Haye has called out pound-for-pound king Manny Pacquiao.

The WBA heavyweight beltholder issued his challenge at a press conference in London. Wearing a T-shirt that depicted him holding a British flag in one hand and a sword in the other while trodding on the Filipino people, Haye declared, "Manny Pacquiao is afraid to fight me. If we ever get into the ring together, I'll show him who's number one in the world."

Informed that Pacquiao had accepted his challenge to fight at a catchweight of 210 pounds, agreed to a fifty-fifty revenue split, and was willing to fight in London, Haye conferred hastily with adviser Adam Booth and told the assembled media, "We don't want to rush into anything. I might fight Ricky Hatton instead."

Reached for comment in Manchester, Hatton replied, "I'm honored, mate. But to be honest with you, I don't think I can make 210 pounds."

★ ★ ★

In response to a wave of media criticism, the World Boxing Council has decided to fight fire with fire and will form a new BWAA.

"The Boxing Writers Association of America is no good," WBC president Jose Sulaiman said at a press conference yesterday. "So for the good of boxing, the WBC is forming the Boxing Writers Association of the Americas. This will be very special because all of the Americas is bigger than just America."

"And there is much more we have that will be an improvement," Sulaiman added. "The old BWAA has full members and auxiliary members. The new BWAA will have full members, auxiliary members, and diamond members. The diamond members will receive a membership card with an itsy-bitsy diamond in it, which, of course, they will pay for."

Sulaiman also declared, "All writers are aware that their membership in the new BWAA will enhance their marketability. Therefore, for the good of boxing, we will require them to remit 10 percent of their annual salary by wire transfer to a special new BWAA bank account that will be supervised by the WBC."

After being informed that most boxing writers don't have an annual salary, Sulaiman gulped and his face turned ashen. Later in the day, he announced, "I have spoken with the WBC board of governors. To accommodate those writers who don't have an annual salary, the new BWAA will charge a flat fee for membership."

* * *

More on the WBC.

WBC president Jose Sulaiman has announced a new line of WBC belts to be bestowed upon fighters.

"The executive board has spoken wisely," Sulaiman declared. "In addition to our green belt, our silver belt, and our diamond belt, we now have belts for every color in the biggest box of Crayola crayons. That gives us 128 belts in each weight division. It is my dream that someday every fight in boxing will be for a WBC belt."

In a related announcement, Sulaiman said that the WBC also has a new weight division.

"I have devoted my life to making boxing a fair sport," Sulaiman proclaimed. "But the way the sport is now, some fighters are at a disadvantage because they are really light-heavyweights but, because they weigh over two hundred pounds, they are forced to fight heavyweights. This is not fair. To fix this injustice, the WBC will now have a Fatso Division."

The WBC "fatso division" will be open to all fighters who weigh more than two hundred pounds and have a body-fat percentage of 30 percent or more.

"Once everything is in place," Sulaiman elaborated, "the WBC will have a fatso champion, an interim fatso champion, and a super-fatso champion."

James Toney has been designated as the WBC fatso champion emeritus.

* * *

The NCAA announced today that it has decided to scrap its tradition elimination-tournament format and adopt a modified Showtime "Super Six" model for its Men's Championship Basketball Tournament.

"March Madness has gotten tired," NCAA president Mark Emmert said. "Initially, we planned to expand the tournament to sixty-eight teams with four play-in games that would narrow the field to sixty-four. Then we looked at what Ken Hershman has done at Showtime and decided, if it's good enough for boxing, it's good enough for us."

Under the new formula, seventy teams will be invited to the tournament. The Atlantic Coast Conference champion will be excluded because neither Duke nor North Carolina is promoted by Gary Shaw. The seventy teams will play each other in a partial round-robin schedule with UCLA refusing to play in any game that isn't scheduled for Pauly Pavilion in Westwood. Teams will drop out of the tournament as their star players flunk out of college or leave school to join the NBA.

"If things get too complicated," Emmert explained, "we'll just ignore the schedule and go right to the Final Four. I have no idea how the Final Four will be chosen, but we'll think of something."

"And there will be other changes," Emmert added. "Under our new format, a team will be able to skip the first few rounds of the tournament, come in as a late entry, and, if it wins one game big, still make the Final Four. Or maybe we'll just have a Final Three. I don't know when we'll crown a champion, but I think it will be sometime in 2013."

* * *

The WBC board of governors announced today that WBC president Jose Sulaiman has been given the additional titles of Super-President,

Super-Duper President, Silver President, Gold President, Platinum President, Diamond President, President Emeritus, and President for Life.

"They also offered to make me Interim President," Sulaiman acknowledged. "But interim I do not like."

Round 3

Issues and Answers

This might have been the most important article that I wrote in 2010.

Mayweather-Pacquiao, PEDs, and Boxing

Two days before Manny Pacquiao fought Miguel Cotto, I talked with Alex Ariza, who has been Pacquiao's strength and conditioning coach since early 2008. When I asked what it was like to work with an athlete of Manny's caliber, Ariza shook his head in wonder.

"It's an extraordinary experience," he said. "Athletes start to backslide around age twenty-eight if they haven't started to decline before then. Manny is thirty and he's getting better. Our records don't lie. Not only is he getting stronger; he's actually getting faster as he moves up in weight. I've worked with some great athletes, but I've never worked with an athlete like Manny."

"But there's one thing that's very frustrating for me," Ariza added. "Manny won't let me do all the tests I want to do with him. There are tests I'd love to do to determine his lung capacity, but they're invasive and he won't let me do them. And there are other measurements, quite a few, that I'd like to take, but I can't because Manny is very protective of his body."

People will read what they want to into Ariza's comments. Those who supported Floyd Mayweather Jr in the debacle that saw Mayweather-Pacquiao go from superfight to no fight will say that Pacquiao is able to defy the laws of nature because he's using performance-enhancing drugs. Manny's partisans will respond that Ariza's remarks confirm their hero's honest aversion to invasive testing.

I don't know whether Pacquiao (or Mayweather) is using performance-enhancing drugs or not. To my knowledge, no one else in the media does either. I do know that both men are entitled to the presumption of innocence in the absence of hard evidence to the contrary. And to date, no one has produced such evidence.

Still, recent events have ended the anonymity (if not immunity) that boxing enjoyed throughout the earlier public debate regarding PEDs and sports. So let's take a look at (1) the nature of steroids and other performance-enhancing drugs; (2) their role in boxing; (3) the instant controversy between the Mayweather and Pacquiao camps; and (4) some lessons that can be drawn from it all.

It's not a pretty story. The situation brings to mind the exchange between Colonel Nathan R. Jessep (played by Jack Nicholson) and Lieutenant Daniel Kaffee (Tom Cruise) in *A Few Good Men:*

> Colonel Jessep: You want answers?
> Lieutenant Kaffee: I want the truth.
> Colonel Jessep: You can't handle the truth.

Does boxing really want to know?

I

The first thing to know about performance-enhancing drugs is that they work. When used in conjunction with proper exercise and training, they create a better athlete.

Steroids decrease inflammation and healing time. "That's how the whole thing started, with legitimate medical usage," says Dr. Flip Homansky (former chief ringside physician for the Nevada State Athletic Commission).

"Anabolic androgenic steroids," Homansky explains, "are synthetic derivatives of the naturally occurring male hormone, testosterone. Testosterone helps the body turn dietary protein into muscle. The utilization of protein is improved and the inhibitory effects of other substances are reduced. This results in increased capacity to train, decreased fatigue, a shorter time for muscle recovery, and the development of muscle tissue. The old theory in weight training was that you worked a certain set of muscles two or three times a week. Steroids allow a user to work them every day."

Human growth hormone (HGH) is naturally produced by the pituitary gland and is now also synthetically made. It was first administered in the 1950s to children with stunted growth and does what its name implies. In Homansky's words, "If your growth plates are already fixed, you won't get taller. But HGH will naturally enlarge your muscles, although the enlargement is in a flabby way so you have to work out to get a strength benefit."

Twenty years ago, the *New England Journal of Medicine* reported that the use of human growth hormone by men over a six-month period decreased the body fat of participants in the study group by 14.4 percent and increased lean muscle by 8.8 percent. More recent studies show a synergistic effect between HGH and anabolic steroids.

Eerythropoietin (EPO) is a synthetic version of a hormone made by the kidneys that stimulates the body's production of red blood cells. Doctors prescribe it for patients suffering from malfunctioning kidneys and anemia and also to treat cancer patients after chemotherapy. Athletes use EPO to boost their endurance, since red blood cells carry oxygen to muscles.

"It's widely understood in the medical community just how dangerous performance-enhancing drugs are," Homansky says. "But appreciation of that danger hasn't filtered down to some athletes and some physical conditioners. We don't know with certainty what all of the longterm side effects are because very few athletes are willing to admit that they use PEDs. What we know for sure is that the number of dangerous performance-enhancing drugs available to athletes is growing daily; that recent developments have focused on making them less detectable and more powerful; and that the side effects are now often worse than before because the drugs are more potent."

"Steroids, if taken long enough, will destroy an athlete's body," Homansky continues. "But one of the problems we face is that no one can be sure how long is too long."

Then Homansky ticks off a list of negative side effects associated with steroid use by men: (1) shrunken testicles, leading to decreased sperm production and impotence; (2) increased cholesterol levels, leading to hardening of the arteries; (3) blood clots, which increase the chance of a heart attack or stroke; (4) kidney disease; (5) liver failure (most commonly from tumors and cysts); (6) hypertension; (7) gynecomastia (enlarged breasts); (8) the weakening of tendons, leading to joint injuries and muscle tears; (9) premature balding; (10) acne; (11) bi-polar, manic-depressive, and delusional behavior; and (12) uncontrollable violent outbursts (known as "roid rage").

Human growth hormone carries its own set of risks. "The heart is a muscle," Homansky explains. "Human growth hormone can cause an enlarged heart, which is a potentially fatal problem."

Other side effects of HGH use can include abnormal enlargement of the kidneys and liver, diabetes, muscle and joint pain, and hypertension. Also, some researchers believe that HGH accelerates the growth of cancer cells.

As for EPO, an increased concentration of red blood cells thickens the blood and has been likened to pumping Jell-O through an athlete's veins. That increases the risk of heart fibrillation and strokes.

Not good.

That's why Todd Chapman of the Nevada State Athletic Commission says of the penalties imposed for the unlawful use of PEDs, "The fighters may think of this as punishment. The doctors think of it as saving your life."

II

Several years ago, Ed Graney wrote in the *Las Vegas Review-Journal,* "Boxing's image has, for the most part, escaped being overly stained by the presence of performance-enhancing drugs. If baseball is king of the juicing empire, boxing is a mere peasant. Imagine that. Boxing has discovered a high moral ground on which to stand above other sports."

However, it would be naïve to think that athletes use steroids in baseball, football, and other sports but don't use them in boxing. More and more in today's world, fighters are reconfiguring their bodies for maximum performance and to compete in weight divisions that once would have been out of reach. With the history of sophisticated designer drugs in the Eastern European sports machine and the impact of steroids on performance in American sports, it was inevitable that PEDs would gain a foothold in boxing.

Fighters (not all fighters, but some fighters) use PEDs because it gives them a competitive edge. A boxer risks his physical well-being and borrows against his future health every time he steps into the ring. This is just one more risk.

A shared risk. As John Ruiz notes, "The only sport in which steroids can kill someone other than the person using them is boxing. You're stronger when you use steroids. You're quicker and faster. If a baseball player uses steroids, he hits more home runs. So what? I'm not saying that it's right, but you're not putting anyone else at risk. When a fighter is juiced, it's dangerous. People go crazy about the effect that steroids have when a bat hits a ball. What about when a fist hits a head?"

A handful of regulatory entities make an occasional effort to test fighters for illegal steroid use. Sometimes these efforts bear fruit. But fighters, like those accused of white-collar crime, rarely say, "Yeah; I did it and you caught me." More often, they say that they didn't know what their physical conditioner was giving them or they were taking a legal over-the-counter nutritional supplement or doing something else legitimate under medical supervision.

Few fighters are as candid as Tommy Morrison, who admitted in a 2005 interview with RingsideReport.com that he used steroids throughout his boxing career.

"You become bigger, faster, and stronger," Morrison said. "It helps with your endurance and recovery time between rounds. I looked around and, from what I saw, everybody was doing the same shit. It wasn't something that was talked about openly; but when you looked around, you could tell. I just looked at it as bettering my chances. Without steroids, I wouldn't have gone as far as I did. I guarantee you that."

The first fighter of note to test positive for steroids after a championship fight was Frans Botha, who decisioned Axel Schulz in Germany to win the vacant IBF heavyweight crown in 1995 but was stripped of the title after a urine test indicated the use of anabolic steroids.

Roy Jones Jr and Richard Hall each tested positive after a May 13, 2000, championship bout in Indianapolis which Jones won on an eleventh-round knockout.

Jake Hall (chairman of the Indiana State Boxing Commission at the time) later told Elisa Harrison of BraggingRightsCorner.com, "The information we received indicated that Mr. Jones failed the drug test for anabolic steroids. Talking to Roy's attorney, Fred Levin, he indicated that Roy had taken a substance called Ripped Fuel, an over-the-counter supplement that is not illegal but is an illegal substance according to the IBF and the other sanctioning bodies. He admits that Roy took that. I have no knowledge whether he took that or some other substance."

On August 2, 2000, Marian Muhammad (then executive secretary of the IBF, the lead sanctioning body for the fight) sent letters to Jones and Hall advising each man that he had tested positive for an unspecified anabolic steroid. No further action was taken.

On September 14, 2002, Fernando Vargas fought Oscar De La Hoya in Las Vegas. Thereafter, Vargas tested positive for the steroid stanozolol, which he said was given to him without his knowledge. The NSAC fined Vargas $100,000 and suspended him for nine months.

Also in Nevada; former WBO bantamweight champion Cruz Carbajal tested positive for the anabolic steroid nandrolone and the diuretic hydrochlorothiazide after losing to Silence Mabuza in a May 13, 2005, IBF bantamweight elimination fight. And Orlando Salido tested positive for nandrolone after beating Robert Guerrero for the IBF featherweight title on November 4, 2006.

James Toney ran afoul of the authorities in New York, when he tested positive for nandrolone after beating John Ruiz in an April 30, 2005, WBA heavyweight championship fight. The outcome of Ruiz-Toney was changed to no decision; James was suspended for ninety day; and Ruiz was reinstated as champion. Two years later, Toney tested positive for boldenone metabolite and stanozolol metabolite after a fight against Danny Batchelder in California.

How prevalent are steroids and other performance-enhancing drugs in boxing today?

Nobody knows.

The truth is that no athletic commission and no world sanctioning organization tests adequately for performance-enhancing drugs. Only a handful of states (Nevada, New York, and California) test for steroids. Their tests are unsophisticated. Relatively few fighters are tested. And the fighters know in advance when they'll be tested, which allows sophisticated users to test "clean."

No state athletic commission tests for human growth hormone. Chemical traces of synthetic EPO can be eliminated by a well-educated user in less than twenty-four hours.

Victor Conte is the founder and president of Bay Area Laboratory Co-Operative (BALCO), which has been at the heart of several much-publicized PED scandals. He spent four months in prison after pleading guilty in 2005 to illegal steroid distribution and tax fraud.

Conte says that PED testing in boxing today is "IQ testing," nothing more. In a recent interview with Steve Kim of Maxboxing.com, he declared, "The loopholes are so big that you could drive a Mack Truck through them. It's really a joke. Traditional testing in boxing is basically worthless other than the detection of some types of stimulant before and after a fight. The testing is, almost by design, inept, and this basic ineptness breeds the use of performance enhancing drugs."

The facts bear Conte out. The most significant revelations regarding the use of performance-enhancing drugs in boxing haven't come from state athletic commission testing. Rather, they've been incidental to federal investigations of other targets that resulted in the ensnarement of fighters who had previously passed state athletic commission tests.

On August 29, 2006, federal Drug Enforcement Agency officials in Alabama raided a compounding pharmacy (a pharmacy that makes its own drugs generically) called Applied Pharmacy Services. Among the documents seized were records stating that, in June 2004, a patient named "Evan Fields" picked up three vials of testosterone and related injection supplies from a doctor in Columbus, Georgia. That same month, Fields received five vials of Saizen (a human growth hormone). In September 2004, according to the documents, Fields underwent treatment for hypogonadism (a condition that results when the sex glands produce little or no hormones). The date of birth, home address, and telephone number listed for Evan Fields in Applied Pharmacy's records were identical to those of Evander Holyfield.

When these facts were made public, Holyfield issued a statement that read in part, "I have never taken an illegal or banned performance-enhancing drug of any kind. The use of such substances runs counter to everything I believe about sports and my place in the athletic world."

The New York Times reported in 1995 that, after Holyfield lost his heavyweight championship to Michael Moorer, Evander was diagnosed as having a non-compliant left ventricle (one of four chambers in the human heart), which caused a dangerous build-up of fluids. That diagnosis, according to the *Times,* was confirmed by two sets of tests, the second round being conducted at Emory University in Atlanta.

Holyfield was tested a number of times for steroids in Nevada. The tests all came back negative. He was not tested by the Nevada commission for human growth hormone or EPO.

Chris Byrd successfully defended his IBF heavyweight title against Jameel McCline in 2004. Five months later, McCline lost a decision to Calvin Brock.

Thereafter, Byrd said of McCline, "His arms were massive. He was ripped. Everything he hit me with hurt. I've been in with some big punchers, but I've never been punched as hard as he punched me. He was strong. The fight right after mine against Calvin Brock, he didn't look nearly as ripped or as strong. I was thinking, 'This isn't the same guy that fought me.'"

On October 13, 2007, the *Palm Beach Post* reported that fifteen drugs (mostly steroids and related substances) costing a total of $12,343 had been shipped to McCline on a near-weekly basis in 2005 and 2006 through a Boca Raton anti-aging clinic. According to the report, "The drugs included seven steroids: testosterone, testosterone enanthate, oxandrolone, testosterone cypionate, stanozolol, nandrolone, and testosterone propionate. Also sent were carbopol (a thickening agent), chorionic gonadotropin (stimulates male hormones), liothyronine (a thyroid hormone), humulin (an insulin), somatotropin (human growth hormone), and spironolactone/hydrochlorothiazide (sometimes used to treat side effects of steroids). Tamoxifen, used by steroid users so they don't develop feminine physical characteristics, also was shipped."

Then there's the case of Shane Mosley.

In September 2007, *Sports Illustrated* reported, "According to multiple sources who attended an international anti-doping conference in Colorado Springs last November, Jeff Novitzky, a lead investigator in the BALCO case, alleged that boxer Shane Mosley started an elaborate doping regimen in the months prior to a September 13, 2003, fight against Oscar De La Hoya. As Novitzky explained in painstaking detail, two months before the fight, Mosley, a client of the BALCO lab, began using 'the clear' and 'the cream,' the designer substances that Barry Bonds, among other athletes, stands accused of using."

"The clear" is an undetectable anabolic steroid. "The cream" contains testosterone and epitestosterone, and is primarily a masking agent.

Novitzky also stated at the conference that Mosley supplemented these drugs with doses of Erythropoietin (EPO). He backed his presentation with records seized from BALCO that detailed a dramatic rise in Mosley's hematocrit level (a measure of red blood cells).

In response, Mosley told Tim Smith of the *New York Daily News* and Dan Rafael of ESPN.com that he had visited BALCO and met with Conte at the insistence of his former conditioning coach (Darryl Hudson) and had taken the drugs after he was misled by Conte, who told him that they were legal nutritional supplements.

Conte answered back, telling Smith, "I've never misled or deceived any athlete. I've always been a man of full disclosure."

Thereafter, Mosley's attorney (Judd Burstein) advised the media that Shane's position was supported by a lie detector test that Shane had passed "with flying colors." Of course, the lie detector test had been unilaterally arranged for by Burstein.

Then, in April 2008, Mosley filed a lawsuit for slander against Conte for stating publicly that he had knowingly used PEDs. "I cannot begin to explain how devastating Conte's false allegations have been to me," Shane declared in court papers. "I believe that I have carved out an important place for myself in the sport's history. All of my life's work is at risk because of Conte's lies. I have a brand based upon the highest reputation for sportsmanship, and that brand is being irreparably tarnished by Conte."

Conte responded with an affidavit from Darryl Hudson, who declared, "I know that Mr. Mosley was aware that the performance-enhancing drugs provided to him by Mr. Conte were banned drugs because I discussed that fact with Mr. Mosley both during and after our visit to BALCO. It was entirely Mr. Mosley's decision to use the banned drugs. I never recommended to Mr. Mosley that he take banned performance enhancing drugs, nor did I 'push' drugs on him in any way."

At that point, the matter receded from public view. It resurfaced in January 2009, when the grand jury testimony of Conte and Mosley was made public. Based on that testimony, Mark Zeigler of the *San Diego Union-Tribune* wrote, "On July 26, 2003, Shane Mosley and strength coach Darryl Hudson flew into Oakland. Conte, according to his account of the meeting, wrote up a doping calendar with the initials 'S.M.' at the top and handwritten notations for what to take on which days. Then he began putting various pills and substances on his desk. Some were legal vitamins and nutritional substances. Three were not."

"There was The Clear, an undetectable anabolic steroid that he had been giving to his track athletes and that one track coach referred to as 'rocket fuel.' There was The Cream, a lotion Conte used as a masking agent. It tricked even the most advanced drug testers by keeping the body's levels of testosterone at normal levels. Then there was the bottle Conte says was labeled 'Procrit.' Conte produced a syringe and showed Mosley how to use it, flicking it and pushing up the plunger to remove air bubbles. Then, Conte says, he handed the syringe to Mosley and watched him inject his first dose."

"Mosley's doping calendar called for injections of EPO, every other day for the first two weeks of the regimen; then once a week after that. His final injection was scheduled for September 8, five days before the [De La Hoya] fight and plenty of time to clear his system for a post-fight drug test."

Thereafter, Michael Rosenthal spoke for many in the boxing community when he authored an article for The Ring Online.

"Shane Mosley," Rosenthal wrote, "has earned the admiration of everyone in the boxing world for his unusual ability and fighting spirit. He's a certain Hall of Famer. He's one of the nicest guys in sports. And he's a cheater. Of course, he said he never intended to gain an unfair advantage when he took performance-enhancing drugs in the weeks before his victory over Oscar De La Hoya in Las Vegas. He said he didn't know what he was taking or that it might be banned by the majority of anti-doping agencies. However, just as we roll our eyes when Barry Bonds and company deny any intentional wrongdoing, it's difficult to believe Mosley."

"Consider these questions," Rosenthal continued. "Why did Mosley have the supposedly legal substances he purchased from BALCO shipped to him instead of taking them back with him on the plane? Why would he taper off his use of the substances as mandatory drug tests got closer? What would Conte stand to gain by misleading Mosley? Why did Mosley stop taking all the supplements, even the harmless vitamins, after the fight? It adds up to a problem with Mosley's credibility."

The presence of performance-enhancing drugs in boxing (whatever the extent of their use) is a stain on the sport.

"The ring should be as fair and honorable as we can make it," Dr. Flip Homansky says. "No fighter should be allowed to gain an unfair advantage over his opponent. PEDs are an artificial aid and no different than tampering with a fighter's gloves."

Still, reality dictates that more than a few fighters will use performance-enhancing drugs if they think they can get away with it. Indeed, the primary reason that many fighters don't use PEDs is that they simply can't afford them.

"I think it's rampant in boxing," Conte says. "Once one person gains that additional edge in speed and power and endurance, then others will do the same. They feel like they're almost forced to use drugs to be on a level playing field. If there was good testing and the athletes themselves believed that the programs were effective, they'd be more inclined not to use drugs. Knowing that the programs are inept; this is what fuels the idea that they gotta do what they gotta do in order to be competitive."

No one knows how many fights have been affected by the use of performance-enhancing drugs.

"Was Andrew Golota on steroids?" Lou DiBella asks. "I don't know. I do know that Golota looked pretty bulked up and had a lot of pimples on his back and exhibited symptoms similar to roid rage when he fought Riddick Bowe. And I also know that Riddick was never the same after he got hit in the head again and again by Golota."

III

That brings us to the aborted superfight between Manny Pacquiao and Floyd Mayweather Jr, also known melodramatically as "the world held hostage," "the end of life as we know it," and "the worst thing that ever happened to boxing (since at least last year)."

Bart Barry recently opined, "Pacquiao is a charismatic action fighter who has created a market for prizefighting in the Philippines and made it as popular as ever throughout Asia. Mayweather is a foul-mouthed defensive specialist whose fights lose more fans than they gain. Pacquiao is good for boxing. Mayweather is good for Mayweather."

Floyd's fans will take issue with that appraisal. But the reality of the situation is that, over the past year, Pacquiao (not Mayweather) has become the standard-bearer for boxing in the United States and the rest of the world.

Two years ago, Carlo Rotella wrote in the *New York Times,* "There are good welterweight boxers to fight, and Mayweather isn't fighting them.

Even when he does deign to box, he has been taking big money fights against relatively easy opponents. At some point, his refusal to fight other top welterweights begins to undercut his claim to superlative greatness as a boxer, and the cachet of Mayweather's brand rests on that claim."

On May 3, 2009, (the day after Pacquiao annihilated Ricky Hatton), Tim Dahlberg of the Associated Press proclaimed, "All Mayweather can do now is get in line. The road to greatness now runs through a fighter who lets his fists do the talking."

Those comments and others like them were hurtful to Mayweather, who has told the world, "I don't consider myself just a boxer. I'm an entertainment superstar." The prevailing view was that Floyd had to fight and beat Pacquiao in order to maintain his superstar status.

In the wake of Pacquiao's November 14, 2009, demolition of Miguel Cotto, calls for a Pacquiao-Mayweather showdown reached a fever pitch. Mayweather's father (Floyd Mayweather Sr) stated publicly that he thought his son would "whup" Manny but advised against his taking the fight because, he claimed, Pacquiao was using performance-enhancing drugs.

That earned a riposte from Freddie Roach (Pacquiao's trainer), who referenced Floyd Sr's criminal past with the observation, "Just because he's a convicted drug dealer doesn't make him a drug expert."

Alex Ariza (Pacquiao's strength and conditioning coach) weighed-in with the observation, "When he first started saying that stuff, I didn't really address it because it was coming from Floyd. But things like that can start to snowball. I'm not saying this to be demeaning, but Floyd never finished high school and I'm not sure he knows the difference between steroids and supplements."

More to the point, Ariza told ESPN.com, "Manny does take supplements. I'm talking about multi-vitamins and trace minerals. He takes other supplements for his kidney and liver because he's on such a high-protein diet. All of them are perfectly legal. I'm completely in control of what goes into Manny. Everything he puts into his body is my responsibility. Manny takes nothing illegal."

Serious negotiations for a Pacquiao-Mayweather fight began against that backdrop. Pacquiao has a contract with Top Rank (Bob Arum's promotional company). Mayweather was represented by Golden Boy (which Richard Schaefer has built into a formidable force in the boxing industry).

Initially, things went smoothly. March 13, 2010, was designated as the likely date for the bout. After minimal posturing, the two sides agreed to a fifty-fifty financial split. The fight would be known as "Mayweather-Pacquiao" (rather than the other way around), but Top Rank would be referenced ahead of Golden Boy in all promotional material.

Mayweather had ignored the 144-pound contract limit for his September 2009 fight against Juan Manuel Marquez and weighed in at 146, paying a $600,000 penalty for the privilege. To ensure that didn't happen against Pacquiao, Top Rank exacted the concession that there would be a $10,000,000 penalty for each pound or fraction thereof that either fighter weighed over 147.

On December 7th, negotiations hit a snag. Arum, Schaefer, and HBO Sports president Ross Greenburg were scheduled to meet with Jerry Jones in Dallas the following day to tour Cowboys Stadium and give Jones the opportunity to outbid the MGM Grand (which had the support of the Las Vegas establishment) for the fight.

Jones was readying to offer a $25,000,000 site fee. HBO estimated internally that publicity resulting from the fight being held in Dallas could engender an additional several hundred thousand pay-per-view buys.

But on the night of December 7th, Schaefer called Arum and told him to cancel the trip because he'd decided against holding the fight in Dallas. That raised numerous questions; foremost among them whether the MGM Grand (with which Golden Boy has a long-term agreement) or AEG (Golden Boy's partner) had killed the Dallas deal. It was also noted that holding the fight in Cowboys Stadium (capacity 100,000) would have enabled fans to buy tickets at reasonable prices instead of putting virtually all of the tickets in the hands of high rollers and ticket scalpers.

Also, by ruling out Dallas during the middle of negotiations, Golden Boy deprived the promotion of additional leverage in its negotiations with the MGM Grand.

Arum called the cancellation "ruinous," pronounced himself "embarrassed," and declared that something was "fishy."

Then things got worse.

With Dallas out of the mix, it was now clear that Mayweather-Pacquiao (if it occurred) would be contested in Las Vegas. But the

Mayweather camp was unwilling to accept drug testing as implemented by the Nevada State Athletic Commission. Team Mayweather was demanding that both fighters be subject to "Olympic-style testing" conducted by the United States Anti-Doping Agency (USADA). That would involve unlimited random urine and blood testing without advance notice from the start of training through the day of the fight.

Pacquiao has an aversion to invasive testing. Indeed, when Shelly Finkel (who now has a "strategic alliance" with Golden Boy) co-managed Manny, he once asked the Nevada State Athletic Commission to waive a required eye test because Pacquiao didn't want to undergo the procedure in proximity to the fight. The commission refused to grant the waiver.

"You gotta understand," Arum said with regard to the demand for USADA testing. "I'm dealing with a Filipino fighter who is superstitious, and I have to tell him they have the power to come into his dressing room before the fight and take his blood. Manny gets freaked out when his blood gets taken and feels that it weakens him. They would put nothing in writing as to any kind of schedule. That is ludicrous."

Pacquiao, for his part, declared, "I'm not going to let them take my blood whenever they want when I'm getting seriously ready for a fight. They can take all the urine they want."

The ensuing days saw a series of proposals (but little real movement) from the Pacquiao side. Essentially, Manny agreed to unlimited urine tests and three blood tests to be conducted (1) in January on the day that the fight was formally announced; (2) thirty days before the fight; and (3) in Manny's dressing room immediately after the fight. Since USADA would not administer the tests on that basis, Arum suggested that they be conducted "by any of the independent agencies that work with the National Football League, the National Basketball Association, or Major League Baseball."

Then things went viral. The Mayweather camp had suggested all along that Pacquiao was averse to random blood tests because he had something to hide. But the suggestions had come from people whose utterances carried little weight with the mainstream media: Floyd Jr, his father, and adviser Leonard Ellerbe.

Three days before Christmas, the landscape changed. Golden Boy issued a press release under the headline, "MAYWEATHER VS PACQUIAO IN JEOPARDY AS PACQUIAO REFUSES TO COMPLY WITH

UNITED STATES ANTI-DOPING DRUG TESTING PROCEDURES."

Among the bon mots the press release offered were:

- Richard Schaefer: "Team Mayweather is certainly surprised that an elite athlete like Manny Pacquiao would refuse drug testing procedures which Floyd has already agreed to and have been agreed to by many other top athletes."

- Floyd Mayweather Jr: "I understand Pacquiao not liking having his blood taken, because frankly I don't know anyone who does. But in a fight of this magnitude, I think it is our responsibility to subject ourselves to sportsmanship at the highest level. I have already agreed to the testing, and it is a shame that he is not willing to do the same. It leaves me with great doubt as to the level of fairness I would be facing in the ring that night."

- Leonard Ellerbe: "We hope that Manny will do the right thing and agree to the testing as it is an egregious act to deny the testing and, hence, deny millions of fans the right to see this amazing fight. We just want to make sure there is a level playing field in a sport that is a man-to-man contest that relies on strength and ability."

One day later, Oscar De La Hoya (who lost to Pacquiao in 2008 and is the primary equity participant in Golden Boy) poured his own cup of poison into the brew in the form of a blog authored for The Ring Online.

"If Pacquiao, the toughest guy on the planet, is afraid of needles and having a few tablespoons of blood drawn from his system," De La Hoya wrote, "then something is wrong. The guy has tattoos everywhere. You're telling me he's afraid of needles? If Pacquiao doesn't want to do this and risks a possible $40 million payday because he's afraid of needles or believes he'll be weakened by blood tests, that raises question marks. Now I have to wonder about him. I'm saying to myself, 'Wow. Those Mosley punches, those Vargas punches, and those Pacquiao punches all felt the same.' I'm not saying yes or no [about whether Pacquiao might be taking performance-enhancing drugs]. I'm just saying that now people have to wonder: 'Why doesn't he want to do this? Why is it such a big deal?' A lot of eyebrows have been raised. This is not good at all. I would say to Pacquiao, 'Do the test. Do it because it's only a couple of tablespoons.

Needles don't hurt. Just look away when they put the needle in your arm.' He'll probably lose more blood in the fight than the blood being drawn for the test. Why don't you want to do it? C'mon. It's only a little bit of blood. If you have nothing to hide, then do the test."

De La Hoya's statement was hypocritical. For starters, there was his claim that Pacquiao's punches felt like those of Shane Mosley and Fernando Vargas (both of whom had used performance-enhancing drugs prior to fighting Oscar). Yet on two prior occasions, De La Hoya had demeaned Pacquiao's punching power. First, he'd stated, "Luckily, he doesn't hit hard. Obviously, if he hit hard, he would have knocked me out with no problem." Later, Oscar had maintained, "Truthfully, he didn't hit hard. He didn't really hurt me. But the punches were so fast and they were coming from everywhere."

Still, after the Golden Boy press release and De La Hoya blog, the suggestion that Pacquiao was using performance-enhancing drugs exploded into the mainstream media. That tarnished Manny, increased enmity between the two camps, and made the issue of drug testing harder to resolve.

Everything that followed was a sad endgame.

On December 25th, Team Pacquiao issued a statement saying that Manny intended to file a lawsuit for defamation within the next few days.

"Enough is enough," Pacquiao was quoted as saying. "These people —Mayweather Sr, Jr, and Golden Boy Promotions—think it is a joke and a right to accuse someone wrongly of using steroids or other performance-enhancing drugs. I have tried to brush it off as a mere pre-fight ploy, but they have gone overboard. I have instructed my promoter, Bob Arum, to help me out in the filing of the case as soon as possible because I have had people coming over to me now, asking if I really take performance-enhancing drugs and have cheated my way into becoming the number-one boxer in the world. I maintain and assure everyone that I have not used any form or kind of steroids. My way to the top is a result of hard work, hard work, hard work, and a lot of blood spilled from my past battles in the ring, not outside of it. I have no idea what steroids look like."

On December 26th, Pacquiao issued another statement. After restating his terms (urine tests anytime; blood tests on the three previously offered dates), he declared, "The truth is, taking blood out of my body does not seem natural to me. Mentally, I feel it will weaken me if blood is taken from me just days before the fight. To all of my fans, I want to say thank you very much for your support and understanding. I always give honor to God first. I would never cheat God; I would never cheat myself; and I would never cheat my country and my fans."

Meanwhile, Arum was pursuing a new tack; that the entire matter should be decided by the Nevada State Athletic Commission.

On December 26th, the promoter declared, "The Nevada commission is paid by the state to oversee this sort of thing. They're the governing body. Let [the Mayweather side] make any petition it wants to the commission. If the commission wants to take blood, fine. If they go to the commission and they ask for blood tests and the commission says yes, we will do whatever the commission says. We will allow Golden Boy to present experts to the commission to explain why additional testing is required and we'll explain our position. Then we'll let the Nevada commission decide. If Nevada says we need to do more testing, we'll do more. But if they don't, we won't. Let the commission tell us how many days in front they want blood. Let the commission pick a date to stop taking blood. If the commission says both fighters have to give blood as they're walking into the ring, we'll do it. But I want the commission saying it."

In response, Schaefer declared, "It does not make sense for this to become a commission matter. This is a contractual matter. The commission did not decide the weights or the purse split or how the foreign television rights would be sold. We are okay to move off USADA. What is important to us is that the tests be random; that they include blood and urine; and the time frame, meaning when do you stop the tests before the fight but know they will still be effective. We have agreed on random, blood, and urine. So now it's a matter of the two sides working out the specifics of the cutoff date to assure it will still be effective. We know that thirty days before is not effective. At thirty days, we might as well not even do it."

Meanwhile, at Top Rank's behest, publicist Fred Sternburg sent out a March 25, 2008, Associated Press article recounting a request by Zab Judah that Shane Mosley agree to blood testing for drugs prior to their May 31, 2008, fight (which was cancelled after Judah suffered a serious cut on his arm).

In response to Judah's request, Schaefer (Shane's promoter) had declared, "Mosley will agree to any tests required by the Nevada Athletic Commission. Whatever tests they want them to take, Shane will submit to that. We are not going to do other tests than the Nevada commission requires."

That revelation was followed by a blast from Arum, who proclaimed, "Shane Mosley was an admitted drug-user. I've had Shane Mosley fight two of the guys that I've promoted in the last few years. One of them was Miguel Cotto and the other was Antonio Margarito. Did I ever ever ever even indicate in any way that Shane Mosley should be subject to special testing? No."

"Floyd, to me, is a coward and he has always been a coward," Arum raged. "Not a physical coward, but a coward because he's afraid to face somebody who could beat him. And believe me, Manny Pacquiao could beat him. So he'll go his way, we'll go our way, and that will be fine. We're not going to keep appeasing this guy for no damn reason, especially over something that would affect, psychologically, my fighter. We're not going to be pushed around by this guy. We're not going to do it."

Asked if he thought the Mayweather camp was playing mind games, Arum declared, "Of course, they are. And they can go screw themselves. I don't care if this fight doesn't happen. Manny is not going to be subjected to blood-testing while he's in training. I have never ever in all the years I have known Manny seen him so angry. He was angry, bitter, and really pissed off."

On December 28th, Richard Schaefer launched a counteroffensive, focusing on Team Pacquiao's claim that it would weaken Pacquiao mentally, if not physically, to have blood taken from him within thirty days of the fight.

"We have actually been able to establish that, two weeks before the Hatton fight, he [Pacquiao] had his blood taken here in Los Angeles," Schaefer told the media.

The basis for Schaefer's claim was footage from HBO's *Pacquiao-Hatton 24/7* series that showed blood being drawn from Pacquiao as part of a routine pre-fight medical examination.

Properly chastised, Arum said that he would consider revisiting the issue with Pacquiao. Then it was determined from a review of medical records that the blood had been taken twenty-four days prior to the fight.

Also on December 28th, the Nevada State Athletic Commission got into the act. Citing its right to require licensed boxers to submit to tests for prohibited substances, the NSAC instructed Pacquiao and Mayweather to submit urine samples within forty-eight hours or face possible fines and suspension.

When advised of the ruling, Arum declared, "That's fine; no problem at all. We are absolutely in favor of it. I really applaud the way the Nevada commission has acted."

Over the next two days, there were breathless "testing updates" and reports in the media of Pacquiao's urine being transported around the world.

"A urine sample of Manny Pacquiao is on its way to Manila," Nick Giongco wrote. "World Anti-Doping Agency (WADA) accredited doctor Alex Pineda, who also works for the Philippine Olympic Committee, personally witnessed the initial phase of testing at Pacquiao's residence in General Santos City."

The sample, Giongco reported had been placed in tubes labeled "A" and "B." These tubes were to be sent "to Thailand, Malaysia, or China" because, according to Pineda, the Philippines doesn't have a WADA-accredited testing laboratory.

On December 29th, Pacquiao issued another statement bemoaning the damage to his reputation caused by allegations that he had used illegal performance-enhancing drugs. "I can't believe these guys can lie without batting an eyelash," Manny said. "Liars go to hell."

On December 30th, Arum declared, "In my opinion, the fight has no chance of happening. We should go and do other things and revisit it later in the year. It's a damn shame, but it's out of my hands. When I think of having to share a dais with those sleazebags, Oscar and Schaefer, after what they've been saying about Manny, it turns my stomach."

That same day, Pacquiao filed a defamation suit in United States District Court in Nevada against Floyd Mayweather Sr, Floyd Mayweather Jr, Roger Mayweather, Mayweather Promotions, Richard Schaefer, and Oscar De La Hoya.

On January 5th, the parties met in a last-ditch effort to resolve their differences through mediation under the guidance of Daniel Weinstein (a retired federal judge, who had successfully mediated a previous dispute between Golden Boy and Top Rank). Arum, Todd DuBoef (Arum's stepson and the president of Top Rank), Schaefer, De La Hoya, Al Haymon (Mayweather's manager), and legal counsel for some of the attendees were in attendance. The mediation was adjourned after nine hours.

On January 6th, the participants met again but still could not resolve their differences over the issue of drug testing. The talks collapsed. The fight was off.

IV

What are the lessons of the Mayweather-Pacquiao debacle?

Let's start by acknowledging that, laying aside their motives and tactics, Mayweather and Golden Boy raised a legitimate issue. Boxing has a PED problem. It's unclear how widespread the problem is, but it's there.

That said; the problem won't be solved by focusing on one or two fighters. That would be like the National Football League coming up with a steroid plan to test Peyton Manning and Tom Brady but nobody else.

In essence, Golden Boy told the world that the Nevada State Athletic Commission couldn't (or wouldn't) test effectively for performance-enhancing drugs. Golden Boy was right. That's not a knock on the NSAC (which tests for PEDs as well as any commission). It's a knock on the system.

Mayweather and Golden Boy were also correct in their assertion that there were loopholes in Pacquiao's final testing offer. As Victor Conte told Maxboxing.com, "The clearance times of most of these drugs that are out there are well-known. Some of these clear in a matter of hours or days. So if you know when you're going to be tested a week out, you go off the use of oral testosterone, for example, and you're going to test negative."

The issue of PEDs in boxing cries out for uniform national medical standards. To make real headway, it should be a condition of granting a license in any state that a fighter can be tested for PEDs at any time. Logistics and cost would make mandatory testing impractical on a broad scale. But unannounced spot testing could be implemented.

Unfortunately (as was the case with Major League Baseball when home run records were being shattered), most of the powers that be in boxing think the status quo is just fine. And looking at the matter realistically, what are the chances that the Nevada State Athletic Commission would cancel a mega-fight three or four days before the bell for round one because a participant tested positive for a banned performance-enhancing drug?

Next thought—

The dialogue that unfolded with regard to PED testing was unfair to Pacquiao. Tim McKeown put it best when he wrote, "Mayweather is demanding that Pacquiao prove himself innocent of a transgression that only Mayweather and his people are alleging. I know what you're thinking: 'If Pacquiao doesn't have anything to hide, why doesn't he agree to blood testing?' That's become the default position in today's society. Stop at this checkpoint; walk through this machine; hold your arms out for the wand. We've become so accustomed to proving our innocence in everyday life that we forgot how the system is supposed to work. This is a guy who is being accused of a crime by the other side, and he's being called upon to prove his innocence despite the complete absence of evidence suggesting guilt."

Okay. What else might someone be thinking? How about the manner in which Pacquiao has moved up in weight and the extraordinary evolution of his destructiveness as a fighter?

Let's start with weight. Between the ages of sixteen and thirty-one, Pacquiao fought at weights ranging from 106 to 144 pounds. Between the ages of sixteen and thirty-one, Mayweather fought at weights ranging from 106 to 150 pounds.

Improvement as a fighter?

"Here are some facts," Al Bernstein recently wrote. "Manny Pacquiao is one of the hardest working and most disciplined fighters in the sport. Manny Pacquiao's success as he moved up in weight has been fueled mostly by a change in style and tactics rather than added strength. One of the most astonishing things to me is the folks who somehow believe that all of a sudden it's reasonable to assume that Pacquiao, above all other boxers, needs a special set of testing rules to participate in a big fight. No performance-enhancing drugs can change your technique. It was not power that made the difference. The difference was speed, ring generalship, combination punching, and a vastly improved defense."

Also; Bob Arum wasn't blowing smoke when he said that Pacquiao is "superstitious" and that doing things a certain way is important to Manny's state of mind.

Pacquiao is a creature of habit when it comes to pre-fight preparation. Although he boards the Team Pacquiao promotional bus for television sound bytes and occasional print interviews, he insists on traveling in his own car ahead of the bus on final pre-fight trips from Los Angeles to Las Vegas. Before every fight in Las Vegas, he stays in the same suite at Mandalay Bay; prays in the same chapel; and works out in the same gym.

Be that as it may; it's clear that events of the past two months have tarnished Pacquiao. In retrospect, Top Rank made a tactical error by publicly engaging with Golden Boy on the issue of PED testing. From a public relations point of view, Arum should have said from that start that this was a commission matter and left it at that.

Now, a sizeable number of people have heard Pacquiao's name mentioned in the same sentence as "steroids" and "performance-enhancing drugs." They've been told that he "must be doing something wrong" because he's "afraid to take the tests."

Meanwhile, the furor over drug testing has obscured what some observers believe to be the essential truth about the collapse of Mayweather-Pacquiao; that Floyd didn't want the fight.

In the past, while laying claim to greatness, Mayweather has avoided the most threatening opponents in his weight class. Indeed, British commentator Steve Bunce recently declared, "Floyd has ducked so many opponents that, when he opens his mouth, I expect him to quack."

Similarly, William Dettloff writes, "If you're going to talk as much as Mayweather does, you simply have to fight the best guys available or you're a fraud."

By that standard, "Money Mayweather" is in danger of becoming known as "Phony Phloyd."

There were times during the past month when the conduct of Team Mayweather had the look of an effort to sabotage the fight. A negotiator who wants to make a deal doesn't go out of his way to antagonize and publicly embarrass the other side. But that's what the Mayweathers and Golden Boy did.

Thus, Al Bernstein opines, "It seems patently obvious to me that Floyd and his minions killed the Pacquiao fight. The bottom line is that the fight was basically a done deal before they decided to inject the demands for blood testing into the picture. Pure and simple, Golden Boy and Floyd and his advisers created the problem, and it ended up killing the fight."

Indeed, there's a school of thought that, had Pacquiao agreed to Mayweather's drug-testing demands, Floyd ultimately would have balked at the $10,000,000-per-pound penalty for failing to make weight or found another way to scuttle the ship.

In any event, the war outside the ring between Mayweather and Pacquiao has hurt boxing. This was a fight that the world wanted to see; one with huge crossover potential that could have made new fans. And instead, the focus fell on an ugly dispute, reinforcing the view that boxing is dirty (i.e. the accusation that its biggest star is using illegal performance-enhancing drugs).

A lot of people are disappointed by the way that Richard Schaefer conducted himself over the past month. They think he's too smart and too classy to act in that manner. Their belief is that Mayweather and Al Haymon (Floyd's de facto manager) have been calling the shots. That view was reinforced when Schaefer told Rick Reeno of BoxingScene.com, "We have been instructed by a client, which is Mayweather and Mayweather's management team, to ensure from the beginning that the proper test, which is blood and urine, be performed. Mayweather wants the proper test to take place. It's as simple as that."

But it isn't that simple. Al Haymon might care about medical issues. But he's also the manager who sent Lamon Brewster to Germany to fight Wladimir Klitschko when Lamon was on medical suspension in the United States. And he manages Andre Berto, who is scheduled to fight Shane Mosley in Las Vegas on January 30th.

As Kevin Iole noted, "It would stand to reason that, if Haymon were truly concerned about Berto's physical well-being, he'd have already requested that Mosley submit to [pre-fight blood and urine] testing. Mosley, after all, actually has used steroids and other performance-enhancing substances, which he testified to in the BALCO case."

Then again, maybe Schaefer (working in collaboration with Haymon) was open to the idea of burying Mayweather-Pacquiao. That way, Golden Boy can put Floyd in against one of its own fighters (like Mosley).

Are the thoughts expressed in the preceding paragraphs unfair to Schaefer? If so, he can prove them wrong.

Golden Boy can take the lead on the issue of PEDs in boxing by requiring its fighters to submit to Olympic-style drug testing before each major fight. And in order to fight on a Golden Boy card (remember; Golden Boy has a lot of dates on HBO), it could require opponents to do the same.

In fact, Golden Boy could start by testing Shane Mosley to protect Shane from unknowingly using PEDs again. It's interesting how Shane looked very old when he fought Ricardo Mayorga in 2008 and then improved with age when he fought Antonio Margarito in 2009.

And speaking of age; let's have a round of applause for another Golden Boy fighter; Bernard Hopkins. People talk a lot about what great shape Bernard is in and how remarkable it is that a fighter well into his forties can perform the way he does.

I consider Hopkins a great fighter. Other fighters have moved up in weight and excelled in the manner of Manny Pacquiao. But there is no precedent for a fighter performing as agelessly as Bernard has. I'm aware of no proof whatsoever that Hopkins has used illegal performance-enhancing drugs at any time in his career. Of course, to my knowledge, Bernard hasn't undergone USADA testing.

WBA heavyweight champion David Haye is another Golden Boy fighter. David was a cruiserweight less than two years ago. His body has filled out nicely since then. Very nicely. Now Haye wants to fight Vitali and Wladimir Klitschko. Vitali tested positive for a banned substance while training for the 1996 Olympics and was removed from the Ukrainian national team. He later acknowledged using steroids, saying that he had done so after aggravating an old leg injury previously sustained during a kick-boxing bout. Wladimir's body is even more imposing than Vitali's.

If Haye fights one of the Klitschko brothers, a Golden Boy–implemented USADA-like testing plan would assure the world that everything is on the up and up.

Will Golden Boy take the lead in across-the-board PED testing?

My guess is that there's a better chance of Tiger Woods becoming Pope.

But there is something very simple that Golden Boy can do to set an example. It involves the Golden Boy himself.

Oscar De La Hoya can show the world how a righteous PED-free fighter acts. In order to fully inform the public on the issues involved (and remove any hint of suspicion that he himself might not have clean hands) Oscar should waive his right to confidentiality and authorize the Nevada State Athletic Commission to release the results of any tests for performance-enhancing drugs that he has taken in the past. The same waiver should authorize all present and past NSAC personnel and any other person with knowledge of the situation to discuss the test results with any media representative who inquires about them.

I'm not talking about Lidocaine (which Oscar acknowledges having taken when he suffered a cut prior to his 2004 fight against Bernard Hopkins). Nor am I talking about creatine (which Lem Satterfield, then of the *Baltimore Sun,* authoritatively reported that Oscar incorporated into his training regimen in 1999 when he was preparing to fight Felix Trinidad).

I'm talking about the possibility of something more.

Let me even suggest wording for the waiver that Oscar can make public and send to the Nevada State Athletic Commission:

"I, Oscar De La Hoya, hereby waive all right of confidentiality with regard to the past testing of my blood and urine for steroids and other performance-enhancing drugs conducted by or on behalf of the Nevada State Athletic Commission. In that regard, I also authorize all present and past Nevada State Athletic Commission personnel and any other person with knowledge of the situation to speak openly with the media about such testing."

To paraphrase: "C'mon, Oscar. If you have nothing to hide, then do it. It's only a piece a paper. Just sign the waiver."

Bob Arum has shaped the business of boxing since the 1960s and will continue to do so in the foreseeable future.

Bob Arum Brings Boxing Back to the Future

Bob Arum is seventy-eight years old. That's an age when most businessmen are well past their prime. Yet Arum remains on the cutting edge of boxing. On March 13, 2010, he promoted Manny Pacquiao vs. Joshua Clottey at Cowboys Stadium in Dallas. On June 5th, he'll promote Yuri Foreman against Miguel Cotto at Yankee Stadium in New York.

Cowboys Stadium and Yankee Stadium are the two highest-profile stadiums in the United States. With these fights, Arum is harkening back to an era when tens of thousands of fans attended championship fights in big-city venues. That has significant implications for the future of boxing.

There was a time when boxing and baseball were America's national sports. 120,757 fans jammed into Sesquicentennial Stadium in Philadelphia on September 23, 1926, to watch Gene Tunney challenge Jack Dempsey for the heavyweight crown. One year later, 104,943 spectators witnessed their rematch at Soldier Field in Chicago. Joe Louis and Max Baer drew 88,150 fans to Yankee Stadium on September 24, 1935, for a non-championship fight.

Sadly, boxing in the United States is now a niche sport. "People say that television killed boxing," Arum notes. "But television didn't kill baseball or football or basketball. Television didn't kill golf or tennis or the Olympics. Most sports in America have thrived because of television. Boxing has been killing boxing."

There are myriad reasons for the decline of the sweet science in America. The proliferation of world sanctioning organizations has stripped the sport of readily identifiable champions. Boxing's economic model has pushed its most attractive fights to pay-per-view, where they're seen by a relatively small number of people. And casino site fees have taken precedence over selling tickets to a national fan base.

"The way things are now," Arum says, "a promoter gets a television date; he makes a deal with a casino; he holds a press conference to announce the fight; and he thinks he's a promoter. And what makes it worse is that boxing's biggest events are all held in the same few arenas again and again."

"We're all busy," Arum elaborates, "so we tend to do what's easy instead of what's innovative and best for the sport. We have fight after fight in casinos, where we don't have to put the same amount of time and effort into promoting them. I live in Las Vegas. It's a great city and it's a great place to have a big fight. But you get stale doing the same thing over and over. And you're not a major sport if all of your big events are in the same place, catering to the same high-rolling customers. If boxing is going to return to being a mainstream sport, it has to put some of its showcase fights in stadiums and big arenas around the country. You'll never be a major sport if you keep going back to the same site in the same town and promoting fights with ticket prices that are too high for most fans and where tickets for your most important events aren't even available to the public. If you do that, you're not a major sport. You're a circus act to bring in casino customers."

In keeping with that theme, Arum pushed hard during the failed negotiations for Manny Pacquiao vs. Floyd Mayweather Jr. to have Cowboys Stadium considered as a possible fight site. Richard Schaefer (the lead negotiator for the Mayweather-Golden Boy team) refused to consider that option and said the fight would be held in Las Vegas or not at all.

That led Steve Kim to write, "If this fight is really about promoting the sport of boxing and really having a transcendent appeal, why in the world would you take it back to the same setting that helped make boxing a niche sport to begin with? When boxing was truly thriving, events like Pacquiao-Mayweather didn't take place in casinos out in the desert. They took place in major cities like Chicago, New York, and Los Angeles, where crowds in excess of 50,000 packed stadiums to watch championship fights. Does a bout the caliber of Pacquiao-Mayweather, which has already garnered unprecedented interest, really belong in an arena that holds less than 20,000 patrons? Put this in a much larger venue and you give fans a real opportunity to enjoy a big-fight atmosphere, which is key in creating and cultivating a new fan base. What other professional sport would even entertain the thought of putting such a seminal event in such a small venue?"

Then Pacquiao-Mayweather imploded, giving Arum the opportunity to test his theory. Pacquiao-Clottey was scheduled for Cowboys Stadium. Instead of 16,000 spectators who paid ticket-scalper prices or were high rollers comped by casinos, everyday fans would be able to buy tickets at face value.

Arum is no stranger to big-stadium fights. In 1966, he promoted the first fight in the history of the Houston Astrodome—Muhammad Ali vs. Cleveland Williams. Ten years later, he promoted the rubber match between Ali and Ken Norton, which was the last fight held in the "old" Yankee Stadium. Then, in 1978, he put the rematch between Ali and Leon Spinks in the New Orleans Superdome. That encounter drew 63,350 fans and remains the largest attendance ever for an indoor fight in the United States.

Four days before Pacquiao-Clottey, Arum spoke of seeing the Astrodome for the first time. "The building just blew me away," he reminisced. "I'd never seen anything like it before. Suites and the amenities; there was nothing like it anywhere in the world."

But that was forty-four years ago. Cowboys Stadium, which opened last year, is now the largest domed stadium on the planet and lives up to its self-description as "the largest, most technologically advanced entertainment venue in the world."

"Words can't describe it," Arum says. "You have to see it in person."

Television doesn't do it justice either.

The stadium, which can seat 100,000 for boxing, is beyond spectacular. It looks like a set created by James Cameron for *Avatar* and is so symmetrically proportioned that it's hard to grasp how big it is unless you're there. There are luxury suites, trendy restaurants, and a high-definition video board (the largest in the world) that cost $40,000,000, weighs 600 tons, and is 160 feet long by 72 feet high.

"I've never had an experience where the venue played such a paramount role in the promotion," Arum told the media. "We had fifty thousand people watching the fight the way a fight should be watched—in person."

Now Arum is on track to become the first man to promote a fight in the "new" Yankee Stadium, which also opened last year.

Unlike Cowboys Stadium, Yankee Stadium (which is modeled on and across the street from the original structure) is steeped in boxing tradition. Sixteen heavyweight championship fights were contested in the old ballpark; most notably, Joe Louis's first-round knockout of Max Schmeling in 1938. Jack Dempsey, Gene Tunney, Rocky Marciano, and Muhammad Ali were all victorious within its hallowed walls. It was there that Sugar Ray Robinson, well ahead of Joey Maxim on points, wilted in the heat and suffered the only knockout loss of his career.

With Arum overseeing the promotion, Yuri Foreman will defend his WBA junior-middleweight title against Miguel Cotto at Yankee Stadium eight days before New York's Puerto Rican Day Parade. In configuring the stadium for boxing, the infield will be off-limits because the baseball season is underway. Thus, the ring will be erected in right field. Arum hopes that 35,000 fans will be there. With full use of the playing field, the stadium could accommodate 75,000 for boxing.

The structure of the deals that Arum made for the use of Cowboys Stadium and Yankee Stadium are similar, although the numbers are different. Both the Cowboys and Yankees guaranteed a certain dollar amount to Arum (just under $7,000,000 in the case of the Cowboys). The stadium recoups its guarantee plus out-of-pocket expenses out of ticket sales. If and when that number is reached, revenue sharing between Top Rank and the stadium on ticket sales comes into play.

The Cowboys and Yankees keep all revenue from on-site concessions and parking, which can be extremely lucrative (e.g. it costs fifty dollars to park at Cowboys Stadium). Arum pays his own expenses (including the fighters' purses), but keeps all pay-per-view revenue, television license fees, and other subsidiary income.

The one cloud on the horizon for Arum's Yankee Stadium promotion is a literal one. Rain on fight night would be a disaster. In the old days, rain simply meant a one or two-day postponement. But that's not feasible when television is driving the economics of a fight, and Foreman-Cotto is slated for *HBO World Championship Boxing.* There will be a canopy over the ring to protect the canvas in the event of precipitation. But that won't protect the live gate.

Arum says that these two big-stadium fights are the beginning of a new era in boxing. He calls them "bringing elite fights back to the people" and proclaims, "This has long-range implications. It takes boxing back into the mainstream and into the future. Going to these large venues and moving these boxing matches around the country will help in branding the sport and make it what it once was and will be again; a major sport in this country."

There's truth in that. Pacquiao-Clottey in Cowboys Stadium received far more coverage in the mainstream media than would have been the case had it been contested in Las Vegas. And it made people who don't often think about boxing curious as to what was going on.

Similarly, Foreman-Cotto in Yankee Stadium will be a much bigger event than the same fight in Madison Square Garden would have been.

In that vein, Arum hopes to promote a second fight card at Cowboys Stadium later this year and a mega-event at the 82,000-seat Meadowlands Stadium in New Jersey in 2011. "You've got to do fights all over the country," he says. "That's how people get energized."

All of which leaves one question: "When the next mega-fight comes (whether it's Pacquiao-Mayweather or something else) will everyone return to Las Vegas?"

Here, the thoughts of Jerry Jones are instructive. Jones is the owner of the Dallas Cowboys and the man who put up the $7,000,000 guarantee for Pacquiao-Clottey. Previously, he'd offered a $25,000,000 guarantee for Pacquiao-Mayweather. Putting that number in perspective, the previous high site fee paid for a fight was $18,000,000 (for De La Hoya-Mayweather).

"I don't want this to sound wrong," Jones said several days before his stadium hosted Pacquiao-Clottey. "But we write checks like that around here all the time. I can compete with Las Vegas. I can and I will."

"Not only can Jerry Jones compete with Las Vegas," Arum added; "he can beat Las Vegas."

The business of boxing is sometimes described as the theater of the absurd. A look at negotiations for the proposed autumn 2010 fight between Manny Pacquiao and Floyd Mayweather Jr demonstrates why.

The Mayweather-Pacquiao Negotiations

Too often, boxing gives the impression that the inmates are running the asylum. That phenomenon has been on display recently in the conflicting, and sometimes absurd, public pronouncements regarding the proposed November 13, 2010, fight between Manny Pacquiao and Floyd Mayweather Jr.

For several months, the public was told that negotiations were proceeding pursuant to a self-imposed gag order that the participants had put in place to avoid incendiary statements that might derail the fight.

On June 10th, Golden Boy president Oscar De La Hoya (Mayweather's co-promoter as of late) broke the silence and told Univision that a deal for the bout was "very close."

On June 30th, Top Rank CEO Bob Arum (Pacquiao's promoter) told SI.com that, with HBO Sports president Ross Greenburg acting as an intermediary, he and Mayweather advisor Al Haymon had reached a tentative agreement for the fight. All that was necessary, Arum said, was for Mayweather to sign off on the deal points.

Mayweather was silent on the issue. Thus, Arum set a deadline of midnight on the night of Friday, July 16th. If there was no response from Floyd by then, rather than keep Pacquiao out of the ring indefinitely, Team Pacquiao would seek another opponent.

Midnight came and went. At 12:01AM, Arum announced on a teleconference call that Mayweather had failed to respond positively or negatively to the terms that had been hammered out by Greenburg, Haymon, and himself. As a result, the promoter said, he would explore other options for Pacquiao.

Then things took a turn evocative of *Alice's Adventures in Wonderland*. On July 19th, Team Mayweather issued a statement from Mayweather advisor Leonard Ellerbe denying that negotiations for Mayweather-Pacquiao had ever taken place.

"Here are the facts," Ellerbe's statement read. "Al Haymon, Richard Schaefer, and myself speak to each other on a regular basis. The truth is, no negotiations have ever taken place nor was there ever a deal agreed upon by Team Mayweather or Floyd Mayweather to fight Manny Pacquiao on November 13th. Either Ross Greenburg or Bob Arum is not telling the truth, but history tells us who is lying."

Of course, there's a third possibility: that Leonard Ellerbe is not telling the truth.

So what really happened?

Greenburg was extremely anxious to make Mayweather-Pacquiao a reality. Multiple sources say that, this spring, he told Arum, "'I want to put this fight together. I can do it with Haymon."

Later, at a June 3rd tribute to Arum at the Friar's Club in New York, Ross assured Bob, "I can get this fight."

"I never talked to Haymon," Arum says. "It was all done through Ross. Ross represented to me that he was talking to the Mayweather side through Haymon, and it was left to Haymon to deal with the rest of the Mayweather people. Based on what Ross told me, I assumed that we had a meeting of the minds on money and drug testing. There was no done deal for a site, but the most likely site was Las Vegas. The MGM Grand wanted the fight. Steve Wynn was interested. Jerry Jones might have given us a blank check and told us to fill in the amount if we went to Dallas. But all the talk about finalizing the venue was premature."

"Haymon never represented to Ross that Floyd had signed off on the deal," Arum continues. "According to Ross, Haymon always said that he had to get final approval from Mayweather. But if Ross is to be believed—and I believe him here—Haymon said that he, meaning Haymon, was satisfied with the terms."

A source at HBO with knowledge of the situation says that there was a time during negotiations when Haymon tried to link Mayweather-Pacquiao to TV dates for several of his other fighters. Greenburg, according to the source, appropriately refused.

It's unclear what role, if any, Golden Boy was to play in the promotion. "That was up to the Mayweather people," Arum says. "Depending on the day, I got mixed signals through Ross. From time to time, Ross would tell me that Haymon was checking certain things with Schaefer. Other times, I got the impression that maybe Golden Boy was out."

As the world knows, July 16th passed with no deal for Mayweather-Pacquiao. Then Ellerbe issued his statement denying the existence of negotiations.

Ellerbe's claim is undermined by the reasonable assumption that he read reports about the negotiations in the media. Yet he never publicly suggested to anyone that the reports were wrong. At the very least, one would have expected him to pick up the phone, call Greenburg, and ask, "What are these reports all about?"

One would also think that, if there were no negotiations, Greenburg would have called Arum to inquire about the reports.

Arum puts it more bluntly, saying, "Is Ellerbe crazy? If there were no negotiations, why was everyone talking about a gag order?"

Al Haymon has refused to comment publicly on the controversy. So has Greenburg. Where Haymon is concerned, that's par for the course. Regarding Greenburg, the view here is that Ross owes Arum the courtesy of a public statement that negotiations did, in fact, occur (the assumption here being that they did).*

As for the future; Arum noted in his midnight statement, "People have asked me, 'Does this mean the Mayweather fight is dead?' Even though Mayweather has not responded by the deadline, the deal is dead when we reach a deal with an opponent for Manny's fight in November. Then we are contractually bound to do that fight. In the interim, if Floyd suddenly emerged and said he wanted to do the fight, there would be nothing opposed to getting together and doing the fight. That is our position, and I hope it is as clear as I can make it."

In that vein, one source says that Haymon met with Greenburg on

* Four days after the above article appeared online, Ross Greenburg issued a statement acknowledging that he had been negotiating a Mayweather-Pacquiao fight with a representative from each fighter's camp from May 2nd through the breakdown of negotiations in mid-July.

Tuesday, July 20th, and told him, "Don't worry. I have everything under control."

Maybe he does. Maybe he doesn't.

The fight will happen if Mayweather wants it. If he's afraid of Pacquiao, it won't.

We're living in the 21st century. Todd DuBoef thinks that boxing should too.

Todd DuBoef and the Future of Boxing

There were whispers when Todd DuBoef started work at Top Rank in 1993.

"Todd is a spoiled rich kid . . . Todd is Bob Arum's valet . . . The only reason Todd has a job at Top Rank is that Arum married Todd's mother."

That was then.

Seventeen years later, DuBoef is recognized throughout the boxing industry as energetic, hard-working, and smart. He understands the economics of the sweet science and its interaction with the new media as well as anyone. Over the next decade, he might be the most important person in boxing. Not the most powerful, but the most important.

"Anyone who says that Todd teethed on a silver spoon is missing the point," Jim Lampley states. "He's passionate about his vision. He's a formidable intellect. You underestimate Todd at your own peril. If anyone can lead a revival of the boxing business in the United States, he's the one."

DuBoef was born on August 18, 1967. He grew up in Las Vegas before attending prep school on the east coast; first at Eaglebrook in Deerfield, Massachusetts; then at The Loomis Chaffee School in Windsor, Connecticut. That was followed by four years at Trinity College in Hartford, six miles from Loomis Chaffee.

At Trinity, DuBoef excelled on the varsity hockey team. "Success as an athlete came easily to me at a certain level," he says. "And sports were important to me. When I wasn't in season, I ate right and stayed in shape." During his four years in college, Trinity notched 83 victories against 19 defeats. Todd scored 59 goals and 74 assists for a total of 133 career points (sixth on the school's all-time points list).

After graduating from Trinity in 1990, DuBoef moved to New York and worked in commercial real estate. Meanwhile, back in Las Vegas,

Arum and Lovee DuBoef had begun dating each other and would marry in 1991.

Arum has three children from his first marriage: Richard (a tenured professor of sociology at NYU), John (an environmental lawyer in Seattle), and Liz (a teacher at St. Ann's School in Brooklyn). Each of them came to fights occasionally. None were interested in the business of boxing.

"I could see right away that Todd was a bright guy," Arum says. "He had no boxing background, but obviously he had a good business mind. I thought he'd be helpful as someone who could relate to the fighters better than I could because of the age factor. I told him, 'Look; except for George [Foreman], these fighters are all more your age than mine. Why don't you come to work for Top Rank?' I had no idea then how innovative he was and how important he'd become to the future of the company."

"My first impression of Bob was personal, not professional," Todd recalls. "I knew him initially as someone who was dating my mother. He was warm and respectful. He had an engaging personality. Then he asked if I'd like to work at Top Rank. Growing up, I'd gone to dozens of big fights with my father. That was when Las Vegas stopped for a big fight. So the idea appealed to me. Being at Top Rank was exciting at first. There was a sexy addictive rush. But there were also times when I said to myself, 'This is the stupidest thing I've ever done.'"

"The first thing that Todd had to do was learn the boxing business," Arum says, picking up the narrative. "I liked his desire to soak up knowledge and his reluctance to push himself forward until he had that knowledge."

DuBoef, for his part, recalls, "There was no pressure on me to do anything except learn. I didn't have to produce. And I had the best teachers imaginable. The best way to learn from Bob is to watch and experience with him. He's not an "X's" and "O's" coach. And my other teachers were people like Teddy Brenner, Mike Malitz, Bruce Trampler, and Lee Samuels. There's no faculty in the world better than that."

"It was a while before we spoke," Top Rank matchmaker Bruce Trampler remembers. "Then, one day, Todd came into my office and started asking questions; and he hasn't stopped asking questions since."

"I first met Todd when Bob began bringing him to meetings at HBO," former Time Warner Sports president Seth Abraham (the architect of HBO's boxing program) says. "He was quiet and respectful. When you sat down with him, it was clear that he wanted to learn what you knew. One of the things that struck me about him was that he put a lot of thought into what he was going to say before he said it. And he had the ability to see the other side's point of view. He didn't necessarily agree with it, but he saw it and understood it, which isn't always true of Bob."

Abraham smiles as he recounts the past.

"After a while, whenever Bob and I had one of our periodic thermonuclear wars, Todd would come in as the peacemaker. One time, Lovee was throwing a birthday party for Bob. I got an invitation and didn't RSVP because HBO was in the middle of a lawsuit that Top Rank had filed against us. Lovee followed up with a telephone call to ask if I'd come, and I said, 'I don't think so.' Two hours later, Todd called and made the point that my being there could begin the process of reconciliation. So I went out to the party and, soon after that, the lawsuit was settled. I'm a fan of Todd's. He gives nepotism a good name."

Over time, DuBoef began to put what he was learning to use. Arum had been one of the first promoters to understand the potential of the international market. "At Top Rank," Bob says, "we've always been proud of our international business." Todd had been tutored in international sales by Mike Malitz. In 1995, he journeyed to Monaco to attended Sportel [the International Sports Convention for Television and New Media] for the first time.

"Back then," Todd recalls, "all of the major promoters in the United States had output deals with international networks that guaranteed them a certain number of dates each year, which in turn guaranteed them a certain income flow. They were luxurious deals from the point of view of the promoters with poor oversight by the networks. Over time, most of the deals expired and weren't renewed. At Top Rank, we made the decision to over-service. That developed a lot of good will, which enabled us to get renewals and also to fill the void that was created when the other deals expired."

Looking back on DuBoef's first few trips to Sportel, Arum says, "I realized then that Todd was good and that there was a whole new generation of foreign television executives, the ones who were making the key decisions, who were his age; not Mike Malitz's age or mine. Todd was talking the same language as these guys, and it was obvious that, sometime in the not-too-distant future, my role would be reduced to telling old war stories."

Mike Heitner (who has been Arum's attorney since the 1960s) concurs, saying, "I understood that Todd could be special when he started developing the foreign business beyond what Mike Malitz had done. Todd wasn't just making good deals; he was outselling HBO."

Summarizing that time, DuBoef says, "Sportel was the start of my maturation process. And it gave me insight into the demand for boxing at the global media companies. They weren't just buying one fight. The volume of what they wanted on an annual basis was staggering. It opened my eyes to the broad appeal, not of one fighter, not of one event, but of the brand of boxing."

Fifteen years later, DuBoef is Top Rank's indispensable man.

"Todd has made it his business to learn, not just the boxing business but every media innovation and new production technology that comes along," Heitner notes. "He's realistic. He has a retentive mind. He's great with numbers. He's fiscally responsible, but he'll spend what he has to spend to do the job right. And he's willing to take financial risks to bring the business to the next level."

"When you're talking with Todd," says Bruce Trampler, "you hear a lot of Todd's opinions. But they're fact-based opinions; not bullshit. And he's knowledgeable about certain areas of boxing where most promoters don't have a clue."

"Todd can take a complicated business situation and distill it to very simple terms," Seth Abraham adds. "He's passionate about the business, but he can also be very dispassionate in a good way. He never lets his emotions rule his intellect. He'll say to himself. 'Here's my problem. Here's my opportunity.' And then he'll think things through to a logical conclusion."

"I'm still the face of Top Rank," Arum acknowledges. "But Todd does more of the essential work."

Part of what DuBoef has done over the past decade is to significantly change Top Rank's business model.

By and large, the business of boxing is a series of one-night stands. Promoters make their money on a fight-by-fight basis. Todd sees things differently. His vision for Top Rank is for a more integrated flow of content that the company will create and transmit to consumers via media platforms that are built for the future.

"Top Rank isn't a boxing promotional company anymore," DuBoef says. "We're a media company. That's a seismic shift in the business model. It used to be that an event on Saturday was over on Sunday, and what do you do with it then? We no longer value the success of what we do based only on one night. We've changed from being in the boxing event business to the new media business. We're creating assets and viewing our content on a long-term basis."

"The greatest growth at Top Rank in recent years has been on the production side of things," Todd continues. "We have our own editors and editing facilities. The Top Rank library [which contains fights promoted by Arum dating back to 1966] is a major asset that we haven't fully exploited yet."

More significantly, Top Rank is capable of producing telecasts of its own fights. Roughly two dozen employees work for the company on a fulltime basis. When HBO televises a Top Rank fight, DuBoef supplements the HBO crew with his own staff and freelancers to form an independent crew of thirty to thirty-five people. Top Rank uses all of HBO's cameras plus a few of its own. Then it cuts the HBO feed with Top Rank's own on-air talent, cameras, graphics, and branding to create a Top Rank telecast for the international market. The company also distributes all of the undercard fights.

For independent pay-per-view shows, Top Rank puts the whole package together with a crew of fifty to sixty people. Its Fox telecasts require a crew of forty.

"I like to think that, when we produce something, we get more bang for our buck than anybody," Todd says. "At Top Rank, we want our people to push the envelope and be in the forefront of innovation. Be creative. Don't have the same repetitious shots and the same format as everyone else. We're always looking to take things to the next level."

"A full HBO production might be a shade better than ours," Arum acknowledges. "But that's like comparing apples with oranges because their producers have so much more money to work with. You have to compare apples with apples. Watch some of our productions and compare them with *ShoBox* or *Friday Night Fights* on ESPN2. Showtime and ESPN might argue the point, but our productions are better."

The fact that Top Rank is capable of producing and distributing its own telecasts is crucial to DuBoef's plans for the future because it gives the company autonomy.

There's a school of thought that HBO wanted to help Golden Boy create UFC-type dominance of boxing within the United States and, through Golden Boy, control the sport at the highest levels with "clean hands." That might be far-fetched. But certainly, the network sought to empower Golden Boy as a counterweight to Top Rank. No one disputes the fact that Golden Boy has been built in large measure on HBO's dime.

Arum is enraged by HBO's tilt toward Golden Boy. Todd's attitude is, "With or without HBO, we'll survive and we'll thrive." Indeed, since Golden Boy signed its output deal with HBO (which gives it a significant advantage over competitors), Top Rank has strengthened its position as the lead promoter in the United States.

"People in boxing value success based on how many television dates they get," DuBoef says. "You're a successful promoter if you have dates. But that means you're completely at the mercy of the doler-out. Our job at Top Rank is to create, to promote, to be autonomous. I don't want our success or failure to be based on what side of bed a television executive woke up on that morning."

"Look at how Top Rank has built Julio Cesar Chavez Jr," Todd continues. "The networks might never want Chavez Jr. We've had zero help from HBO, Showtime, or ESPN where he's concerned. But if the public has an appetite for Chavez, why not feed the public what it wants instead of saying, 'Sorry; you can't fight because the television executives won't give us dates.'"

Individual Top Rank "Latin Fury" cards featuring Chavez Jr have generated as many as 90,000 pay-per-view buys, making them a profitable venture.

After HBO and Showtime turned down comeback fights for Kelly Pavlik and Miguel Cotto in early 2009, Top Rank mounted a two-site show on its own. The Pavlik-Cotto doubleheader sold out in Youngstown (where Kelly fought), did nicely at Madison Square Garden (where Miguel performed), and engendered a reported 140,000 buys.

"Todd taught me that complaining and moaning about not getting dates gets you nowhere," Arum says. "So now, when we can't get dates, we do our own shows."

At the same time, DuBoef has continued to build Top Rank's international business. "When we do a big event like a Manny Pacquiao fight," he says "it's distributed live in about one hundred fifty countries. We have pan-regional deals in Latin America, Africa, Asia, and Europe; so many of the same countries get other Top Rank shows on a live or delay basis."

Top Rank is now the world's biggest provider of content to the international market. Moreover, unlike other American promoters, it has drawn a line in the sand with HBO and successfully insisted on keeping foreign rights to all of its fights.

What would happen if HBO demanded international rights and said that the issue was a deal-breaker?

"HBO is a service in the United States," Todd answers. "Its subscribers are in the United States. International rights constitute a revenue stream that belongs to the promoter. We understand each other on the international side. Top Rank is in that space."

Meanwhile, DuBoef is an evangelist for the new media. "There was a time when everyone in boxing was completely engaged with the conventional media," he notes. "When online came around, it was an afterthought. MMA had no penetration with the conventional media, but it was cyberyears ahead of us with the new media. I'm not an expert on it, but I have guys who are. I've hired young media managers and given them free reign with the Twitters, the YouTubes, MySpace. The symbiosis between boxing and the new media is growing and will be increasingly important to us in the future."

As for what that future will be; DuBoef believes in what he calls "the brand of boxing."

"There was a point where I became very frustrated," he says. "All I heard was 'the sport is dead.' It was morbid and depressing. Then I had an epiphany. I said, 'Wait a minute. We get six thousand people for a weigh-in in Las Vegas. When Manny Pacquiao is on terrestrial television in the Philippines, we do a 98 percent share. Wladimir Klitschko did a 51 percent share in Germany against Eddie Chambers. Boxing is not dead.'"

"One of boxing's problems," Todd continues, "is that, unlike other major sports, we have no public relations effort keyed to promote boxing as a whole. The NBA has 'I love this game' and 'Amazing!' Major League Baseball tells you that it's "fantastic" and a life-long bond between fathers and their children. In boxing, virtually all of the publicity is keyed to a specific fight and, on a few occasions, to a specific fighter."

"If you ride the coattails of the sport, you'll be fine. It's like the movie business. Stars are important; sometimes sequels work. But stars come and go. The brand is movies. Top Rank built Oscar De La Hoya. Top Rank built Floyd Mayweather Jr. We did well with them and we're doing well without them. The brand is boxing. Every fight has the potential to be memorable. There's incredible drama in the moment when a fighter walks to the ring for a major fight. That feeling, that energy, is unique to boxing."

Now DuBoef is on a roll.

"One of the things we have to do—all of us in boxing—is put an end to the infighting. People in boxing are horrible when it comes to infighting and vicious behavior in the press. We're constantly demeaning the brand by demeaning each other's product. Bob does it too. It's stupid and it hurts the sport. Jerry Jones doesn't say, 'Don't watch the Giants against the Eagles; that game sucks.' David Stern doesn't run around saying, "This is a miserable fucking business.' I love it when someone puts fifty thousand people in an arena in Germany to watch Vitali Klitschko against Kevin Johnson. I don't say, 'That was a lousy fight.' If the people who run boxing are negative, how can we expect the public to react positively to our product?"

One of the keys in DuBoef's mind to building the brand of boxing is to turn each fight into the best "event" possible. Part of that involves enhancing the overall in-arena experience.

"I've learned a lot from watching UFC," Todd says. "They do a great job of energizing the crowd and keeping it engaged. We have to do more of that in boxing. Other sports have changed their presentation. Baseball added mascots and music. Cheerleaders in the NFL are different from what cheerleaders used to be. Too many promoters today ignore the on-site fan. And too many television executives don't understand that part of a great telecast is having a live audience that's involved in the action and having a great time."

DuBoef is committed to making the experience of watching a fight in the arena more entertaining than it has been in recent years. He spent $150,000 to rent a light board for the MGM Grand Garden Arena when Manny Pacquiao fought Miguel Cotto. When Pacquiao fought Joshua Clottey in Cowboys Stadium, the arena was bathed in a futuristic silver-blue light.

"Todd is a showman," HBO Sports president Ross Greenburg acknowledges. "There's no doubt that he has elevated the big-event feeling for boxing to a new level. For Pacquiao-Clottey, we gave him what we usually allocate for sound and lighting and told him that, if he wanted to spend more, he could supplement it out of Top Rank's pocket. With the big screen and sound and blue-lit lighting, he made the event feel like a mini-Super Bowl."

DuBoef's work with Miguel Cotto is also indicative of his thought processes.

Cotto was the first major fighter that he brought into Top Rank. "Todd scouted him at the Olympics," Arum recalls. "He worked hard to sign him. He looked at Miguel as his fighter, and I pretty much gave him free reign to do what he wanted to do as far as Miguel was concerned. The idea for an annual fight at Madison Square Garden featuring Miguel on the eve of the Puerto Rican Day Parade originated with Todd."

And it became an event.

"I've dealt with Todd a lot," says Madison Square Garden executive vice president Joel Fisher. "He's not your typical promoter, who comes in, puts up a boxing ring, and has fights. He wants to give the fans more. When he came to us with the idea of creating a franchise with Miguel Cotto and the Garden around the Puerto Rican Day Parade, he said, 'It will be good for Cotto; it will be good for Top Rank; and it will be good for the Garden.' So we started with Cotto against Muhammad Abdullaev. Then we had Cotto and Paulie Malignaggi; and after that, Cotto and Zab Judah. This year, Top Rank put Cotto in Yankee Stadium. But Todd was very up-front and honest with us when he started negotiations with the Yankees; and I appreciated that too."

How good is DuBoef at selling his product?

Dana White is the public face of UFC. One wouldn't expect him to look kindly on Top Rank given the fact that, last year, Arum called UFC fans "a bunch of skinhead white guys watching people in the ring who also look like skinhead white guys rolling around like homosexuals on the ground."

Add to that the fact that, in the mid-1990s, White wanted to go to work for Top Rank. "They didn't offer me a job," he recalls. "In the end, that worked out well for me."

"Todd is a sharp guy," White says. "Todd gets it. Boxing is all about 'let me get as much money as I can right here right now and stuff it in my pocket.' Todd is different. He knows how to build a product. I like the way he presents his product. The Dallas thing [Pacquiao-Clottey] was incredible. I'm a huge Manny Pacquiao fan. I love watching him fight. Todd invited me to Dallas and gave me some tickets and I tweeted about it. There are 1.2 million people who follow me on Twitter, so it was good for both of us."

Meanwhile, DuBoef is constantly looking for ways to expand business opportunities for Top Rank.

"Boxing has an almost exclusively event-based merchandise business," he notes. "There's no sustainability from fight to fight. The NFL has Super Bowl merchandise, but most NFL merchandise has a much longer shelf life. The same is true of Major League Baseball and NBA merchandise. We have to look outside of the box we're in."

"Sponsorships are another area where we're just coming out of the dark ages. People were dismissive of boxing on a corporate level, and that assumption had been built into our economic models. Golden Boy successfully challenged that notion. Richard [Schaefer] and Oscar [De La Hoya] did a good job of leveraging Oscar to get corporate America to look at boxing. Everyone in boxing can benefit from that."

"But the biggest problem that boxing faces," DuBoef continues, "is that we're cutting off the flow of content to the consumer. If you go back in history, media rode the shoulders of boxing content. Boxing was on the cutting edge of newspapers, magazines, radio, and television; all of which brought boxing to more and more people. Now we're locked into a business model where fewer and fewer people see our best content. The contraction started when HBO paid large license fees to lure boxing away from free broadcast television. HBO is in the subscriber business; not the boxing business. It took a product that was in ninety million homes and put it on a much smaller platform. And the demographic was further diminished when HBO put boxing on a pay-per-view platform. That took the product away from even more consumers and further marginalized the sport. Now we've lost the flow of big fights to consumers. We've lost regularly scheduled big fights. We've lost our foundation for the sport. We have to loosen the grip of the current economic model and expose more people to the sport."

"The current economic model is about appealing to a handful of television executives, not fans," DuBoef elaborates. "And the lack of vision, the lack of knowledge, and the behavior of some of these executives is very disappointing to me. Maybe I was naïve, but I expected more. Once upon a time, I assumed that the people who bought fights for the networks understood the business. Many of them don't. And I thought that they'd be guided by a desire for the best content because that's the best way to sell their product and serve their subscribers. But that's not necessarily the way they operate. Let's be honest. Most of these guys are in the job-preservation business. Bob gets angry when he talks about it. I say, the television networks are what they are, just like the world sanctioning bodies are what they are. They're part of our world, and we'll deal with it."

"I'm very proud of Pacquiao-Clottey," DuBoef says. "I think what we did in seven weeks to create that event was amazing. But I should have explored making a deal with ESPN for that fight. HBO brought nothing to the promotion. They wouldn't even do a *24/7* series. They did *The Road to Dallas* as a promo piece. One show. ESPN would have given us four "Roads to Dallas" in 90,000,000 homes. Bob is a creature of habit. He likes things that are familiar and the way they are. But if I had it to do over again; absolutely, I'd discuss Pacquiao-Clottey with ESPN, with CBS, with Showtime. I'm not looking to rock the boat. But I am looking to grow the audience."

"When Top Rank and Main Events co-promoted Holyfield-Foreman [in 1991], there were 16,000,000 homes that were addressable for pay-per-view. The fight did 1,400,000 buys. That's a 9 percent buy rate. Now we have 77,000,000 homes that are addressable for pay-per-view. A 9 percent buy rate would translate into 6,900,000 buys. How do we get to that 9 percent number again? On what platform? At what price? Suppose, for a full month, every time you went to Google, you saw banner that said,

'Click here to order Pacquiao-Mayweather'? That would be a lot bigger than *24/7*."

"The media world is changing by the month and year now; not by the year and decade. Before long, people will be watching pay-per-view on the Internet on a regular basis. There will be a conversion. That's inevitable. The question is, 'Who will be the gatekeeper?' Will it be Google? AT&T? Yahoo? AOL? YouTube? Apple? You can put anything you want online, but you have to create awareness. Once we decide how to create major awareness for pay-per-view online, the technology will take over."

"But we also have to get boxing back into people's homes without it being too expensive for our prospective fan base. CBS, NBC, ABC, and Fox are in 110,000,000 homes. That would be nice. But if we could get a platform like TNT or TBS to put its arm around boxing the way Spike did with UFC, that would be enough. That would give us 90,000,000 homes; three times as many homes as HBO; almost six times as many homes as Showtime."

There are things that DuBoef likes to do besides work. "The most important thing to me," he says, "and it's not always easy to do, is to balance my life. People in this business are so obsessed and so consumed by it all that they never take a step back. I have a hectic travel schedule. I live in Las Vegas, but I'm on the road a lot. In and of itself, the travel doesn't bother me, but being away from my wife and son does. Family is more important to me than business. I love skiing, hiking, and mountain biking. We have a home in Aspen that's my sanctuary."

On occasion, DuBoef ruffles feathers. One rival promoter complains, "He's an elitist. He's arrogant. He talks down to you. He grew up in privilege, which very few of us did. With Todd, it's, 'You don't understand' and I just flew in from Aspen, where I was skiing.' He's not one of the guys."

"Todd has a good business mind," Ross Greenburg says. "He's very smart. But there are times when he thinks he knows more than he does and more than you do. Sometimes he pontificates. I asked him once, 'Are you lecturing me?'"

He was.

"When I come up with an idea and want to execute it," DuBoef says, "I'm frustrated when people try to hold me back. I'm open to suggestion. But once I've established my position, vetted it out, and feel that I'm right, I don't like being told that I can't do it or that it can't be done."

DuBoef's detractors also point to January 6, 2004, when a dozen FBI agents raided Top Rank's offices pursuant to a sealed search warrant. Rumors swirled regarding tax fraud, the submission of fraudulent medical documents to state athletic commissions, fixed fights, and cocaine trafficking. But no charges against Todd or anyone else at Top Rank were filed.

Six years later, Top Rank is the number-one promoter in boxing and DuBoef is firmly ensconced as a major force in the sweet science.

"Todd is truly the president of Top Rank." Mike Heitner says. "It's not an empty title. He hires; he makes deals. He has the power to act independently. He most definitely has found a place outside of Bob's shadow. And he complements Bob in ways that are good for the company. Bob is impatient; Todd is the opposite. Todd is a conciliator; Bob is more confrontational. And Todd has developed expertise in technological areas that will serve Top Rank well in the years ahead."

"Todd has matured into an executive with much broader shoulders than he had when he started," adds HBO senior vice president Mark Taffet. "He addresses issues and problems and differences of opinion constructively rather than by just blowing up. If you disagree with Todd, he'll listen to your point of view, genuinely think about what you said, and come back with a thoughtful response."

"I was most impressed with Todd when we were trying to hold Mayweather-Pacquiao together in late-2009 and early this year," Ross Greenburg notes. "He was the voice of reason in that whole mess."

DuBoef sees the big picture. He doesn't just look at things in the moment. He's always asking, "Where will Top Rank be in five years? What will boxing be like ten years from now?"

"I have a vision of the future," Todd says. "Not all the pieces of the puzzle are in place. I'm still trying to figure some of it out. I might be dead wrong in my approach, but I don't think so."

Meanwhile, the biggest beneficiary of DuBoef's emergence and growth as an executive has been the man who brought him into Top Rank.

"I can stay active longer because I have Todd," Bob Arum says. "He's really the one who runs things now. My involvement on any given fight is as intense or as limited as I want it to be. It might appear to the outside world that I'm as active as I ever was, but I'm not. More and more, Todd is taking over the company and moving it in the direction that he wants to move it."

"There are so many issues that people in boxing will have to face in the years ahead," Arum continues. "Nobody knows with any certainty where the technology is going and how fast we'll get there. Will we do 3-D boxing in theaters? If so, will Saturday night be the right night? How will Internet distribution, which is bound to come, affect pay-per-view? Todd is better equipped to deal with these issues and others like them than anyone else I know. And there are other things, like delegating authority, that Todd does better than I ever did. As Top Rank gets bigger and bigger, it's essential to do that. He's the right guy in the right place at the right time. I can't tell you how lucky I am to have him."

Then there's the legacy factor. Arum has spent almost five decades of his life building a promotional empire. Is it comforting to him to know that Todd will carry on after he's gone?

"Not really," Arum answers. "I'm a very practical guy. For me, dead is dead. After I pass on, as long as the people I love are happy, I'm fine. Tex Rickard left his mark on boxing, and there was no Tex Rickard Jr in boxing after him. I have three children; each of them very accomplished and fulfilled professionally. They're happy in what they do and none of them would be happy in boxing. Just because I made my life through boxing doesn't mean that Todd has to. Right now, being in boxing is satisfying to him. If there comes a time when it isn't and he wants to do something else, that's fine. If Todd leaves boxing when I'm not around and there's an afterlife and I can look down, I'll be thinking, 'Good for you. You did a great job in boxing while you were in it, and I hope you're happy in whatever else you do.'"

These "Notes" chronicled bits and pieces of the boxing scene in 2010.

Fistic Notes

The first three weeks of January 2010 could be summarized as: "Pacquiao-Mayweather off . . . Hopkins-Jones II on, probably . . . Mosley-Berto off . . . Mayweather-Mosley, maybe."

Finally, on January 23rd, boxing fans got to see some actual fights.

There was a buzz at Madison Square Garden for the first important fight card of the year. Juan Manuel Lopez vs. Steven Luevano and Yuriorkis Gamboa against Rogers Mtagwa were co-featured on HBO's *Boxing After Dark*. They were preceded by a non-televised seven-bout undercard. And for those who wanted to follow the festivities on Twitter, Top Rank (which promoted the action) arranged for a pre-fight "tweet-up" from the basement of Stout Restaurant and Bar, one block from the Garden.

"I'm not going to the tweet-up," Top Rank CEO Bob Arum confessed earlier in the week. "I'm old school. Tweeting and twittering in a bar sounds dirty to me."

The near-capacity crowd of 5,142 came to the WaMu Theater at Madison Square Garden early and was into the undercard contests. But the loudest cheers were reserved for Gamboa and Lopez.

Gamboa (a Cuban expatriate now living in Miami) won a gold medal in the flyweight division at the 2004 Athens Olympics. Prior to facing Mtagwa, his record stood at 16 victories against no losses with 14 knockouts. He's one of two WBA featherweight (126-pound) champions. Chris John is the other.

For the uninitiated, multiple champions (and the multiple sanctioning fees they generate) are a common WBA phenomenon. "Idiocy" and "greed" are words that could be added to this paragraph.

Seconds into Gamboa-Mtagwa, it was clear that Gamboa was too fast and too strong for his opponent. He dominated from the start with devastating speed and power, hitting Rogers at will and rocking him when he did.

Mtagwa's only defense was his chin, which had served him well in previous fights. But his chin was no match for the fury of Gamboa's fists, and Gamboa's speed befuddled him. Yuriorkis battered his hapless foe, landing 60 percent (52 out of 87) of his power punches. A sharp left hook put Rogers down late in round one. A second knockdown ended matters at the 2:35 mark of round two, when referee Steve Smoger wisely stopped the carnage. It wasn't much of a fight but it was an impressive performance.

Gamboa's destruction of Mtagwa cast a long shadow over Lopez as "Juanma" entered the ring.

Lopez finds himself in an odd situation. Four months ago, he was undefeated with 24 knockouts in 26 fights, Arum was marketing him as Puerto Rico's next boxing idol and a superstar in the making. His name appeared on quite a few "pound-for-pound" lists. He was also the WBO's 122-pound champion.

Then, on October 10, 2009, Lopez fought Mtagwa. He won a decision, but was in desperate trouble and one punch away from being knocked out in the twelfth round.

There are few instances of a champion's stock falling so far so fast after a win as Juanma's fell after the Mtagwa fight. Lopez said that one reason for his poor performance was that he'd been weakened by the struggle to make weight. But comparisons with Gamboa were inevitable. After all, Lopez had lost by decision in the first round of the bantamweight competition at the same Olympics that saw Gamboa win a gold medal.

The manner in which Lopez-Luevano was styled was also an oddity. Luevano was the champion at 126 pounds. Juanma was coming up in weight to challenge for Steven's title. But at the December 3rd kick-off press conference, it was Luevano who thanked Juanma for the opportunity to fight him.

Later, Luevano seemed less thankful. "It's like he's already won the fight," Steven grumbled during fight week. "That's how they're treating it; like he's already champion at 126. He has all those knockouts and a country behind him, and they think they can make more money off him than they can off me. I don't really think much of him as a fighter."

When the bell for Lopez-Luevano rang, both men fought cautiously in the opening stanza. Then they began letting their punches go, with

Juanma landing harder and more often. Luevano hung tough and kept Lopez working, but Juanma was clearly the better fighter. The only issue was whether he would run out of steam as had happened against Mtagwa. Twelve rounds is a long time; particularly in a fast-paced fight.

It wasn't to be. Early in round seven, a straight left put Luevano in trouble and a right uppercut deposited him on the canvas. He rose, but referee Benji Esteves called a halt to the proceedings. At the time of the stoppage, the judges had Lopez ahead 60–54, 60–54, 59–55.

Gamboa and Lopez now appear to be on a collision course. But those who want Bob Arum to put the final pieces of the puzzle in place will have to wait.

"Any moron could put Lopez and Gamboa in against each other now," the promoter says. "Would it be a big fight? Absolutely. But the way a real promoter does it is to have them beat everybody else in the featherweight division. Then, when they finally meet, it will be the biggest featherweight fight of all time."

At the moment, it's Gamboa, rather than Lopez, who's creating great expectations and looks like a superstar in the making. But don't sell Juanma short. He's still undefeated. His own encounter with Mtagwa showed that he's willing and able to walk through fire to win after being badly hurt. And he just knocked out a pretty good fighter.

The wheel of fortune turns quickly in boxing.

* * *

Steve Cunningham (promoted by Don King Productions) and Matt Godfrey (promoted by Jimmy Burchfield) were supposed to fight on March 26, 2010, for the vacant IBF cruiserweight title on *ESPN2 Friday Night Fights.* The match-up had gone to purse bid with the winning bid ($65,200) coming from King.

Then King and ESPN reached a contractual impasse over clauses in the network's standard form contract that give ESPN foreign rights and income from ring-mat advertising. On March 17th, DKP announced that the fight was off. That left King in default. After some confusion within the IBF, it was determined that the right to promote Cunningham-Godfrey resided with Main Events (the runner-up bidder), which had ninety days to promote the fight.

Rather than wait, Main Events quickly put the pieces of a new puzzle together. It applied for a promotional license in Illinois; received approval for the fight from the Illinois State Athletic Commission; arranged with local promoter Dominic Pesoli to put the fight at the top of an already-scheduled night of boxing that Peroli was promoting in Chicago; and arranged with ESPN2 to televise the fight.

That left one problem. While Cunningham had continued to train for the March 26th match-up, Godfrey hadn't. On Friday, March 19th (or Saturday, March 20th depending on one's version of events), Godfrey was told that the fight was back on. And Matt said "no, thank you."

Thereafter, IBF president Marian Muhammad announced that the IBF was dropping Godfrey from its rankings and replacing him with Troy Ross (who presumably will fight Cunningham at some point in the future). Godfrey has been pilloried in the boxing media.

But it's not that simple.

Matt Godfrey didn't fight professionally for six years and train hard for a championship bout with the intention of blowing that bout off without cause.

Two days off from training (and not watching one's diet during those two days) in close proximity to a fight can make it exponentially harder for a fighter to make weight.

Also, whether one approves or not, fighters have been known to relax by taking a puff or two when there's no fight on the horizon. I have no idea what Matt Godrey's habits are. But it's not beyond the realm of possibility that he put something in his system that might have shown up in a urine test and thus rendered fighting on March 26th impractical.

Nor will punishing Godfrey help Steve Cunningham, who's the other victim in this mess. The culprit is Don King, who failed to make good on his contractual obligation to promote the fight. Under IBF Rules, King has forfeited the 20 percent deposit ($13,040) on his purse bid. That money will be divided equally between Godfrey and Cunningham. Further penalties by way of litigation might be in order.

Meanwhile, the March 27th rematch between Ali Funeka and Joan Guzman should have been called off but wasn't. That fight, televised by HBO on *Boxing After Dark,* was for the vacant 135-pound IBF title.

Guzman has a history of weight problems. Eighteen months ago, his title fight against Nate Campbell was cancelled when he came in 3½ pounds overweight. So it was no surprise when Joan failed to make weight for Funeka II. What was surprising was that he weighed in for his latest 135-pound fight at 144 pounds.

The always-eager-for-sanctioning-fees IBF decreed that the fight could proceed as long as Guzman didn't weigh more than 150 pounds at seven o'clock on Saturday morning. If Funeka won, he would be the IBF champion. If Guzman prevailed, the title would remain vacant.

Then the Nevada State Athletic Commission (which has become a prime enabler of misconduct) gave its blessing to the bout after announcing that Guzman would be fined 25 percent of his purse (with half of the fine going to Funeka and the other half enriching the state's coffers).

At that point, HBO should have pulled the plug on the telecast. Presumably, its contract allowed it to do so. If not, HBO needs better contracts. After all; HBO contracted for a competitive fight between in-shape fighters at 135 pounds.

Instead, HBO presented a farce to its subscribers. The fighters weighed in again on Saturday morning. Guzman tipped the scales at 148 pounds; Funeka at 143. In all likelihood, Guzman entered the ring one, and possibly two, weight classes above Funeka. We don't know what the final weight differential was because, when fight night arrived, HBO didn't ask the combatants to get on "the unofficial HBO scale." Guzman won a split decision.

HBO should state plainly and simply that it will not televise Joan Guzman in the future. That would send a message and go a long way toward eliminating the growing problem of fighters blowing off their contractual obligations with regard to making weight.

* * *

Billy Conn, the legendary light-heavyweight champion, turned pro seventy-five years ago. Conn is best known for his heroic 1941 effort to dethrone Joe Louis. Ahead on points after twelve rounds, he got "too brave" and was knocked out in the thirteenth stanza.

"Billy was great last night," Conn's manager, Johnny Ray, said the day after. "But Louis was just a little greater."

Conn had a way with words. Before fighting Louis, he told reporters, "Joe's a nice guy. I ain't mad at him. I just want that title of his."

Speaking of his wife's sartorial tastes, Conn observed, "The first time I got to know about women's clothes was when I married Mary Louise. I found out what they cost. And I found out that you had to like them or else she'd buy some new ones."

And at age sixty-eight when asked if he'd like to be young again, Conn noted philosophically, "You only pass through here one time. If you play your cards right, once is enough."

★ ★ ★

Hasim Rahman, we're advised via press release, made a triumphant return to the ring on March 27, 2010, when he knocked out Clinton Boldridge in the first round of a "special attraction" bout in Kansas City.

Question: Who is Clinton Boldridge?

Answer: He's a forty-three-year-old heavyweight with a 9-and-16 record. What makes this record remarkable is that all sixteen of Boldridge's losses have come by way of knockout.

Rahman-Boldridge was a grotesque mismatch. The state of Missouri should not have approved it.

★ ★ ★

In the 1880's John L. Sullivan established an enduring tradition. He realized that, as heavyweight champion, he could make large sums of money by appearing on stage in legitimate theatrical and vaudeville shows.

A half-century later, Jack Dempsey signed a contract to star in ten Hollywood films for a minimum guarantee of $1,000,000.

In the 1960s and 1970s, Muhammad Ali starred on Broadway in *Buck White* and played himself in a feature film entitled *The Greatest*.

Doug DeWitt was never a match for Sullivan, Dempsey, or Ali in the ring. But he hopes to outdo them as an actor.

DeWitt was born in Youngstown in 1961 and grew up in Yonkers (on the outskirts of New York City). At age eighteen, he turned pro. After five years, he had 25 wins, 1 loss, and 2 draws. Then the competition got tougher. Doug lost decisions to the likes of Thomas Hearns and Milton McCrory and was stopped by Sambu Kalambay in his first bid for a world title. He rebounded in his next outing to decision Robbie Sims and win the inaugural WBO middleweight crown. After that, he knocked out Matthew Hilton before losing his title to Nigel Benn. He retired in 1992 with a record of 33 wins, 8 losses, and 5 draws.

Four months after his ring career ended, DeWitt began studying acting at the Lee Strasburg Theatre and Film Institute in New York.

"My first day at the Strasburg Institute, I fell in love with acting," Doug recalls. It was the same kind of feeling I had when I found boxing. I've been pursuing a career as an actor ever since. When I do it well, it's the most euphoric feeling in the world."

Over the years, DeWitt has been in twenty plays. He devoted a year to stand-up comedy ("I always got laughs, but I decided I didn't want to be a stand-up comic"). And he had a role in *Bullet;* a 1996 feature film starring Mickey Rourke.

"In *Bullet,* I was a cop yelling at someone who was painting graffiti on a wall," Doug says. "I had one line: 'Hey, fucknuts. Come on down from there.' It wasn't Shakespeare, but it got me into SAG [the Screen Actors Guild]. I'm a member of Actors Equity too. And I had one other film role, in a movie called *The Florentine.* I played a thug and had a good scene with Chris Penn, but it got cut. That pissed me off. It would have been a good showcase for me."

"Film is what I really want to do," DeWitt continues. "But I haven't been able to get film roles, so I'm doing theater. If a guy in the gym says he's a boxer but he just hits the heavy-bag and doesn't fight, he isn't a boxer. It's the same thing with acting. An actor who doesn't act isn't an actor."

DeWitt is currently appearing in *The Cutting Den;* a drama set in a Brooklyn barbershop that doubles as a bookie parlor. He plays the role of Eddie Armstrong (a former fighter who's battling dementia and works as an enforcer for a local crime family).

The play was written by Ron Scott Stevens (former chairman of the New York State Athletic Commission). "Doug auditioned; he earned the role," Stevens says. "He takes his acting very seriously and he's good."

Ray Mancini (who fought at the same time as DeWitt) also took up acting when his ring career ended. He now has two dozen feature film and television roles to his credit.

"Ray tells me that, if I want to do film, I should move to Los Angeles," Doug says. "But I'm not moving to LA. My life is in Scarsdale [an upscale New York City suburb] now. I work as a personal trainer and make a good buck. And the most important thing is that my son is here. He's three years old. I see him every day. His mother is my girlfriend. We have keys to each other's apartments. The best thing I am in my life is a father."

As for the future, DeWitt notes, "I have a name from boxing. A lot of people in theater and film know me. Getting good roles is hard. Let's be honest; I'm not young anymore. I'm a middle-aged character actor in a business where being young is important. But I still think I can make it."

* * *

Andre Dirrell finally fought like he's capable of fighting when he faced Arthur Abraham on March 27th in round two of Showtime's super-middleweight championship tournament.

Dirrell, boxing fans will recall, lost a decision to Carl Froch when he turned their first-round tournament bout into a track meet.

Against Abraham, Dirrell moved, he boxed; but he didn't run. Referee Laurence Cole confused matters a bit by inappropriately helping Andre out of a corner in round eight and missing several knockdowns. Bottom line: In round eleven, Dirrell was comfortably ahead on the judges' scorecards but tiring. Could King Arthur score another late-round knockout?

Yes and no.

One minute into round eleven, Dirrell slipped on a beer logo that had been painted on the ring canvas and went down. At that point, Abraham whacked his defenseless opponent on the jaw with a crushing righthand, knocking Andre unconscious.

Abraham was appropriately disqualified. But there's a larger issue involved.

Time and time again, we've seen fighters slip on corporate logos that have been painted on the ring canvas. Often, these logos are slippery to begin with. They're like ice when they become wet.

There are ways, for a few extra dollars, that a promoter can make these logos less slippery. It's not rocket science. Get it right.

* * *

When a fighter is in the ring, he hits and gets hit. But when a fighter and writer interact, almost always, the fighter is on the receiving end of the questions.

What would it be like if the tables were turned? In search of an answer, I asked seven fighters what questions they'd like to put to the men and women who write about them. Their questions follow:

Paulie Malignaggi: "If we switched places, who would do a better job. You in the ring or me as a writer?"

Yuri Foreman: "What fight were you watching?"

Kelly Pavlik: "Why do you have to put something negative in every article you write?"

Lennox Lewis: "Do you have a framework that you want your story to fit in? And then do you distort reality so you can put what you saw and heard inside your framework? Because sometimes it seems like you do."

John Duddy: "I wanted to be a fighter when I was growing up. I'm living my dream. What did you want to be?"

Freddie Roach: "How many fights have you had?"

Larry Holmes: "That's a good question. What I'd ask the other writers is, 'Why do most of you guys ask the same questions again and again. Can't you come up with some new questions?'"

* * *

In the past, I've recounted the memories of various boxing personalities regarding the first professional fight they ever saw. The recollections of three more people who have left their mark on the sweet science follow:

Pat Lynch

It was Bobby Czyz against Mustafa Hamsho at Convention Hall in Atlantic City [on November 20, 1982]. I had a friend named Oscar Saffrin, who was thirty years older than I was. He and his wife gambled a lot, so they'd been comped by Bally's and invited me and my girlfriend to the fight. I was a boxing fan, but I'd never been to a live fight before. We got there during the preliminaries and sat in the second row. To be that close, to see the punches that way, to hear the punches; I was like, "Wow! This is different from television." I was in awe.

The place was packed. Czyz was undefeated, and his fans had come by the busload to see him. They went berserk when he got in the ring. Then the bell rang and Hamsho put a beating on him. Bobby was never in the fight. He lost a ten-round decision. Mustafa manhandled him. But what impressed me most was the punishment each guy took. Watching a fight on television, you see the impact of the big punches but not punch after punch after punch. That afternoon completely changed my understanding of boxing and my appreciation for what fighters go through."

Seven or eight years after that, I got into boxing on my own. Joe Gatti was the first fighter I managed. Then I managed Arturo. Oscar Saffrin died before I got in the business, which is a shame. I would have loved to have taken him to one of Arturo's fights, sat him in the second row, and said, "Thank you. You got me hooked on this. I am where I am in boxing now because of you."

Ray Mancini

I was nine years old. I'd grown up with boxing because of my father and been to amateur fights before. I knew in my heart that I'd be fighting professionally some day.

There was a guy from Buffalo named Dick Topinko, who was fighting in the semi-final at the Struthers Field House [in Mancini's hometown of Youngstown, Ohio, on March 31, 1970]. My uncle was working his corner. Topinko came in for the weigh-in on the morning of the fight and spent the day at our house. Part of that time, he took a nap in my bed. Then my father took me to the fights. Topinko won. A heavyweight from Youngstown named Ted Gullick won in the main event. And nine years later, I made my pro debut at Struthers Field House.

Kevin Iole

My dad was a big boxing fan. He'd boxed in the Army. His favorite fighters were Rocky Marciano and Sugar Ray Robinson. He asked what

I wanted for my sixth birthday, and I told him I wanted to see Sugar Ray Robinson [Robinson was fighting Joey Archer at Civic Arena in Pittsburgh on November 10, 1965, in what would be the last fight of his career].

My memory of that night is overwhelming. The arena was dark. Bright light was shining on this grand stage, this alter, that men were fighting on. Ray came down the aisle for the main event and the crowd was roaring. I don't remember much about the fight itself. I know from reading about it later on that Ray was knocked down, but I don't remember that happening. I do remember being disappointed that he lost. And I remember that his hair, which had been so perfect when he entered the ring, was tousled afterward.

My father died in 2003, so he lived to see me covering boxing. He'd ask me from time to time, "Does Oscar De La Hoya know your name? Does Mike Tyson know your name?" I'd tell him yes, and he loved it. The first time I met Ali, I called my father to tell him about it. Both of us were excited. But seeing Sugar Ray Robinson fight that night has always been hugely significant to me because I saw the Babe Ruth of our sport.

* * *

Wladimir Klitschko has been quite vocal recently about David Haye.

Wladimir is upset that Haye pulled out of proposed title fights against each of the Klitschko brothers. To make his point, he posted a video on YouTube in which he declared, "[Haye] bitched out on me and then he bitched out on my brother. He lied about his injury, and then he lied to the last moment and pulled out of the fight with my brother to take the Valuev fight. I really don't like anything about him. He lies; he's sneaky. This is a personal issue to me."

Wladimir is also offended by David's penchant for trash talking. In that regard, he's particularly angered by a T-shirt David has worn that depicts him holding the bloody severed heads of the Klitschko brothers.

"He did terrible things the way he presented himself," Wladimir states. "I didn't like that and neither did my brother."

I'm not a fan of Haye's mouth. But let's look at the record.

Yes; Haye pulled out of his fight against Wladimir, claiming a back injury of questionable provenance. But Setanta (the television network slated to carry Klitschko-Haye in the UK) was teetering on the edge of bankruptcy. Given the way David's fight contract had been structured, he was to receive most of his purse from Setanta. It was unrealistic to expect him to go through with the bout given the likelihood that he wouldn't be paid.

And yes; Haye abruptly cut off negotiations for a fight against Vitali in favor of challenging Nikolay Valuev, who was the WBA heavyweight champion at the time.

Poor manners?

Absolutely. But not unprecedented.

Let's not forget that Shannon Briggs thought he had a deal to fight Wladimir at Madison Square Garden in late 2007. Klitschko adviser Shelly Finkel assured the Briggs camp that the bout was "one thousand percent certain." Then Klitschko left Briggs standing at the alter and fought Sultan Ibragimov instead.

As for Haye's poor manners; I agree with Wladimir that part of being a champion is treating people, and particularly fellow athletes, with respect. That's why I was disheartened that, as part of his diatribe against Haye, Wladimir labeled Nikolay Valuev "a freak show."

Let me quote something that Nikolay said to me several years ago:

"I am not a machine. I am not a piece of meat. I am not a circus show. I am a normal human being. I have human feelings. I have a beautiful family. I have many friends. I like good music, classical music. I read books. People sometimes do not treat me like a human being because of my size. They make a sensation. I try to not take it personally because they do not know me as a person. But there are times when it hurts me inside."

Nikolay Valuev has always conducted himself in the athletic arena with dignity and personal grace. Wladimir Klitschko owes him an apology.

* * *

How silly is the WBC silver belt?

On July 24, 2010, Oscar Ibarra will fight Carlos Melo for the vacant WBC silver flyweight belt in Campeche, Mexico.

Ibarra's record is 22-and 4. Two years ago, he was knocked out by Giovanni Caro and Jose Alberto Cuadros (two fighters who had a combined total of 17 wins in 34 career fights at the time Ibarra fought them).

Now we get to the really embarrassing part.

Carlos Melo (the other half of this "silver belt" travesty) has won only one of his last six fights. And the guy that Melo beat (Alfonso De la Hoz) is winless in his last sixteen outings.

WBC president Jose Sulaiman and his son (WBC executive secretary Mauricio Sulaiman) should change the name of their bauble to the "tarnished silver" belt.

* * *

Amir Khan vs. Marcos Maidana at Mandalay Bay on December 11, 2010, was a scintillating fight. Khan has a world of talent, and Maidana fights like an Argentinean Arturo Gatti. Unfortunately, referee Joe Cortez was overly involved in the action.

This isn't the first time that Cortez has forced his imprint on a high-profile bout. When Floyd Mayweather Jr and Ricky Hatton met in December 2007, Hatton would work his way inside; Mayweather tried to tie him up; and Cortez broke them apart even though Ricky was still punching. By his conduct of the fight, Cortez denied Hatton the chance to impose his physical strength and forced him to fight much of the battle at long range, where Ricky was at a decided disadvantage.

History repeated itself in Khan-Maidana. There were no clinches in round one. But as the fight progressed, it was clear that Maidana wanted to fight inside and Khan didn't. Whenever Marcos got inside, Amir tried to tie him up by holding on to his right arm. When that happened, Maidana would pump left hooks to Khan's body and head. Instead of doing nothing or saying "punch your way out," Cortez broke the fighters.

Over the course of the fight, Cortez broke the fighters prematurely on THIRTY-SIX occasions.

On one of these premature breaks in round five, the referee spun Maidana around. Marcos's right elbow brushed against Cortez's chest, and he deducted a point from the fighter. That brought back memories of round six in Mayweather-Hatton, when Cortez took a point away from Hatton under odd circumstances.

Also, throughout Khan-Maidana whenever Maidana got inside, Khan would push down hard on the back of Marcos's head and neck. Cortez never did anything more than warn him. After round six, Miguel Diaz

(Maidana's chief second) shouted at the referee, "You take a point on us. Take a point on him, please." But it was to no avail.

Given the way the action unfolded, the narrow verdict in Khan's favor was justified. But with a different referee, Maidana might have won the fight.

★ ★ ★

A champion shouldn't retain his title when he wins three of twelve rounds in a title fight. But that's the gift that two judges bestowed upon Jean Pascal in Quebec City on December 18, 2010.

Watching a fight on television is different from being there. I viewed Pascal-Hopkins from the comfort of my living room. One presumes that the judges had a better view of the action than I did. That said; I think Bernard won the fight.

Pascal scored flash knockdowns in the first and third rounds. Take away those knockdowns, and Hopkins would have won both of those rounds on my scorecard. Rounds ten and twelve were close from where I sat. Other than that, I thought that Bernard clearly won every round.

Hopkins fought more aggressively than expected. Pascal attacks when his opponent isn't attacking. Bernard went into the fight knowing that constant pressure was the key to keeping Jean from launching his own lunging assault. Hopkins was the aggressor throughout the night, raking hooks to the body augmented by occasional overhand rights. By the middle rounds, the fight had the look of Bernard's 2006 beatdown of Antonio Tarver.

People talk about Pascal having a "granite" chin (which is overstating the case). He certainly doesn't have a granite body. By round seven, Jean was a gun-shy, safety-first fighter. As Hopkins said afterward, "We saw a young guy running from an old grandpa."

Giving Pascal rounds one, three, ten, and twelve plus an extra point for each knockdown would have left him with a 114–112 deficit. I had it 115–111 for Hopkins.

Judge Steve Morrow scored the fight 114–112 for Bernard. Claude Paquette and Daniel Van de Wiele had it even. That's strange scoring, given the fact that Hopkins had a 171-to-105 edge in punches landed and appeared to land the more damaging blows.

Prior to fighting Pascal, Hopkins was asked how he felt about fighting in Jean's home province of Quebec.

"I'd rather be fighting in Canada than Ecuador," Bernard answered.

That was a reference to 1994, the last time that Hopkins journeyed outside the United States, when he fought to a draw against Segundo Mercado in Quito.

Next time, Bernard might rather fight in Ecuador.

★ ★ ★

The boxing community recently said goodbye to two of its finest.

Don and Lorraine Chargin were married on December 28, 1961. She was the building manager at the Olympic Auditorium in Los Angeles. He'd just started matchmaking there for promoter Aileen Eaton. The best match that either of them ever made was with each other.

Don and Lorraine were involved in various aspects of the fight game for a half-century. In 2001, the Boxing Writers Association of America honored them with the James J. Walker Award for long and meritorious service to boxing.

Lorraine died of cancer on April 6th. I vividly remember her holding hands with Don one afternoon as they left the media center at the MGM Grand in Las Vegas. They were boxing's nicest couple. It will always be impossible for me think of one of them without the other.

Arthur Mercante refereed his first world title fight (Benny Paret versus Federico Thompson) in 1954. Over the next half-century, he was the third man in the ring for 145 championship bouts including, most famously, the March 8, 1971, "Fight of the Century" at Madison Square Garden between Muhammad Ali and Joe Frazier.

Arthur was a master at positioning in the ring. He had a thorough knowledge of boxing's rules and regulations, which he coupled with sound judgment and the ability to act decisively in a crisis. He ruled without fear or favor. Late in life, he left the confines of the ring to judge fights from the outside. His place within the ropes was taken by his son, Arthur Jr.

The younger Mercante once explained why he didn't think it would be a good idea for his father to judge a fight that he refereed. "Number one," Arthur noted, "some people might think it was a conflict of interest.

And number two, I know my father. He'd be critiquing my performance instead of concentrating on scoring the fight."

Arthur Mercante died on April 10th at age ninety. He was a gentleman.

Boxing has the greatest literary tradition of any sport.

Notes from the Literary Front

There are hundreds of books about Muhammad Ali, but very little good writing about Sonny Liston. *Liston and Ali* by Bob Mee (Mainstream Publishing) is very good writing about Liston.

Liston's résumé before he began boxing included incarceration for a long string of violent offenses (including armed robbery) and work as a strike breaker for the St. Louis mob. His resume after incarceration included more run-ins with the law (one of which sent him back to prison for nine months) and repeated arrests for offenses that ranged from driving while intoxicated to the unlawful possession of a firearm.

He was menacing and monosyllabic; what Mee calls "the flip side of Ali; with no apparent political or religious beliefs, no apparent interest in the well-being of anybody outside his own household."

But Mee also writes, "I found a sad man made suspicious by a world that gave with one hand and snatched away with both; a man who sought redemption and acceptance by winning the heavyweight championship of the world, but who found only disappointment, rejection, and constant reminders of the moral debt it was felt he owed his country. In the end, I found a disillusioned man, who became what it seemed the world wanted him to be."

Mee would have done well to pare down the material about Ali in his book. Some of it is shopworn and, in a few instances (such as the recounting of Ali's travails with the military draft), inaccurate. But when the author turns his spotlight on Liston, his work shines.

Liston began boxing in prison, was paroled in 1952, and turned pro after eleven months as an amateur. The prevailing view is that he was backed by the mob from the start of his career and that what followed was just a matter of Sonny being upgraded from little mob bosses to big mob bosses.

Mee writes extensively about Liston's ties to organized crime and the role of the mob in boxing midway through the twentieth century. He also traces Sonny's ring exploits, highlighting his two championship victories over Floyd Patterson (both first-round knockouts) followed by his losses to Cassius Clay (in Miami Beach) and Muhammad Ali (in the unlikely venue of Lewiston, Maine).

Liston-Patterson II is notable in Mee's eyes, in part, because Patterson failed to land a single punch. Bob Cannobio of CompuBox (who studied the bout on tape) demurs, saying that Floyd landed one of seven blows, compared to 25 of 58 for Liston. Whatever the number, after disposing of Patterson twice, Sonny was widely regarded as the reincarnation of Godzilla. The presumption was that he would reign as champion for years.

Mee's book is styled as a study of both Ali and Liston. But its strength is as a portrait of the latter.

Sonny conducted himself as though he had a grudge against the world.

Mee is sympathetic toward Liston because of his origins. There's good material in his review of Sonny's early life in an impoverished area of rural Arkansas. But nothing is more telling than Liston's own testimony before a United States Senate subcommittee that was investigating the influence of organized crime in boxing:

> Senator Estes Kefauver: How much education did you get?
> Liston: I didn't get any.
> Q: You didn't go to school at all?
> Liston: No, sir. Too many kids.
> Q: How many kids were there?
> Liston: Well, my father had twenty-five.
> Q: Did you have to work to help support the other twenty-four children?
> Liston: That's right.
> Q: What did you do?
> Liston: Pick cotton.
> Q: Do you read at all?
> Liston: No, sir; I don't.
> Q: Do you sign your name?
> Liston: Yes, sir.
> Q: Can you sign your address?
> Liston: No, sir.
> Q: Suppose your share of a fight purse was $25,000 and they handed you a check for it. Could you tell whether they were giving you a check for $25,000?
> Liston: Not exactly.
> Q: You would have to depend on somebody else?
> Liston: Yes, sir.

Jack Nilon (who served for several years as Liston's manager) later elaborated on that theme. "Sonny is frustrated because he can't read," Nilon told a companion while sitting at the swimming pool at The Thunderbird Hotel and Casino in Las Vegas. "See that sign over there: 'Please register with lifeguard.' Sonny doesn't know what that says. For all he knows, it might say 'Free Drinks.'"

In that vein, Liston was also sensitive about his age (which was widely thought to be older than reported). That's because he didn't know for sure how old he was.

"I only got one man to thank for what happened to me," Liston said after annihilating Patterson for the second time. "Me. I done it the hard way. Nobody never gave me nothing. There haven't been too many people that meant anything in my life. I've done some rough things, and I've had some rough things done to me."

Mee is honest enough that, despite his sympathy for his subject, Liston emerges in the pages of *Liston & Ali* as a surly bullying violent man. As an adult, Sonny moved from St. Louis to Philadelphia to Denver to Las Vegas, and found trouble every step of the way. He had a ravenous appetite for women, and there were times when he abused them. While champion, he drank more than he had before. Then his substance abuse problems grew.

Could he have been saved?

Before the first Patterson fight, Liston invited a group of boys from a local reform school to watch him train. That same day, he told the media, "If I win this fight, you'll be able to see there is good and bad in everybody. The way things stand now, everybody thinks there is only bad in me."

At that point, Sonny believed that, if he defeated Patterson, he'd be embraced by society by virtue of his being heavyweight champion of the world.

He wasn't. And it hurt. From that point on, Mee notes, "Liston did not really see the need to bother with niceties. And bad became worse."

On January 6, 1971, Liston was found sprawled across the bed in his Las Vegas home. His body was bloated and decomposing. He'd been dead for approximately eight days. Theories as to the cause of death ranged from a mob rub-out to an accidental overdose of heroin. A coroner's inquest left the issue unresolved.

* * *

Rick Folstad is a former fighter who writes for several outlets, including TheSweetScience.com. Fighting out of Minneapolis as a junior-welterweight in the 1970s, he compiled a 20-and-2 record as a pro. The guys he beat were far from world-class. But unlike most writers (myself included), Folstad has been on the hard side of the ropes.

Cornered is Folstad's first novel. Set in Miami in the 1970s, it's told in the first person by middleweight prospect Boone Connors. There's a plot involving the mob that's serviceable. But Folstad is at his best (and his best is very good) when he's recreating the gritty realism of boxing.

Rather than characterize what Folstad says, I'll let his writing speak for itself:

- "If you fight, you don't want to live in Beverly Hills and be surrounded with pretty flowers and clean white walls and marble fountains with fairy statues pissing into the water. If you fight, you want to go to gyms where the windows are dirty and cracked, the water pipes are leaking, and the floors are stained with blood. You want to go where the winos stand outside the door begging for a quarter. A good gym's got to be in the bad part of town. It's got to be crowded with a lot of guys down on their luck, guys who don't give a damn about anything but their next fight and when they're going to get paid. At least that's how I feel."

- "If you can take a good punch, you're going to end up taking a lot of them and that's when you get hurt. The fighters who can't take a punch; they don't go too far or get paid too much. But they don't get hurt either. They don't turn forty and suddenly forget their name or where they live or how to get to the grocery store. They just lose a lot of fights. But Teddy wasn't like that. You could hit him across the head with a Louisville Slugger and all he'd do was flinch and smile and then try to take your head off. I figured either he'd win the title by the time he was thirty or have trouble counting to ten by the time he was forty."

- "He lay on his back shivering under the hot ring lights, and the stupid-ass referee stood over him and started counting. The only sounds were Spider's heels banging on the canvas and the referee counting him out . . . one . . . two . . . three . . . four . . . like Spider might actually get up and beat the count. It looked like the referee was standing over a corpse that was still twitching. I think the referee was so scared, he did the only thing he knew how to do."

• "Callahan isn't a fighter. You have to have balls and a heart for that. He's just a fat miserable sonofabitch looking for an easy ride. He's always trying to suck out a little blood, a pimp working the fight game instead of the streets. I think it made Callahan feel good about himself, seeing fighters who could have kicked his ass when they were younger, drool and stutter."

• "[On the women a fighter meets] If they've been drinking the night you meet them, you never know what's going to happen when you call them. They wake up sober the next day and they might have forgotten what happened the night before, even if nothing did happen. Then you call them and they tell you to get lost without really coming out and telling you to get lost. They can't remember what you look like. That's the worst, them not remembering you."

• "Mel smeared a little more Vaseline on my face and asked how I felt. 'Fine,' I told him. 'Got my mouthpiece?' He started looking around to make sure he had everything before we left to go to the ring. I could tell he didn't think I was gonna win."

• "I stood in the dark toward the back and looked at the ring, which always calmed me down before a fight. It was a familiar place, like your living room or your own backyard. They could do a lot of things to screw up boxing, but they could only change the ring so much. The ring still had to be square with ropes and corners and a canvas."

• "The bell rang. Copper Daniels and I met in the center of the ring and stood there a second, looking at each other like you might look at someone you just met at a party. It was hot and bright under the ring lights and any remaining butterflies were gone. I started circling to my right, which is the wrong way to go when you're fighting a southpaw because you're moving into his power. But I was trying to find that feeling you get when you know right away you can beat the guy standing in front of you, when you know you can knock him on his ass whenever you want. But when you don't get that feeling, when you're not so sure, everything gets kind of tight and turned around."

• "You dream of fighting for the title most of your life, but you can't get carried away with the dream. You got to be honest with yourself. How many guys get a chance to be a world champion? So you keep the dream tucked somewhere safe in the back of your head. You hold onto it without getting carried away. For most fighters, it's not going to happen. It's like living in the projects when you're a little kid and wishing for a pony for Christmas. You know you're not going to get a pony because your parents can't afford one. And where are you going to put it, in the kitchen?"

* * *

Biographies of boxing's early gloved champions tend to be lacking when discussing their subject away from the prize ring. *James J. Corbett* by Armond Fields (McFarland & Company) is an intriguing book, in large part because it breaks that mold.

Fields (who died in 2008) was a social historian who wrote extensively about the early days of popular American theater. *James J. Corbett* is as much about Corbett the actor as it is about Corbett the fighter.

Beginning in 1892 (the year that he defeated John L. Sullivan), Corbett embarked on a theatrical career that was noteworthy for its success, variety, and longevity. He began in vaudeville, made numerous forays into legitimate theater, and worked hard to develop his craft as a stage performer. Later in life, he appeared in feature films.

At times, Fields's recitation of Corbett's acting credits is repetitious. Corbett was onstage for thirty-nine of his sixty-six years, and there are moments when it seems as though the author is determined to recite the particulars of every performance. Be that as it may; vaudeville and theater in Corbett's era and his place within that realm come to life in the pages of this book.

Fields also offers readers an engaging look at the San Francisco that Corbett grew up in as well as Corbett's personal life. Of particular interest here are the break-up of the fighter's marriage to Olive Lake in 1895 as a consequence of his affair with Vera Stanwood (who he later married to the delight of the tabloid press) and the deteriorating mental condition of his father. Patrick Corbett ultimately shot Jim's mother to death as she slept and then turned the gun on himself.

As far as boxing is concerned, Fields crafts an interesting portrait of Corbett's amateur career and his relationship with the Olympic Club in San Francisco, where his ring skills matured. But the author falls short of capturing the drama of big fights; especially fights for the heavyweight championship of the world.

That said; Fields succeeds in portraying Corbett as a full flesh-and-blood figure, rather than a cardboard cutout from the distant past. He is on firm ground when he writes, "Corbett changed the public role of a champion, dressing like a gentleman, behaving like a college graduate, and greeting the world with a smile instead of a scowl." And the words resonate when he quotes W. O. McGeehan (one of the premier sportswriters of his time), who wrote upon Corbett's passing in 1933, "With the death of James J. Corbett, another figure of the romantic era of the American prize ring passes into the twilight of the modern demigods."

★ ★ ★

On July 4, 1923, Jack Dempsey defended the heavyweight championship of the world against Tommy Gibbons in Shelby, Montana. Dempsey-Gibbons is the only championship bout that's remembered more for the site than the fight itself. *Shelby's Folly* by Jason Kelly explains why.

Shelby was one of the most improbable and ill-considered venues ever to host a major championship fight. As Kelly notes, "Shelby consisted of a few commercial buildings, some homes, and a train depot; all visible with hardly a turn of the head. Beyond that, Montana's high plains loomed, an earthen barrier barren of civilization. If there was a middle of nowhere, this was it. They had no arena, no transportation infrastructure, no restaurants, and no hotel rooms to accommodate even a fraction of the crowd a heavyweight championship fight would attract."

The promotional venture began as a publicity stunt orchestrated by civic leaders who wanted to draw attention to Shelby and raise local real estate prices. They had no intention of actually hosting a fight. Then they got caught up in the flow of events that led to financial disaster.

The promotion was doomed from the start. Nothing prepares one for the business of boxing except the business of boxing. The fight organizers, many of whom were established businessmen, knew nothing about the boxing business. The regional economy was fragile to begin with, and their bumbling made it worse. Shortly after the bout was contested, three local banks whose presidents had been involved with the promotion shut down.

Kelly writes well. And he researches well, which makes his writing even better. *Shelby's Folly* has vivid portraits of idiots and scoundrels plus a solid recounting of the fight itself.

To most people, Tommy Gibbons is just a line in boxing's record book. But in Kelly's hands, he comes alive as someone we want to know.

By contrast, "Doc" Kearns (Dempsey's manager) is fun to read about, but decent people might not have wanted to spend time in his presence. Kelly describes Kearns as "a symbol of boxing excess and ethical flexibility . . . as coldly persistent as a glacier and even more slippery."

"Boxing is a business," Kearns said proudly. "And its main stock in trade is the double-cross, the runaround, and the two-face."

It's hard to imagine that there's much worth knowing about Dempsey-Gibbons and Shelby, Montana, that isn't in *Shelby's Folly.*

★ ★ ★

"Peter Close lost most of his fights. He had just lost for the ninth time in a row and it showed. It was not the longest losing streak in the history of the ring, but it was nothing to brag about. It looked like a child had drawn a pair of cartoon goggles on his face. One eye was black, a general term that always does the trick when talking about damage to an eye, and one was closed. Blood stuck to six dark stitches on his bottom lip. A red tissue dropped from his nose. He was not a bad fighter or father or husband. He was just a bit too brave for his own health. And in professional boxing, that made him stupid. He was a nice guy with a bravery problem."

"A few hours earlier at the Wembley Conference Centre, Close had been dropped and stopped in three rounds. It was his 43rd defeat in 52 fights. He was a journeyman from the old school. He lost fights for a living and was a necessary and kosher part of the boxing business. Close was an idiot in boxing terms because he still fought like a winner. Lester had tried to talk sense into him countless times and it was a waste. How do you tell a man to forget his pride and to just lose when he still thinks he can win?"

"Lester" is Ray Lester, the cynical protagonist in Steve Bunce's new novel, *The Fixer.* The paragraphs above are Bunce's way of introducing readers to Lester and the underside of professional boxing.

Lester is a one-time boxing writer turned booking agent, promoter's representative, and adviser to anyone who will pay for his services. Bunce defines him with the observation, "Boxing is a lonely planet for anyone unlucky enough to have a conscience. Ray Lester was not a bad man, but he had his moments."

The Fixer reads like a William Goldman thriller (think *Marathon Man*) set in the world of boxing with some refugees from *The Godfather* thrown in. Much against his will, Lester is sucked into a violent war between two organized crime figures. There are times when the plot is a bit contrived; particularly when Lester (who seems like a savvy guy) ignores his own safety to play the game out. But as one reads on, tension and drama overtake skepticism.

Bunce mixes real-life people and events into his plot in a way that makes the narrative stronger. The scene moves from London to Las Vegas (for Mayweather-Hatton). Referencing the agony that Ricky felt after his loss, the author observes, "It was the type of suffering that only the very best prizefighters ever get to experience. It's the end of something inside; the end of a life they have been living away from all thoughts of defeat. They believe they will never lose, and the hurt is staggering."

Then it's on to Atlantic City (for a world-sanctioning body convention), back to London, and finally to Blackpool.

Even the bit characters are vividly portrayed. One longtime denizen of the fight game is "an old man living with splendid memories and his own hate. He spent his days in loneliness, making phone calls to people who didn't really want to speak to him. He liked to state the obvious and imagine he was spreading wisdom."

At the other end of the spectrum, a Las Vegas hostess has "eyes which she had obviously plucked from a dead Barbie."

Kudos to Steve Bunce for a good and entertaining novel.

Lines were blurred when Alexander Povetkin and Bruce Seldon exchanged punches.

The Povetkin-Seldon "Sparring Session"

On July 28, 2010, Alexander Povetkin and Bruce Seldon met in the ring at the South Philly Arena. Teddy Atlas, who trains Povetkin, says that the meeting was a "glorified sparring session" and that efforts were made "to replicate the atmosphere of a real fight even though it was just a training session."

The facts are as follows.

Earlier this year, Povetkin was the designated mandatory challenger for Wladimir Klitschko's IBF heavyweight crown. The two sides could not agree on contract terms. Klitschko's promotional company won rights to the bout with a purse bid of $8,313,000. Twenty-five percent of that amount was to go to Team Povetkin. Then Alexander pulled out of the fight.

On July 22nd, Atlas told ESPN.com, "I think he [Povetkin] deserves the chance to develop. I'm in the middle of training this kid, which is obviously an important time in his life for the future of his career. My job is to do the best job I can for the fighter and to make sure he's the best he can be when he's in a situation to fight. I'm not controlled or dictated by anything other than that. I was never really for the fight right now. Let me have more time with him. I decided the most important thing was to do what was the best for the fighter. My opinion was, more time would be good."

Six days later, Povetkin entered the ring to face Seldon. The event, scheduled for 8:00 PM, was closed to the public. Between seventy and one hundred invited guests were in attendance.

The event was set up to simulate a regulation fight.

Conversations with multiple sources who were in attendance confirm that Povetkin and Seldon wore ten-ounce gloves.

There was no headgear.

The referee was Luis Rivera.

The judges were Russell Peltz, Adam Berlin, and Don Steinberg.

The ring announcer was Larry Tournambe.

The timekeeper was Fred Blumstein.

Rivera, Peltz, Berlin, Steinberg, Tournambe, and Blumstein were paid for their services. So was Don Elbaum.

Elbaum did the nuts-and-bolts work of putting everything together. He negotiated with Seldon's management team and the venue and arranged for an ambulance to be on site.

Bruce Seldon was paid $10,000 for his participation in the event. He brought his own cornermen with him from Atlantic City.

Teddy Atlas served as Povetkin's chief second.

Joey Intrieri was Povetkin's cutman.

The money to pay for the event came from Povetkin's management team. Refreshments (such as pizza and hot dogs) were sold. There was no beer.

The event was scheduled for ten rounds. Seldon won the first round on each judge's scorecard but suffered a cut above one of his eyes. The second round could have gone either way, but all of the judges scored it for Povetkin. Round three belonged to Alexander. In round four, Povetkin knocked Seldon down three times. There was no three-knockdown rule, but Seldon was badly hurt and bleeding from the mouth after the third knockdown. At that point, referee Luis Rivera stopped the event.

A Fight Fax report states that Seldon, age forty-three, has been on suspension since August 13, 2009, because of a failed drug test administered in conjunction with a ninth-round knockout loss to Fres Oquendo in Illinois on July 24, 2009.

Povetkin engaged in at least one similar "sparring session" with Robert Daniels at the Front Street Gym in Philadelphia on October 17, 2009. That encounter was also stopped short of its scheduled duration by referee Luis Rivera.

Greg Sirb is executive director of the Pennsylvania State Athletic Commission. As a general rule, Sirb is outgoing and informative when talking with reporters. That wasn't the case when he talked last week with Lem Satterfield of BoxingScene.com. Satterfield recounts the following exchange:

Sirb: We checked into it and we classified it as a glorified sparring session.
Satterfield: Can you give me any details?
Sirb: Nope.
Satterfield: Was there any headgear used?
Sirb: Glorified sparring session, part of a training program.
Satterfield: But the guy got knocked out, didn't he?
Sirb: Glorified sparring session, part of the training program.
Satterfield: Was Teddy Atlas there?
Sirb: Yep.
Satterfield: Was he working Povetkin's corner?
Sirb: He was at the event.
Satterfield: There's no sanctions or anything like that?
Sirb: Part of a training program.

Speaking with this writer today (August 23rd), Sirb said, "This is a big to-do about nothing. Things like this happen every day in gyms in Philly. If it's part of a regimented training session, there's no problem. This is silly. I'm not going to discuss it anymore."

However, the Povetkin-Seldon encounter appears to have been different from a "gym war." In a sparring session, if a fighter is hurt, his adversary backs off. In this "sparring session," when Seldon was hurt, Povetkin hurt him some more.

Fights are regulated by the state for several reasons. The most important of these is to safeguard the health and safety of fighters. That involves ensuring that (1) the participants are sufficiently skilled and in appropriate condition to participate and (2) the combat is overseen by qualified licensed personnel.

The state is responsible for making these determinations. Not any individual trainer, manager, or promoter. Teddy Atlas and Don Elbaum are good boxing people. They can regulate a fight far more capably than most state athletic commissions. But there are a lot of bozos in boxing with a towel over their shoulder and a pencil in their hand. A state can't have one set of rules for Teddy Atlas and Don Elbaum and a different set of rules for someone else who wants to arrange a "glorified sparring session."

Where should a state athletic commission draw the line? Suppose the Povetkin-Seldon encounter had taken place at a black-tie event with spectators paying two hundred dollars each for a gourmet dinner? Suppose there were six "glorified sparring sessions" at the event instead of one? Suppose one of the participants suffered a brain bleed or lost an eye?

I don't have a problem with fighters sparring without headgear and with small gloves. It's fine with me if fighters go hard in sparring. And I'll accept the premise that, from Povetkin's point of view, this was a training exercise. But no matter how the Povetkin-Seldon encounter is styled, it appears to have been a fight.

Was it?

If it looks like a duck, walks like a duck, and quacks like a duck; most likely, it's a duck.

When Antonio Margarito became the focal point of a boxing morality play, a lot of people considered him a bad actor.

Antonio Margarito and the Handwrap Issue

A fighter's fists are his weapons. Tampering with a fighter's gloved fists is one of the worst offenses imaginable in boxing. It subverts the notion of a fair fight and puts the opposing fighter at exponentially greater risk of serious injury or death.

On January 24, 2009, Antonio Margarito fought Shane Mosley at the Staples Center in Los Angeles. In the dressing room prior to the fight, an illegal insert was found in each of Margarito's knucklepads. The inserts were removed and the fight proceeded as planned. Mosley knocked Margarito out in the ninth round.

Margarito's license was subsequently revoked by the California State Athletic Commission. On August 18, 2010, the CSAC will consider his application for reinstatement. That is expected to open the door for a proposed November 13th fight between Margarito and Manny Pacquiao.

There has been considerable debate during the past eighteen months regarding the Margarito handwrap issue. But the lines have been blurred by inaccurate reporting and the tendency of some observers to take sides based on their fondness or antipathy for Margarito's promoter, Top Rank.

Let's put the nonsense aside and view the Margarito handwrap issue in perspective.

The taping of a fighter's fist begins with a roll of gauze being wrapped several times around his hand. Then a pad that has been previously fashioned from multiple layers of gauze is placed over the fighter's knuckles. That's followed by the application of more gauze and tape. California rules allow for the use of gauze and surgical adhesive tape when wrapping a fighter's hands; nothing else. The application of water or any other liquid to the gauze or tape is prohibited.

Margarito's hands were wrapped in his dressing room prior to the Mosley fight by his longtime trainer, Javier Capetillo. The task began under the supervision of inspector Che Guevara with Naazim Richardson (Mosley's trainer) looking on.

Before a big fight, Richardson usually objects to the manner in which an opponent's hands are being taped if for no other reason than to upset the opposing fighter. Here, he lodged numerous objections to the taping of Margarito's right hand. Several more inspectors, including chief inspector Dean Lohuis, came into the dressing room. Richardson's objections were overruled.

Then Capetillo began taping Margarito's left hand, and Richardson asked if he could physically inspect the knucklepad. Lohuis instructed Capetillo to pass the pad to Richardson. Naazim felt it and said that it seemed unusually hard. He then handed the pad to Lohuis, who agreed that it felt stiffer than is normally the case.

CSAC inspector David Pereda, who was in the room, later testified, "Naazim opened the gauze and pulled something out of it. He showed us what appeared to be an old gauze which had been used before and hardened from perhaps being sweaty and wet many times."

Inspector Guevara testified, "It [the knucklepad] was a clean new bandage. But within it, in the inner layers of it, was another bandage wrap. It was not as white as a new bandage wrap would be. It was used and it looked almost like it was sweat-soaked and that's what caused it to have the discoloration. It was harder in certain areas than it should be for pure gauze. It was definitely firm and hard. I believe there was a little bit of, it looked like old blood, on it."

Mike Bray (an inspector who entered the dressing room during the dispute) recalled, "I observed what appeared to be a blood stain on the corner of the pad. I also noticed that it was moist and dirty-looking. The pad had the appearance that it had been used before. After looking at the pad closer, I could see a white substance smeared across the face of the pad and into the gauze. I touched the white substance, and it was hard to touch. It looked like a cast plaster or maybe a thicker type of white out that you would put on paper."

Lohuis confiscated the knucklepad and instructed Capetillo to make a new one. Capetillo did so and wrapped Margarito's left hand. Richardson then asked the inspectors to examine the knucklepad on Margarito's already-wrapped right hand. Lohuis instructed Capetillo to remove the right handwrap and a similar insert was discovered inside the pad. Lohuis confiscated that pad as well and ordered Capetillo to prepare a new right-hand knucklepad.

After the pads were confiscated, Mike Bray (at Richardson's request) brought them to Mosley's dressing room, where three members of Mosley's team were allowed to touch them under the inspector's supervision. An undetermined number of commission personnel also touched them.

Three days after the fight, the California State Athletic Commission temporarily suspended Margarito's boxing license and Capetillo's trainer's license, and set February 10, 2009, for a hearing on the status of both men.

Capetillo testified at the hearing that he prepared Margarito's knucklepads in the dressing room at the Staples Center and put them on top of the contents in his training bag. Then, when it was time to wrap, he pulled the wrong knucklepads out of his bag by mistake. He further testified that the confiscated pads had most likely been used by another boxer while hitting the heavy bag in the gym.

"They just throw their things in my bag," Capetillo told the commission.

The following colloquy exemplifies his testimony:

> Q: Is this the kind of pad you usually use in a championship fight?
> Capetillo: No, sir.
> Q: Have you ever used a pad like that in a professional boxing fight?
> Capetillo: No, sir.
> Q: So is it your testimony that, when you wrapped Mr. Margarito's hands, you reached into your training bag and grabbed the wrong pad?
> Capetillo: That is correct . . . I put my hand in my bag to pull out, they are like little pads. And by mistake, that I had those in my bag, I put them on and I wrapped them on without realizing that it had been a big mistake.

There was no direct evidence that Margarito knew about the inserts inside the knucklepads; only inference. Antonio denied any knowledge of the inserts, and Capetillo testified, "I commit a big mistake and I acknowledge it. I don't want that this young man have any problem because he is not at fault. He didn't realize what I had put on."

Prior to the hearing, the California State Athletic Commission sent one of the inserts to the Bureau of Forensic Services at the California Department of Justice for testing. The Commission rejected a request by Margarito's attorney to allow his own expert to analyze the inserts. The lab results were not in before the hearing. On March 19, 2009, the Bureau of Forensic Services forwarded a report to the CSAC that read, "Calcium and sulphur, two elements found in plaster of Paris, were found on the submitted gauze pad using an X-ray fluorescence [XRF] spectrometer. The elements calcium, sulphur, and oxygen are found in plaster of Paris. These three elements are also found in substances other than plaster. Oxygen is not detectable by XRF."

Margarito's defense team contends that calcium and sulphur are also common elements in hand cream and salves.

The options available to the California State Athletic Commission ranged from taking no action against Margarito and Capetillo to a fine, suspension, or revocation of their respective licenses (the maximum penalty under law). In the event of revocation, either man would be free to reapply after one year with no guarantee of reinstatement. An irrevocable permanent ban was not an available option.

At the close of the February 10, 2009, hearing, the commission voted to revoke each man's license. It made no finding that Margarito had knowledge of the inserts, but held him responsible for Capetillo's actions. In so doing, it relied on Boxing Rule 390 of the California Code of Regulations, which states, "Any licensee who conducts himself or herself at any time or place in a manner which is deemed by the commission to reflect discredit to boxing may have his or her license revoked, or may be fined, suspended, or otherwise disciplined in such manner as the commission may direct."

In making its determination, the CSAC imposed a doctrine of "strict liability" upon Margarito. That's similar to the position that most commissions take when a fighter tests positive for an illegal performance-enhancing drug. A fighter, the theory goes, is a professional athlete. He's responsible for his body and his equipment. If someone who works for him puts something illegal into his body or on his hands, the fighter should be held ultimately responsible.

After Margarito's license was revoked, he filed a lawsuit to overturn the commission's decision. The matter is currently pending in the Second Appellate District of the California state court system.

Meanwhile, on February 10, 2010 (one year after his license was revoked), Margarito became eligible to fight in any state that would grant him a license. There was talk of his fighting in Dallas on the undercard of the March 13th fight between Manny Pacquiao and Joshua Clottey. Indeed, on January 20th, Tim Lueckenhoff (president of the Association of Boxing Commissions) sent an email to Dickie Cole (administrator of combat sports for the Texas Department of Licensing and Regulation) that read, "The State of Texas may accept an application from Margarito and determine if a boxing contestant license will be issued based upon the laws of Texas."

Instead, Margarito returned to the ring in Aguascalientes, Mexico, on May 8, 2010, and hammered out an unimpressive ten-round decision victory over Roberto Garcia.

Then, with negotiations for a fight between Pacquiao and Floyd Mayweather Jr on the verge of failure, Margarito applied for a license to box in Nevada. On July 9th, the Nevada State Athletic Commission voted 4-to-1 to table a decision on the application until after Margarito applied for reinstatement in California.

Initially, the California State Athletic Commission said that it didn't have time to hear an application from Margarito until September and suggested that he first abandon his appeal from its original order of revocation. That struck some (including the leadership of the Association of Boxing Commissions) as a violation of due process. In any event, the CSAC subsequently reversed course and agreed to hold a hearing on Margarito's application on August 18th. After the hearing, regardless of the CSAC's decision, Antonio can apply for a license in any state.

During the past year, some commentators have likened Margarito's situation to the decades-old scandal involving Panama Lewis, Luis Resto (who was trained by Lewis), and Billy Collins. On June 18, 1983, Resto won a unanimous decision over Collins at Madison Square Garden. Thereafter, it was determined that, in the dressing room before the fight, Lewis had removed padding from the striking surface of his fighter's gloves. Collins suffered serious eye damage in the fight, never fought again, and died in a car crash nine months later. Resto and Lewis were criminally convicted, imprisoned for several years, and banned from boxing for life.

The Margarito handwraps controversy has also become one of many proxy wars being fought between Top Rank and Golden Boy.

On January 26, 2010, Golden Boy president Oscar De La Hoya criticized the prospect of Margarito being licensed to box again and declared, "I'm very disgusted by it. When you're messing with somebody's life in that ring, you should be banned for life. That's my opinion."

That infuriated Top Rank CEO Bob Arum, who saw rampant hypocrisy in De La Hoya's position that Shane Mosley (a Golden Boy fighter) shouldn't be punished for his past use of illegal performance-enhancing drugs because Shane did so "unknowingly," whereas Margarito should be banned for life without any direct evidence that Antonio had prior knowledge of wrongdoing.

Arum (who promoted De La Hoya for over a decade) also stated that Oscar should sign a waiver of confidentiality with regard to his own medical history "and let's find out if there was ever any proof of Oscar using performance-enhancing drugs. People who live in glass houses should not throw stones."

Six months later, Arum and De La Hoya were at each other's throat again. On July 28th, Oscar declared, "Why should any fighter who's been banned because he was wearing plaster of Paris in his gloves be allowed to fight? A lot of people are against it, including myself. There's no reason why he should be licensed to fight."

Arum countered with, "Oscar is not the brightest penny on the block. There is all of this misinformation out there that people like Oscar eagerly cling to because he's a man who has no discernment. He doesn't read and he doesn't study. Oscar is an advertisement for this movie that's coming out on Friday night that's called *Dinner for Schmucks.*"

Now; putting all of that aside . . .

Let's look at the real issues in the Margarito handwrap controversy, starting with Javier Capetillo.

Capetillo shredded his credibility by maintaining that the use of the inserts was accidental. A trainer doesn't reach into his bag and make a mistake like that. To say that's what happened here is nonsense.

Moreover, if (as Capetillo claims) the knucklepads he pulled out of his bag "by mistake" had been used by another fighter in the gym, why was the gauze that surrounded the illegal inserts squeaky-clean?

There has been near-universal condemnation of Capetillo for his role in the handwrap scandal, and justly so.

The case against Margarito is more difficult to construct. Essentially, Antonio's detractors say, "Stop with the bullshit. A fighter who has fought for as long as Margarito has fought would be aware that his handwraps felt different."

They hypothesize that one reason Margarito fell apart so dramatically during the Mosley fight was that, when the illegal inserts were discovered, Antonio lost both his physical advantage and his self-belief.

They maintain that Capetillo can't be believed when he says Margarito didn't know about the inserts, because Capetillo lied when he said that using the illegal knucklepads was an innocent mistake.

"And by the way," they add. "If Margarito didn't know about the inserts, then he also doesn't know if the inserts were in his handwraps for other fights, including his brutal beatdown of Miguel Cotto. Do you remember what Cotto's face looked like after he fought Margarito? And suppose the inserts hadn't been discovered before the Mosley fight? Take the hypothetical one step further and suppose that Margarito put Mosley in a coma and the inserts were discovered after the fight. There still wouldn't be firm proof that Margarito 'knew' about the inserts. What would the appropriate punishment be then?"

The fact that the illegal inserts were previously used also raises the question: "Who used them?"

Were the inserts molded to Margarito's knuckles? Is the stain on one of the inserts dried blood? If so, is it Antonio's blood?

Margarito's blood on the insert would be viewed by some as the equivalent of Bill Clinton's semen on Monica Lewinsky's blue dress. Certainly, it would be an interesting piece of the puzzle.

Meanwhile, Margarito's position boils down to the following: "Capetillo was solely responsible for acquiring the gauze to make the knucklepads. Margarito was not present when Capetillo prepared the knucklepads. Margarito was totally unaware that anything improper had been inserted in the knucklepads."

Is that possible?

Yes.

The inserts certainly weren't visible to Margarito. We know that because Naazim Richardson (who was looking for irregularities) saw no visual evidence of them.

Nor is it a given that Margarito would have felt them.

Emanuel Steward, Freddie Roach, Don Turner, and Dan Birmingham have been honored as "Trainer of the Year" nine times by the Boxing Writers Association of America. Pat Burns trained Jermain Taylor for both of his victories over Bernard Hopkins and is a former police detective. Naazim Richardson trains Shane Mosley and is the man who discovered the illegal inserts in Margarito's knucklepads.

Their thoughts are instructive:

Dan Birmingham: "My guys watch me closely when I wrap. But what you're talking about here happens pretty quickly. The pad goes on and then you put more gauze over it. So sure; it's possible that the fighter wouldn't know."

Pat Burns: "Some fighters don't pay attention when their hands are being wrapped. They're listening to music or talking to someone or watching a television monitor. And even if they're watching, they're not wondering what's in the knucklepad. If I wanted to put a few layers of hardened gauze inside a fighter's knucklepads, I could and the fighter would never know."

Freddie Roach: "If I did something like that, which I wouldn't, I think I could do it without my fighter knowing. And if I was the fighter; Eddie Futch [who trained Roach] would never have done something like that. But if he had, I think he could have kept it secret from me."

Don Turner: "I wouldn't do it. I don't cheat. But if I wanted to, unless what I was putting into the knucklepad was very heavy, I could do it in a way that the fighter wouldn't know. Even if the fighter is watching me wrap, he might not know because he wouldn't see or feel the difference."

Emanuel Steward: "My experience has been that a fighter watches very closely when his hands are being taped. But in a situation like this, it's definitely possible that a trainer could put an insert in the knucklepad without the fighter knowing. When I get in the dressing room before a fight, one of the first things I do is make two knucklepads and put them on the table. I don't put them in my bag. I leave them out on the table, and so does every other trainer I know of. So I have a hard time believing that Capetillo took the wrong knucklepads out of his bag by mistake. But the fighter doesn't watch me make the knucklepads. A lot of times, the fighter isn't even there when I make them. So the fighter wouldn't know if I put something inside the pads unless I told him or the pads were heavy enough that he could feel a difference."

Naazim Richardson: "I'm the wrong person to ask about this. If a guy is driving a truck and tries to run my daughter over and misses, don't ask me what the punishment should be. But to be fair, yes, a fighter might not know."

Could Antonio Margarito have been complicit in the handwrap scandal?

Yes; but we don't know that he was. And there's no way that a fighter in his situation can prove his innocence.

If Margarito knew that his knucklepads contained illegal inserts, a lifetime ban from boxing would be warranted. But a fighter's career shouldn't be terminated on a guess.

A FURTHER NOTE ON THE ANTONIO MARGARITO HANDWRAP ISSUE

It's now official. Antonio Margarito has been licensed by the Texas Department of Licensing and Regulation and will fight Manny Pacquiao at Cowboys Stadium on November 13th. There will be a lot gnashing of teeth about Margarito's transgressions between now and fight time. Let's look at where things stand.

Last year, the California State Athletic Commission revoked Margarito's license after illegal inserts were found in his knucklepads prior to his January 24, 2009, fight against Shane Mosley. On August 18, 2010, the CSAC denied Margarito's request for reinstatement of his license by a 5–1 vote.

The statements made by members of the California State Athletic Commission make it clear that they think Margarito knew his handwraps were loaded. Just as obviously, they can't prove it. Nor has the state attorney general's office seriously tried to prove it with any sort of in-depth investigation.

Instead, California has asked Margarito to supply the proof by expressing "remorse" for taking part in a scheme to load his gloves and promising that he'll never do it again because he has been "rehabilitated." The problem with this line of thinking is that Margarito says he didn't know that his knucklepads contained illegal inserts.

In other words, the California State Athletic Commission has updated Joseph Heller's classic World War II novel, *Catch-22.* In that book, crew members at a United States Army air force base would be exempt from life-threatening combat missions if they were insane. All they had to do was ask to be grounded. But as Heller explained, "There was one catch. That was Catch-22, which specified that a concern for one's safety in the face of dangers that were real and immediate was the process of a rational mind. Orr was crazy and could be grounded. All he had to do was ask. And as soon as he did, he would no longer be crazy and would have to fly more missions."

Hence, the California State Athletic Commission's own "Catch-22." If Margarito is innocent, then there is nothing to express remorse for and no need for rehabilitation. But absent remorse and rehabilitation, the CSAC won't give him a license. And if Margarito is guilty, then he has previously perjured himself in addition to having committed an offense that merits more than a one-year suspension.

The California State Athletic Commission also chastised Margarito and his new trainer, Robert Garcia, for violating an obscure California rule that requires a "sparring permit." Margarito sparred in California in preparation for a May 8, 2010, fight in Mexico without having such a permit. The problem with the CSAC's position on this issue is that hundreds, if not thousands, of fighters (including Manny Pacquiao) spar in California without a permit.

It's also worth noting that, according to the Association of Boxing Commissions, forty-five boxers fought during the past twelve months while on medical suspension or without the required federal identification card. That's a clear violation of federal and state law. Seventeen of these boxers fought in California under the auspices of the California State Athletic Commission. That's the worst record of compliance of any state in the country.

California should get its own house in order.

By late 2010, Floyd Mayweather Jr was in danger of becoming a caricature of himself.

Floyd Mayweather Jr: When Is Enough?

Manny Pacquiao isn't given to trash-talking. He rarely says a bad word about anyone and is particularly careful when talking about other boxers. Thus, it was significant when Pacquiao said recently, "[Floyd] Mayweather thinks he's better than anybody else. In the ring, it's good for a fighter to think that way, to have confidence. But Mayweather thinks that way about other people outside of boxing. I don't like that."

A lot of people don't like it, and their numbers are growing.

To many in the sweet science, loyalty is a four-letter word: c-a-s-h. Based on that principle, Mayweather has become what Keith Idec calls "boxing's most spoiled child, a smug multi-millionaire accustomed to getting his way with the help of an army of enablers."

These enablers, Kevin Iole writes, "have whored themselves out and ignored Mayweather's increasingly irrational behavior because of his ability to generate money. They've turned their heads to his often bizarre and distasteful behavior because he could increase the bottom line in their checking accounts. For far too long, he has been allowed to run unchecked. The result is a man who has become out of touch with reality, who has lived a fairy tale to stroke his own ego."

Mayweather has chosen to make his life very public, so it's fair for the media to comment on that life. He's an exceptionally talented fighter. Even his most severe critics acknowledge that. And he has promoted himself very skillfully to maximize his earning potential. What he has not done is conduct himself as a responsible adult. His repeated abuse of women, his racist comments, and his constant demeaning of ring opponents stand testament to that. Last month, there were ominous signs that he is imploding and that his world might come crashing down.

Mayweather's latest troubles began on September 2, 2010, when he was seen worldwide on a UStream.com video. The kick-off press tour for

Pacquiao-Margarito was underway. Floyd might have been jealous of the attention that Manny was getting. Regardless of his motive, he spewed venom.

During the video, Mayweather called Pacquiao a "little yellow chump," a "whore," and a "faggot." He also said, "Once I stomp the midget, I'll make that motherfucker make me a sushi roll and cook me some rice." For good measure, he added, "Motherfucker Pacquiao, he can't speak no English."

Some things are too disgusting even for boxing.

Jeff MacGregor suggested on ESPN.com that the video should be preceded by the legend, "WARNING! Fantastically immature mature content, bad language, poor grammar, brainless not-safe-for-work-or-play racism, miserable homophobia, smug condescension, and irredeemable self-regard."

Jerry Izenberg wrote, "Now Mayweather has become as offensive as he is boring. You can add dumb to that. None of this is very complicated. He said what he said. He is what he is."

Others condemned Floyd's remarks as hateful and grotesque. The general consensus was that a village somewhere was missing an idiot.

A new parlor game arose: "Floyd Mayweather Jr's comments were so dumb that . . ."

"Floyd Mayweather Jr's comments were so dumb that Floyd Sr is complaining that his son is disgracing the family name."

"Floyd Mayweather Jr's comments were so dumb that his initials stand for FuckerMother."

"Floyd Mayweather Jr's comments were so dumb that James Toney condemned him for trash-talking."

"Floyd Mayweather Jr's comments were so dumb that the WBC is turning down the sanctioning fee for his next fight."

"Floyd Mayweather Jr's comments were so dumb that John Rocker issued a statement demanding that Floyd apologize."

"Floyd Mayweather Jr's comments were so dumb that Danny Milano couldn't stop the bleeding."

"Floyd Mayweather Jr's comments were so dumb that Michael Buffer lost his cool when he heard them."

"Floyd Mayweather Jr's comments were so dumb that Reebok is paying him to wear Nike."

"Floyd Mayweather Jr's comments were so dumb that Bernard Hopkins was speechless."

"Floyd Mayweather Jr's comments were so dumb that Roger is now known as the intelligent Mayweather."

"He's not the sharpest tool in the shed," Dan Rafael wrote. "He's also too dumb to realize that he's not even promoting an actual fight, since he won't sign for it. I wonder if his mother is proud of him? How about his young children? They'll be able to watch that video someday because it will be on the Internet forever."

On September 5th, Mayweather spoke out again on UStream.com. This time, he offered a rambling stream of consciousness about a variety of subjects. Toward the end, he said, "I do want to apologize for what happened the other night. I want to apologize to everybody because everybody thought that it was a racist comment that I said. I don't have a racist bone in my body. I have nothing but love for everybody. Some of my guys are Muslim. Some of my guys are Jews, Puerto Ricans, Dominicans, whites. I got nothing but love in my heart. All I want to say is, if anybody was affected from what I said the other day, I apologize as a man. I was just having fun. I didn't really mean it."

Having fun?

Meanwhile, the storm was moving beyond the boxing community.

On September 6th, the National Federation of Filipino American Associations condemned Mayweather's remarks as "blatantly racist and homophobic." National chairperson Greg Macabenta declared, "This disgusting diatribe against Pacquiao is a racial slur against all Filipinos and Filipino Americans and an embarrassment, not only to the boxing community but to all Americans. We are asking all civil rights organizations to stand in solidarity with us in denouncing this racist and homophobic rant. At a time when immigrant communities are being viewed with increasing suspicion and mistrust, Mayweather's cruel, abusive, and hurtful remarks can only stoke more hostility, derision, and resentment. Mayweather's shameless and reckless conduct seriously undermines America's core values of inclusivity and racial tolerance."

AT&T and Reebok (which had featured Mayweather in earlier advertising campaigns) announced that their relationship with the fighter had expired.

HBO's initial response was muted. The network's *24/7* series has been a crucial building block in the construction of Mayweather's celebrity image. Rightly or wrongly, the powers that be at HBO Sports feel that, to a degree, their fortunes are tied to Floyd.

On a September 11th *Boxing After Dark* telecast, blow-by-blow commentator Bob Papa referenced Mayweather's comments in a prepared script, but did not tell viewers what Floyd had said and would not categorize the remarks other than to say that they were "racially insensitive." It was left to HBO Sports president Ross Greenburg to more forthrightly tell this writer, "I think I speak for everybody at HBO when I say that we were appalled by Floyd's comments. There's no place for that type of racist rant in our society, and I hope it never happens again."

Mayweather, of course, has played the race card in the past when he felt that it worked to his advantage. Once, during contract negotiations, he publicly denounced an HBO offer as "slave wages." Two years ago, he said that HBO's announcing team was "racist" and singled out Jim Lampley (a committed advocate of equal rights) for criticism.

Floyd's racist homophobic rant against Pacquiao offered a window onto his thinking where the dignity of others is concerned. It also led some to connect the dots to another incident where ethnicity was an issue.

On March 4, 2010, Mayweather appeared at the Nokia Theater in Los Angeles for a press conference to promote his May 1st fight against Shane Mosley. Afterward, several Filipino writers complained that they had been barred from interviewing Floyd because they're Filipino.

Chino Trinidad (who covered the press conference for the GMA network) recounted, "We were waiting for our opportunity to talk to Floyd, and other journalists kept being taken to him ahead of us. Finally, we got up to the stage and a woman named Kelly Swanson [Mayweather's publicist] said to me, 'You're Filipino, right?' I told her yes, and she said, "Floyd Mayweather will not do interviews with the Filipino media."

Swanson denied the allegation. On March 5th, she told Paula Duffy of Examiner.com, "Two individuals approached me about talking with Floyd after all the other television crews had finished. Floyd was already off the stage, signing autographs with fans. They arrived after the other TV crews were gone. I told them that Floyd was not going to answer questions related to Manny Pacquiao and drug testing. I at no time refused them the opportunity to speak with Floyd Mayweather. They were welcome to go down to where he was with the fans and wait to see if he would give them an interview."

That denial infuriates Trinidad, who says, "The statement of Kelly Swanson is false. They did this to us only because we are Filipino. She told us that we could not interview Mayweather because we are Filipino. This is something that cannot be ignored."

No tape of the incident is known to exist. Thus, the controversy lingers.

Meanwhile, Mayweather was careening toward an even more dangerous confrontation.

Over the years, Floyd has had significant issues with women and the criminal justice system in Nevada. In 2002, he pled guilty to two counts of domestic violence. In 2004, he was found guilty on two counts of misdemeanor battery for assaulting two women in a Las Vegas nightclub.

On another front, Mayweather was on the fringes of an August 2009 shooting incident that took place outside a Las Vegas skating rink. His Rolls Royce was spotted at the shooting scene and one of his associates, Ocie Harris, was indicted on attempted murder charges for shooting at two passengers in another car. After the shooting, police searched Mayweather's house, looking for evidence. Harris's lawyer has said that his client is being used as a pawn by police and prosecutors in an effort to link the shooting to Mayweather.

Additionally, in February 2005, Floyd was fined and ordered to perform community service after pleading no contest to misdemeanor assault and battery charges in conjunction with an altercation that took place in a bar in Grand Rapids, Michigan.

Thirty-year-old Josie Harris is the mother of three of Mayweather's children, ages ten through seven. She and Floyd have had a tumultuous on-again-off-again relationship for years.

In the early morning hours of Thursday, September 9th, according to a Las Vegas Metropolitan Police Department report, Harris was out at the Red Rock Casino. She returned home at 2:30 AM to find that Mayweather had "let himself in" to her residence and was talking with their three children. Why children between the ages of seven and ten were up at 2:30 in the morning is another matter.

At that point, according to Harris, Mayweather began searching through her belongings and accused her of dating another man. He was loud and abusive. She called the police. The officers arrived. She told them that she wanted Mayweather to leave. He said that he owned the house and wanted to evict her. The officers advised him that, to do so, he would have to go through a lawful eviction process. At approximately 3:00 AM, the officers escorted Floyd from Harris's home.

That should have been the end of it. But according to the police report, Mayweather returned at approximately 5:00 AM with a friend named James McNair. One of the children opened the door and let them in. Harris was asleep on a couch. She woke up when Mayweather, who was holding her cell phone and reading text messages, began yelling at her, "Are you having sex with C. J.?"

Knowing Floyd, one might speculate that what he really asked was "Are you fucking C. J.?" Be that as it may; Harris says that she answered, "Yes; that's who I'm seeing now."

"C.J." has been identified in several media reports as C. J. Watson, who plays for the Chicago Bulls. Watson has denied that a sexual relationship exists between Harris and himself.

Harris says that Mayweather then pulled her off the couch, assaulted her in front of their children, and threatened to kill her. More specifically, she told police that Floyd struck her "multiple times in the head with his fist," was "pulling me by my hair and throwing me on the ground in my living room," began "dragging me on the floor and twisting my arm back; continued to beat me in front of the children," and shouted, "I'm going to kill you and the man you're messing around with. I'm going to have you both disappear."

Harris screamed for the children to call the police or run to the security guard station outside their home. Mayweather, she says, told the children that he'd beat their ass if they did.

Koraun (the couple's ten year-old son) told police that he saw his father hitting and kicking his mother. McNair was blocking the front entrance, so he ran out the back door and summoned a friend of his mother's named Georgia Parker. Parker called the police. Koraun then went to the security guard station and told the guard what was happening.

Mayweather took Harris's cell phone and cell phones belonging to two of their children and left.

Police officers responded to the call and brought Harris to Southern Hills Hospital, where she was treated for minor facial injuries and a sore left arm.

When the Clark County District Attorney's office reviewed Harris's complaint, it had a problem. Seven years earlier, she'd lodged similar allegations against Mayweather, accusing him of hitting and kicking her during an argument outside a Las Vegas nightclub. Then, at trial in 2005, she recanted, testifying under oath that Floyd was a "teddy bear" who "would never lay a hand" on her and that she had lied to police officers because she was angry he'd left her for another woman. Mayweather was acquitted.

Given that history, a good defense lawyer could be expected to decimate Harris on cross-examination.

This time, though, the District Attorney's office had an ace in the hole. Two aces, actually.

Two of the cute little children who Mayweather put before the cameras on *24/7* to establish his credentials as a good father corroborated Harris's story.

On September 16th, after some preliminary legal maneuvering, Mayweather was formally charged pursuant to an eight-count criminal complaint that alleges he committed the following crimes:

(1) Battery constituting domestic violence (Nevada Revised Statutes, sections 200.481 and 200.485) for grabbing Josie Harris by the hair, throwing her to the floor, striking her with his fist, and twisting her arm.

(2) Harassment (200.571) for threatening to kill Josie Harris and her boyfriend or make her and her boyfriend "disappear."

(3) Coercion (207.190) for threatening to beat Koraun and Zion if they telephoned 911.

(4) Harassment (200.571) for threatening to "beat" Koraun's and Zion's "ass."

(5) Robbery (200.380) and grand larceny (205.222, a less serious property offense) for taking Josie Harris's cell phone;

A court appearance is scheduled for November 9th, at which time Mayweather must enter a plea in response to the charges against him.

If Harris provides prosecutors with evidence that she was paid to recant her 2003 allegations of domestic violence or recanted because she was threatened with personal injury, there could be additional charges for witness tampering and other crimes relating to the obstruction of justice.

Mayweather's defense attorney is Richard Wright, who represented him at the 2005 trial. In the months ahead, one can expect Wright to say all the things that defense lawyers say in the course of representing a client.

Unfortunately, two of Floyd's most prominent associates seem to be adhering to a similar standard.

Golden Boy CEO Richard Schaefer (Mayweather's most recent promoter) and Al Haymon (Floyd's de facto manager) are two of the most powerful people in boxing. Earlier this year, Schaefer spent months talking about the need for Olympic-style testing to eliminate the use of performance-enhancing drugs from the sport. Those months coincided with the build-up to Mayweather vs. Shane Mosley (promoted by Golden Boy) and the efforts of Team Mayweather to brand Manny Pacquiao as a user.

Once Mayweather-Mosley was over, the issue of Olympic-style drug testing seemed to vanish from Schaefer's agenda. Later, Richard supported the bizarre claim of Leonard Ellerbe (Floyd's business manager) that there had been no negotiations earlier this year aimed at consummating a Pacquiao-Mayweather fight.

Haymon tiptoed around the PED and negotiations issues, although Ross Greenburg says that Al was Mayweather's representative in the negotiations.

Then Mayweather went viral with his racist homophobic rant.

Let's change the paradigm a bit. Suppose Mayweather went on UStream.com and declared, "Richard Schaefer is a faggot foreigner, who should go back to where he came from. Make me some wiener schnitzel, Richard."

Or suppose one of Al Haymon's enemies (he has a few) took to the air and raged, "Al Haymon is a shiftless lazy watermelon-eating parasite."

Those insults would outrage their targets, and justifiably so. Schaefer and Haymon would expect others to condemn anyone who made them, as well they should.

So why are they silent on this issue? The fact that they have a business relationship with Mayweather is not a valid excuse. By their silence, they've turned away from the responsibility that good citizens have to rebut bigoted utterances.

It should also be noted that, when Oscar De La Hoya fought Ricardo Mayorga in 2006, Mayorga spewed ugly insults and homophobic venom.

At that time, Schaefer declared, "I'm not pleased to be associated with a person like Mayorga, but this is boxing so I guess we have to do it."

De La Hoya was more pointed in his condemnation of "all this anger and hatred," saying, "Mayorga started disrespecting me, He insulted my heritage. I personally think he's bad for boxing."

But that was then. Now is now.

Schaefer and De La Hoya said nothing publicly about Mayweather's bigoted rant. Then, when Floyd was arrested following his confrontation with Josie Harris, Richard suggested that the cure for what ails him is a return to the ring (presumably under Golden Boy's promotional guidance).

"The spotlight is a glorious light at times," Schaefer told the *Los Angeles Times.* "But it can be a hard light too. For many, their athletic environment is a kingdom, a real place to find refuge from outside influences. The same is true for Floyd. He's a gym rat. Maybe he needs to get back in there and fight again, so we can all enjoy his amazing talents."

"That squared circle is the best thing that can ever happen to a fighter," De La Hoya added. "The squared circle is what saves you from everything. If it's Mayweather fighting as often as three, four times a year, maybe that's what he has to do."

Or maybe, like Mike Tyson, Mayweather has to deal with his problems away from the ring before he self-destructs completely.

Thus, the question: "When is enough?" For Mayweather and for boxing.

There are still a lot of people who think that the sweet science needs Floyd Mayweather and, in particular, Mayweather vs. Manny Pacquiao. Jeff MacGregor (a sage observer of the sporting scene) takes a contrary view. "If that's what it takes to save boxing," MacGregor writes, "let it die. In fact, grab that pillow and help me smother it on its deathbed."

Ironically, there's a school of thought that Mayweather's recent troubles increase the chances that Pacquiao-Mayweather will happen. Floyd, this reasoning goes, now needs the fight to rehabilitate his image. Moreover, if he were to signal his intention to fight Pacquiao in Las Vegas, some significant power brokers might put pressure on the Clark County district attorney's office to plea-bargain in a lenient way.

Mayweather's "fuck you" to the world would be beating Pacquiao. The world's "fuck you" to Mayweather would be telling him, "Whether or not boxing thinks it needs you, the rest of us don't."

HBO styles itself as "the heart and soul of boxing." But the heartbeat was a bit faint in 2010.

HBO and the State of Boxing

There was a time when the sweet science was governed by the axiom, "As the heavyweight division goes, so goes boxing." Now, in the United States, the rule of thumb is, "As HBO goes, so goes boxing."

No network has ever been associated with a sport to the degree that HBO is associated with boxing. And no network has ever set the agenda for a sport to the extent that HBO sets the agenda for boxing.

HBO has the single biggest boxing budget in the world.

It's one of the few places that a fighter and promoter can go to make big money in the United States and, for many Americans, their only exposure to boxing. Indeed, most of the public and media are unaware of a fighter's existence unless he fights on HBO.

Most big fights in the United States happen if and when HBO chooses to televise them.

In most sports, athletes with talent succeed. In boxing, a good or bad manager, a powerful or weak promoter, a competent or incompetent matchmaker can spell the difference between success and failure. But the most dominant force of all is HBO.

That sort of power demands scrutiny. Indeed, one can make a case that, while HBO's primary obligations are to its subscribers and Time Warner shareholders, it also has a fiduciary obligation to boxing by virtue of its power.

This article is long. No one is required to read it. Anyone who's concerned about the future of boxing might take the time to do so.

I

Much has been written lately about how boxing is struggling in the United States. It's not just boxing. Dozens of MMA companies have folded in recent years. Even UFC, despite perpetually rose-colored pronouncements, has seen a dip in key economic indicators as of late.

Boxing has been a staple of HBO's programming since 1973. For a quarter-century, the network has been the best brand in boxing. But in recent years, HBO's boxing programming has drawn a smaller and increasingly older fan base. One reason this demographic is older is that many viewers first subscribed to the network when HBO boxing was special. They're staying on out of habit. But HBO boxing is attracting relatively few new subscribers.

The best thing to happen to HBO Sports in recent years was the success of *24/7,* both as a marketing vehicle for pay-per-view buys and a passageway to young male viewers. The network continues to have success with its *Sports of the 20th Century* documentary series. *Hard Knocks* enjoyed high ratings this summer, courtesy in part of a foul-mouthed New York–based head coach.

But ratings for HBO's live fights have been disappointing. And HBO CEO Bill Nelson is said to be particularly troubled by the fact that, in recent years, African-American viewership of HBO Sports programming has dropped significantly beyond the drop for other demographic groups.

Nelson rarely gets involved with the sports department budget; but this year, he has. Sources say that, on September 16, 2010, HBO Sports president Ross Greenburg made a presentation to the CEO and outlined a plan to raise ratings among African-American viewers. Greenburg's suggestions included the idea that HBO spend more money on advertising and promotion targeted at the African-American community. But Nelson is a numbers guy and wary of simply throwing more money at problems.

Sources also say that Greenburg has told Nelson and HBO president Richard Plepler that boxing is struggling because (1) despite HBO's best efforts, it was unable to consummate a deal for Manny Pacquiao to fight Floyd Mayweather Jr this year; (2) there are no stars because promoters aren't developing them; and (3) there are no good American heavyweights.

Nelson and Plepler are ambivalent toward boxing. They know there are problems with HBO's boxing program, but they rely in large part on Greenburg for input regarding the sweet science. Also, in recent years, they've had concerns that are more pressing than boxing, such as the need to rebuild HBO's programming staff on the West Coast after Chris Albrecht's abrupt departure, replace *Sex and the City* and *The Sopranos,* and deal with the challenges posed every day by an ever-changing new media.

HBO Sports operates within this framework. That said; there's no escaping the fact that the fights shown on HBO during the first ten months of 2010 have been disappointing. The network's subscribers bankroll its fights. Thirty million subscribers pay HBO well over one billion dollars each year, so the network has total freedom to buy and televise what it wants. Armed with this freedom and the largest budget in boxing, HBO's 2010 offerings to date as part of its premium package have been:

Boxing After Dark: Juan Manuel Lopez vs. Steven Luevano, Yuriorkis Gamboa vs. Rogers Mtagwa, Devon Alexander vs. Juan Urango, Marcos Maidana vs. Victor Cayo, Ali Funeka vs. Joan Guzman, Chris Arreola vs. Tomasz Adamek, Alfredo Angulo vs. Joel Julio, Amir Khan vs. Paulie Malignaggi, Victor Ortiz vs. Nate Campbell, Timothy Bradley vs. Carlos Abregu, Alfredo Angulo vs. Joachim Alcine, Devon Alexander vs. Andres Kotelnik, Tavoris Cloud vs. Glen Johnson, Yuriorkis Gamboa vs. Orlando Salido, and Anthony Peterson vs. Brandon Rios.

HBO World Championship Boxing: Kelly Pavlik vs. Sergio Martinez, Lucian Bute vs. Edison Miranda, Andre Berto vs. Carlos Quintana, Celestino Caballero vs. Daud Yordan, Paul Williams vs. Kermit Cintron, Yuri Foreman vs. Miguel Cotto, Vanes Martirosyan vs. Joe Greene, and Chad Dawson vs. Jean Pascal.

How many of these twenty-three fights would boxing fans want to see again?

HBO simply isn't giving its subscribers fights that fight fans want to see. One way of measuring that is ratings. Another way of measuring it is that fans aren't buying tickets to many of the fights that HBO televises. By way of example, Andre Berto vs. Carlos Quintana (for which HBO paid a $2,150,000 license fee) sold 972 tickets.

"The people at HBO still don't understand what makes a fight entertaining," Bob Arum says. "I have to understand because I'm a promoter. I don't have tens of millions of subscribers sending me money each month. I wish I did, but I don't. I have to sell tickets to fights. I have to give the public fights that it wants. HBO goes to the public and says, 'These are the fights that we're telling you to want,' and the public is smarter than that."

Boxing generates excitement when the best fight the best. Very few fights on HBO this year have matched elite fighters against one another. Too often, the network tries to justify a match-up by saying, "We're putting this on to get to a good fight." Why not say, "We're only going to televise what we think will be good fights."

Luis Cortes recently wrote, "I work in a marketing department. One of the first things I learned is that you can package things and market them as good quality and convince the public all you want. Except when it comes to sports."

Allan Scotto adds, "Nothing turns a fan off quicker then watching someone purported to be a great fighter fighting yet another fight against a human heavy bag. The real excitement comes watching that same fighter when he's actually challenged and faces someone with some skills."

Fans want to see *dangerous* fights. HBO should be looking for competitive action-filled match-ups, preferably involving one or more vibrant personalities. When these factors are combined, stars are born.

"The problem," says hall-of-fame promoter Russell Peltz, "is that HBO is more interested in guys with good records than they are in guys who are good fighters. They think they're building stars, and they aren't. Fighters become stars when they win exciting fights."

But the prevailing ethic at HBO today seems to be, let's get him an alphabet-soup title and then find out if he's any good. "The way things are," says trainer Don Turner, "as long as you're beating up on a stiff, everything is fine. But the fighters aren't learning how to fight. Then they get to a big fight and stink out the joint because they haven't earned their way. There's a difference between padding your record and developing as a fighter."

Taking into account fights that have been scheduled through the end of 2010, the fighters who will have appeared live most often on *HBO World Championship Boxing* and *Boxing After Dark* from 2008 through 2010 are Andre Berto and Alfredo Angulo with seven appearances each. Berto will be dealt with later in this article. Let's take a look at Angulo.

Alfredo is an entertaining fighter. He's a big strong guy who throws punches and gets hit. He had zero name recognition before he appeared on HBO. The network could have insisted that he go in tough. Instead, it was clear before the opening bell that each of his first three opponents (Richard Gutierrez, Andrey Tsurkan, and Cosme Rivera) was woefully overmatched. Then Angulo went in tough against Kermit Cintron and lost, so it was back to less threatening opponents (Harry Yorgey, Joel Julio, and Joachim Alcine).

Why are fighters like Alfredo Angulo consistently on HBO if they're not willing to fight the best?

Fighters, as previously noted, become stars by going in tough. But they have little incentive to go in tough when HBO keeps overpaying them to fight weak opponents. By way of example, Angulo turned down a $750,000 purse to fight Sergio Martinez in November. Martinez would have been favored in that fight.

"It's idiotic to throw money at unproven fighters to fight second-rate opponents," says Bob Arum. "But that's what HBO does, and then they're surprised when they can't make the fights they want. They've created a totally artificial market based entirely on how much money Ross and Kery [HBO senior vice president for sports programming Kery Davis] are willing to pay for a fight. We [Top Rank] got a $2,750,000 license fee for Foreman-Cotto, which is HBO's highest-rated show of the year so far. Look at how often they've paid the same amount of money or more for dogshit. The license fees that HBO pays, and I've said this before, are totally arbitrary. They remind me of when people were selling tulip bulbs in Holland for ridiculous amounts of money. Then, one day, people woke up and said, 'What, are we crazy? These are tulip bulbs!' And the market collapsed overnight."

As a general rule, the economic model for boxing should equate making the most money with making the most entertaining, most competitive fights. Similarly, HBO should pay its highest license fees for the most entertaining, most competitive fights.

But it doesn't seem to happen that way.

HBO paid $3,200,000 for a rematch between Chad Dawson and Antonio Tarver last year (their first fight drew 911 paying fans) because it wanted Dawson in its stable. Dawson-Tarver II sold 1,426 tickets. Then HBO paid millions more for a rematch between Dawson and Glen Johnson before Dawson lost to Jean Pascal.

"That's what happens when a network tries to create a star out of nothing," says Arum. "If the people at HBO bought fights like intelligent people, do you realize what they could have bought for five million dollars?

And more to the point; how many fights has Chad Dawson been in that boxing fans were excited about? What are the chances that anyone outside of Dawson's immediate family has said, "Gee; I think I'll pop in a DVD of Chad's two fights against Antonio Tarver."

The National Basketball Association entered a new era when it began marketing around Magic Johnson and Larry Bird. *HBO World Championship Boxing* and *Boxing After Dark* have entered a new era by marketing around Andre Berto, Alfredo Angulo, Chad Dawson, and company.

"They just don't get it," says Kathy Duva, who has been at the helm of Main Events for the past fourteen years. "The thing that's totally missing from HBO's boxing programming today is passion. If you look at all the superstars in boxing—Ali, Ray Leonard, Tyson, George Foreman, Oscar—they inspired passion. Arturo Gatti wasn't a great fighter, but he inspired passion. Passion is what makes sports entertaining. People aren't making an emotional connection with the fighters they see on HBO anymore."

"Let's be honest," Duva continues. "HBO doesn't understand the importance of passion in boxing anymore because the people who run boxing there have no passion for boxing. That's clear from the fights they make. They keep telling the public, 'You should watch this fighter; he's the best.' And they're not connecting with the public because, whether or not their fighters are the best, they're not entertaining to watch and people don't care about them."

"Kery and Ross should pay fighters based on how much money they'd take out of their own pocket to see them fight," Duva says. "Would they pay their own money to watch Chad Dawson? How many people care if Andre Berto wins or loses? And how can you get excited watching Andre Berto and Chad Dawson when there's no passion in the arena? The only time there was passion in the arena for a Chad Dawson fight was when he went to Canada and fought Jean Pascal. Ross and Kery are television programmers trying to be promoters and they aren't listening to the fans. Kery's vision of the world is very small. He doesn't understand that there's more than HBO involved in a promotion. In the real world of boxing where I have to balance a budget based on how many fans buy tickets for a fight, entertainment matters. Arturo Gatti lost three fights in a row, but he always gave the public great fights. Go to a Tomasz

Adamek fight. Tomasz's fan base isn't as broad as Arturo's was, but it's just as passionate. Tomasz's fans come to his fights wearing red and white. Their faces are painted. They scream all night. His fights are exciting. And the only way he can get on HBO is to go out to California and fight an Al Haymon fighter in a half-empty arena. There was a time when HBO created icons with its boxing programming. Where are the icons of tomorrow?"

It has been said that, to do great things, a person must have passion about what he or she doing. Often, when HBO hosts an on-site party on fight night, the party takes place during the undercard and extends into one or more of the televised fights.

What message does that send?

In recent years, HBO has consistently come up short in identifying young fighters with the potential to become both true champions in the ring and marketable outside it. Berto, Angulo, and Dawson have already been referenced. Chris Arreola, Victor Ortiz, Robert Guerrero, and Danny Jacobs stumbled. Now the network is said to be pushing a fight between Tomasz Adamek and Wladimir Klitschko in the hope of breathing life into the heavyweight division.

There are some extremely entertaining fights involving Tomasz Adamek that HBO could televise. Adamek against Klitschko is not one of them. It would be one-sided beatdown.

Kery Davis is HBO's primary programmer for boxing. "I report to Ross," Davis explains. "My responsibility is to determine when fights are made and which fights we buy, negotiate deals for those fights on behalf of the company, and strategize with marketing before and after the deals are made. I'm not a matchmaker. We buy fights that promoters offer us. The criteria we use are: We want the best fighting the best. We want exciting fights. We're in the business of identifying and developing stars, so we want fighters who have star potential. And the fight should fit within an overall strategy, such as our decision this year to get heavily involved in the 140-pound division because that division has exciting talent that runs deep and can be matched up in competitive fights."

"Kery runs the boxing program on a day-to-day basis," says Greenburg. "He's the one who does most of the dealing with promoters and is primarily responsible for the matchmaking on *HBO World Championship*

Boxing and *Boxing After Dark*. Mark Taffet works the pay-per-view world."

A number of promoters have complained about misinformation that they say flows from Davis's lips during negotiations; misinformation regarding the license fees that HBO pays to other promoters, HBO's arrangements on subsidiary rights with other promoters, the amount of money that HBO receives for foreign rights on a given fight, the availability of dates, and the money that's available to license a fight on a given date.

"I don't give misinformation," Davis says when the issue is put to him. "I give people the most accurate information I have at the time. Sometimes things change."

"That's very Kery," one promoter says in response. "He has zero credibility with some of us, but he and Ross hold our livelihood in their hands."

Bob Arum points to what he believes is a larger problem at HBO.

"The larger your organization," Arum says, "the more you have to rely on other people. There are things I don't know about the new media because I'm not a new media guy; so for those things, I rely on Todd [Top Rank president Todd DuBoef]. On other things, I might rely on someone else. Ross has no one who he can rely on when it comes to making decisions about boxing."

"Kery isn't a boxing guy," Arum continues. "To do that job, you have to love boxing and be part of boxing and get boxing. Lou [DiBella], for all his craziness, was a very very good boxing guy. Kery has no feel for the sport. He would dispute that, but I've been in boxing for a long time and I know what I'm talking about. The biggest need that Ross has right now is for someone to advise him who knows fighters, knows what makes a good fight, and knows what's really going on in boxing. Otherwise, HBO will keep making the same mistakes again and again."

"Ross needs someone with his finger on the pulse of boxing," says another promoter. "HBO got burned last month when it came out that Alfredo Angulo is in the United States illegally. A lot of us have known that for a long time. I mean, come on; Angulo drove cross-country for an HBO fight because he couldn't get on a plane. Why didn't anyone at HBO know?"

Another factor to be considered in HBO's boxing programming is the influence of Al Haymon.

Haymon has roots in the concert-promotion business and, over the past decade, has become the most powerful manager in boxing. His roster of fighters includes Floyd Mayweather Jr, Paul Williams, Andre Berto, Chris Arreola, Antonio Tarver, Andre Dirrell, and many young prospects. In the past, he has represented Jermain Taylor, Vernon Forrest, and Lamon Brewster.

Haymon's reach extends into Showtime, although not to the same degree that he has penetrated HBO. Also, his relationship with Showtime might have been irrevocably damaged as a consequence of his handling of the aborted "super-six" tournament bout between Andre Dirrell and Andre Ward. One of the featured bouts in the tournament next year could be Showtime versus Dirrell in federal court, with a jury asked to decide whether or not Andre was really physically unable to continue in the tournament and what Haymon knew when about the situation.

HBO Sports has entered into contracts for bouts involving Haymon's fighters that seem to defy logic. Ross Greenburg says, "I've tried to dispel the notion that Al has some sort of special influence at HBO. He's a very powerful manager with a lot of good fighters, who conducts himself in the style of Mike Trainer with Sugar Ray Leonard in the 1980s. We talk with Al, but he doesn't wield the power that people think he does."

But sources say that Haymon has influence beyond the skills of his fighters and that it comes from a series of personal alliances as well as his ability to assist in providing talent for HBO entertainment specials.

Sports is in a subsidiary position at HBO. No one leans on Michael Lombardo (the president of HBO programming) to give Chris Arreola a cameo appearance on *Boardwalk Empire.* But the sports department gets leaned on from time to time.

By way of example; when HBO televises a *24/7* series that relates to a fight, the promoter foots the bill. Top Rank paid $1,300,000 for *Pacquiao-Cotto 24/7* and is paying a comparable amount for *Pacquiao-Margarito 24/7.* Golden Boy has incurred similar costs for *24/7* shows that involved its fights.

However *Jimmie Johnson 24/7: Race to Daytona* was subject to a different set of rules. Creative Artists Agency (one of Hollywood's top talent agencies) represents the likes of Brad Pitt, George Clooney, Tom Cruise, Will Smith, Tom Hanks, Robert DeNiro, Julia Roberts, Oprah Winfrey, Steven Spielberg, and James Cameron. Jimmie Johnson is one of its clients.

Sources say that, at the request of CAA, Lombardo asked HBO Sports to produce the Jimmie Johnson show. Greenburg, these sources say, was lukewarm to the idea. But he reports to Lombardo and a deal was struck. HBO paid the production costs for *Jimmie Johnson 24/7* and also a license fee to Johnson. As part of the horse-trading, Lombardo agreed that the money wouldn't come out of the sports department budget.

Al Haymon is a very powerful concert promoter. Among his many ventures, he promoted Beyoncé's *I Am . . . Tour.*

Beyoncé, like other Haymon clients in the musical world, has appeared on HBO.

"If I had Beyoncé," Kathy Duva says, "I could get dates on HBO too."

Kery Davis rejects the notion that Haymon leverages his non-sports relationships to gain favor from HBO Sports. "No person at HBO outside of sports has ever spoken to me about Al Haymon," Davis says. "And the music business is different from the boxing business. In the music business, Al is a promoter, not a manager. And in the music business, the person who would sell a concert to HBO is the artist's agent or manager, not the promoter."

But in the music business, an artist's promoter often works closely with the artist's agent or manager.

Haymon isn't Mother Teresa for long-suffering fighters. He likes the power he wields within the boxing industry and also the money he makes from his share of numerous pies. He's also believed to have made millions of dollars by reselling tickets for big fights; most notably on De La Hoya vs. Mayweather and Mayweather vs. Ricky Hatton (where Alan Haymon Development Inc. had the right to purchase $3,100,000 worth of tickets at face value).

A look at HBO's dealings with Andre Berto (one of Haymon's fighters) is instructive. Berto is a talented boxer, who is currently the WBC 147-pound beltholder.

Fans don't buy many tickets for Berto's fights. As noted earlier, his last championship bout (against Carlos Quintana on April 10th of this year) drew 972 paying customers. And the ratings indicate that HBO's subscribers aren't particularly interested in Andre, which raises the question of why the network paid a $2,150,000 license fee that night.

No one knows how good Berto might be (including Andre) because HBO keeps paying him large amounts of money to appear against ordinary opponents.

Berto will be fighting Freddie Hernandez as part of an HBO tripleheader on November 27th. HBO is paying a license fee of $1,200,000 for Berto-Hernandez.

Hernandez is an ESPN-level fighter. Recently, Dan Rafael of ESPN.com wrote, "Berto-Hernandez is a dog. Al Haymon, Berto's adviser, has manipulated, leveraged, and bamboozled HBO into overpaying and coddling Berto for years, and it continues here. HBO is paying $1.2 million for trash."

Berto-Hernandez will be Andre's tenth fight on HBO over a four-year period. His first nine opponents were:

Miguel Figueroa (December 9, 2006), who took the bout for one last paycheck before retiring.

Norberto Bravo (February 17, 2007); a hopelessly outclassed opponent, who has now lost seven of his last twelve fights.

David Estrada (September 29, 2007); a credible opponent, but one who was beginning a downward slide that has seen him lose in three of his last six outings.

Michel Trabant (February 9, 2008)—In his first fight after being knocked out by Berto, Trabant lost a unanimous decision to Roman Seliverstov (who had lost seven of his previous nine bouts). That gave Trabant a five-fight run of one win, two losses, a draw, and one no-contest (relating to a positive test for steroids).

Miguel Rodriguez (June 21, 2008)—This one was for the WBC welterweight belt. Rodriguez, as of this writing, hasn't won a fight since September 2007.

Stevie Forbes (September 27, 2008), who was known as "Little Stevie Forbes." And that's when he was fighting at 135 pounds. Forbes had no business fighting Berto at 147. He has lost five of seven fights since February 2006.

Luis Collazo (January 17, 2009). This was a good fight. But Collazo had lifestyle issues when he fought Berto and has continued to have them since then. He has fought only once during the past twenty-one months (against a club fighter with a 9-and-16 record, whose nine wins came against fighters with a total of five victories to their credit).

Juan Urango (May 30, 2009)—Urango is another smaller guy who came up in weight to fight Berto. He lost a decision to Andre and got knocked out by Devon Alexander at 140 pounds in his next fight.

Berto was scheduled to fight Shane Mosley in January 2010, but pulled out of the bout because of concern for his family in the aftermath of the earthquake in Haiti. That was understandable. But then, rather than proceed with Mosley-Berto at a later date, HBO paid Andre the equivalent of step aside money in the form of an inflated license fee for Berto-Quintana so the network could proceed with Mayweather-Mosley on May 1st.

Then Berto fought Quintana. Carlos is well past his prime and has won only two fights during the past thirty-three months. Those victories came against Joshua Onyango (4–17–1 in his past twenty-two bouts) and Jesse Feliciano (who hasn't won in forty-four months and is 0-and-5 during that time).

Has Al Haymon done a good job for Andre Berto? Absolutely.

Has HBO fulfilled its responsibility to its subscribers by televising the Andre Berto fights referenced above? Absolutely not.

There are also complaints that HBO has empowered Haymon to act as an unlicensed promoter.

Because of his relationship with HBO, Haymon is in a position whereby he rarely has to give a promoter long-term contractual rights to one of his fighters. Often, the promoter has little more than a handshake and Haymon's word that, where this particular fighter is concerned, the promoter is Al's guy. That gives Haymon enormous leverage over the promoter in terms of how income generated from each fight is split. Promoters put up with the arrangement because, over the years, HBO has been remarkably generous when giving out dates and paying license fees for fights involving Haymon's fighters.

Haymon works with five primary promoters: Dan Goossen, Lou DiBella, Richard Schaefer, Gary Shaw, and Brian Young. Despite their involvement, he acts in many respects as the de facto promoter for the fighters that he manages. Often, he deals directly with Ross Greenburg and Kery Davis during fight negotiations, while the promoter of record is minimally involved and reduced to doing the nuts-and-bolts work on the conduct of the fight.

"Al Haymon functions in large measure as a promoter," says Bob Arum. "Part of a promoter's job is to speak directly with the television networks and put fights together, and that's what he does. States should require him to be licensed as a promoter, but they don't."

Promoters with Al Haymon fighters are more afraid to talk about Haymon on the record than they are to talk about HBO. But several of them have complained that they're often bypassed by Kery Davis, who talks directly with Haymon regarding the details of match-ups for fighters that Al manages and they promote.

Davis disputes that point, saying, "If a fighter has a licensed promoter, I deal with the promoter; not Al Haymon. It presents itself on a case-by-case basis. When we were hoping to buy Paul Williams against Sergio Martinez [which HBO will televise on November 20th], Dan [Goossen] didn't have an agreement with Paul until late in the negotiations, so I negotiated with Lou [DiBella] on behalf of Martinez and with Al on behalf of Paul."

"Almost everyone who promotes an Al Haymon fighter has been neutered by HBO," says another promoter. "The things that they do for him are absurd. He's difficult to work with and he squeezes me hard. But I have to say; I think he's good for the fighters he manages."

As for the *HBO World Championship Boxing* and *Boxing After Dark* schedule over the next three months; Martinez-Williams shapes up as an exciting competitive fight between two elite fighters. It's also a model in many respects for how HBO should do business in the future. The network demanded that each fighter go in tough, offered a $3,000,000 license fee, held firm during negotiations, and got what it wanted. The fighters were free to go elsewhere, but no one else was offering them nearly as much money for any fight. For once, HBO didn't bid against itself.

Amir Khan vs. Marcos Maidana on December 11th is an interesting fight. The assumption is that Khan will outbox Maidana for two minutes and fifty-five seconds of every round. The question is, "What happens in those other five seconds?"

At the other end of the spectrum, HBO's November 27th offering leaves much to be desired. Juan Manuel Marquez vs. Michael Katsidis will be an entertaining mismatch unless Marquez gets old overnight. Berto-Hernandez has already been discussed. Celestino Caballero against Jason Litzau is what Lou DiBella would call a "death match" if Caballero wasn't his fighter.

The other fights on *HBO World Championship Boxing* and *Boxing After Dark* before the end of the year tie into HBO's obligations to Golden Boy, which will be discussed later in this article.

Looking ahead to 2011, Greenburg anticipates nine or ten *World Championship Boxing* cards; eight or nine *Boxing After Dark* shows; and three or four pay-per-view events. He says that there won't be a firm cap on license fees, but that he expects a downward "market correction."

Since HBO is the market, he can make that happen. HBO should hold firm on quality and price. If promoters and fighters balk and HBO boxing goes dark for a few months (as Major League Baseball and the National Basketball Association have done in the past), the world won't end. Eventually, elite fighters will return in competitive fights for reasonable license fees because there's nowhere else for them to go.

"We're going to go back to basics next year," Greenburg promises. "The best fighters and the best fights."

That sounds good. But one has to remember:

Ross Greenburg (2007): "We intend to dig our feet in a little more on mismatches and not give in to promoters, managers, and fighters who don't want to take a risk."

Ross Greenburg (2008): "This year, if a fighter wants to be on HBO, we'll expect him to go in tough."

Ross Greenburg (2009): "This year, we intend to televise the best fighters in meaningful competitive fights."

Ideally, Greenburg means it when he says, "We have to look at the things we did to make the rematch between Martinez and Williams and learn from that experience."

Much of HBO's focus in 2011 will be on the 140-pound division. Depending on the results of Zab Judah vs. Lucas Matthysse on November 6th, Victor Ortiz vs. Lamont Peterson on December 11th, and Khan-Maidana on the same date, the network plans to pick and choose among

Timothy Bradley, Devon Alexander, and the just-mentioned 140-pounders with a few more fighters thrown into the mix.

HBO's first fight in 2011 is slated to be Bradley vs. Alexander on January 29th. The network stumbled in setting up the fight. First, it put Alexander in soft against Juan Urango. Alexander looked good. Then it put Bradley in soft against Carlos Abregu at 147 pounds and Timothy looked lackluster. After that, it put Alexander in what was thought to be a relatively easy fight against Andreas Kotelnik. Devon looked ordinary and almost lost. Thereafter, Bart Barry wrote, "Alexander needs to eschew the greatness track and get back on the Andre Berto track, blasting former champions from smaller weight divisions and outpointing predictable South Americans for good money."

Bradley-Abregu and Alexander-Kotelnik took the edge off Bradley-Alexander. But it's still an intriguing fight. HBO is paying a $2,750,000 license fee for the bout. Timothy is on track to become a promotional free agent on May 8, 2011. Devon becomes a promotional free agent on June 23rd. Gary Shaw and Don King (their respective promoters) wanted contract extensions. There was a compromise whereby, win or lose, each fighter will fight one more fight with his current promoter on HBO. The network can require a rematch of Bradley-Alexander if it so chooses. Otherwise, Bradley and Alexander will be in separate fights against different opponents chosen by mutual agreement between each fighter's camp and HBO. The license fee for each of these fights will be $3,000,000 for Bradley-Alexander II or, if there is no rematch, $1,500,000 for Bradley and Shaw plus $1,500,000 for Alexander and King plus what it costs to sign up the opponents and their respective promoters.

HBO hopes that its 140-pound festival will evoke memories of the glory years when Sugar Ray Leonard, Thomas Hearns, Roberto Duran, and Marvelous Marvin Hagler fought each other. Unfortunately, Bradley, Alexander, Khan, and Ortiz aren't Leonard, Hearns, Duran, and Hagler.

But whatever happens in the 140-pound division, one thing that HBO should avoid in 2011 is allowing Pacquiao-Mayweather (or the absence thereof) to overshadow the entire year.

There were times in 2010 when HBO Sports looked like a kidnap victim tied to some railroad tracks, hoping that Manny and Floyd would come to the rescue. Ask a fight fan today, "What fights do you want to see?" and chances are that, after Pacquiao-Mayweather, the answer will be, "I don't know."

There's danger when talk of one fight, even if it happens, sucks the air out of everything else. Pacquiao-Mayweather, if it takes place, will make a lot of money for two fighters and a handful of corporate entities. But that money won't trickle down to others in the boxing world any more than the money from De La Hoya-Mayweather did. If boxing and boxing on HBO are to become healthy again (as opposed to a single fight generating one big score), it won't be on a pay-per-view basis. Fans need a more satisfying product across the board.

Another reason for the drop in ratings experienced by HBO's boxing programming is that its presentation of fights has gotten stale. The network has a great deal of creative talent. It should use it more.

HBO should find a way to tie Martinez-Williams in Atlantic City into its critically acclaimed *Boardwalk Empire* series. Has anybody thought of asking James Gandolfini to host a pre-fight show on an HBO-PPV card? Or creating a pre-fight panel with some combination of Sylvester Stallone, Robert DeNiro, Jack Nicholson, and Denzel Washington (all knowledgeable fight fans)? Throw Mike Tyson into the mix. That would get some ink and attract viewers. I'd move heaven and hell to have J. K. Rowling talking on camera at a big HBO fight. Ditto for Oprah Winfrey. That would broaden the viewer demographic.

24/7 has proven to be an important tool in building the audience for pay-per-view fights. Why not use it to build the brand of boxing? Take four good young evenly matched fighters in the same weight division. One each promoted by Golden Boy, Top Rank, Main Events, Lou DiBella, Dan Goossen, and Gary Shaw.

That's six promoters, you say; not four.

Right. You'd have the promoters competing against each other and offering their best product so as not to get left out. Set the promoters loose on one another and put the four chosen fighters in an elimination tournament. If you think that watching Roger Mayweather shop for a Thanksgiving turkey on *24/7* is fun, how about that battle royale?

Boxing After Dark was originally conceived as a platform for exciting young fighters to showcase their talents in competitive fights, while a date on *HBO World Championship Boxing* meant that a fighter had made it to the bigtime. Now viewers see some match-ups with aging fighters on *BAD* and some very ordinary events on *WCB*. At times, the programming is indistinguishable. So drop the *BAD* label. All it does is connote lesser fights. The announcing teams are the primary difference between the two franchises, and even that distinction has been blurred.

That leads to another problem. HBO will have televised twenty-two shows by the end of this year; five pay-per-view, eight *World Championship Boxing,* and nine *Boxing After Dark* telecasts. Max Kellerman will have been on the air for fifteen of these shows; Jim Lampley thirteen; Bob Papa nine; and Larry Merchant six. If I'm running a boxing program for a major television network, I want Jim Lampley to be my go-to branding guy; not Max (who, by the way, will also have more "face time" on HBO this year than Lampley).

Next point. HBO has to think outside the box. One way it can do so (and I suggested this last year) is to focus its choice of fights and the marketing of these fights on the issue of "WHO'S #1?'"

Championship fights used to excite fans. Not anymore. The absurd proliferation of title belts has destroyed the idea of lineal succession. As Patrick Kehoe wrote, "The nature of a championship as a marketing tool for gaining network television money has become a championship's primary function, divorcing it from the historic concept of symbolic superiority. Champions have become fighters with belts who are no longer required to defeat the very best within their division. Essentially, titleholders need to defend titles against network-sanctioned opponents and make a yearly mandatory defense; politics not merit, determining that status."

Last year, Eric Raskin analyzed some statistical data and observed, "In the spring of 1998, there were twenty-one American-born fighters who wore IBF, WBA or WBC belts. In the spring of 2008, that number was down to fourteen. Right now, in the spring of 2009, the total is seven."

By my calculations, including the WBO (which Raskin left off his list), the present total is six.

Stop the nonsense! HBO should identify the most credible rankings possible. That might mean convening its own independent panel of experts. I've offered suggestions in the past as to how that might be done. Then, as the network moves through the 140-pound division, it can tell viewers, "This fight is between #1 and #2. This fight is between #3 and #5."

"WHO'S #1" works in other sports. It can work in boxing. But the key to it all is the fights themselves, not how they're packaged. Every fight that HBO televises should have two fighters that the public wants to see; not one. Instead of telling its subscribers, "We're giving you great fights," HBO should give its subscribers great fights.

II

Despite its difficulties, HBO remains the dominant force in boxing today because of the size of its checkbook. But no financial transaction takes place in a vacuum. For every pile of money somewhere, there's a larger pile somewhere else. When two financial powers interact and one helps the other, it can skew the balance of power in an industry. Nothing that HBO has done over the past few years has shaped boxing as much as its strategic alliance with Golden Boy Promotions.

Boxing is a playground that's largely without rules. You want fair in boxing? Fair is a place where people eat cotton candy and go on rides.

When Golden Boy joined the ranks of promoters at the dawn of the new millennium, the company was hailed as a council of white knights who would do their best to clean up boxing. Oscar De La Hoya was the sport's #1 star. Golden Boy CEO Richard Schaefer was a former Swiss banker, who was expected to provide the business acumen necessary for success.

"They all say they're going to come in and clean up boxing," Craig Hamilton, an astute observer of the boxing scene, said at the time. "And they all wind up wanting to control things the way that Don King used to control them."

In recent years, the industry perception of Golden Boy has changed. There's no precise marker of when that happened. But the evening in September 2006, when De La Hoya met Manny Pacquiao at Los Angeles International Airport and offered him a briefcase containing $300,000 in cash in an effort to lure him away from Top Rank was a seminal moment.

Within the boxing industry, Schaefer (not De La Hoya) is now the face of Golden Boy. And one rarely hears him referred to these days as a "Swiss banker." He's a boxing promoter.

Schaefer brilliantly leveraged De La Hoya's appeal while Oscar was fighting. Over the past seven years, the most tested route to stardom in the

United States has been beating De La Hoya. Manny Pacquiao, Floyd Mayweather Jr, Bernard Hopkins, and Shane Mosley all took that route. All but Pacquiao wound up fighting for Golden Boy. And Golden Boy now receives a percentage of Top Rank's profits from Manny's fights as a consequence of a litigation settlement that followed Pacquiao's acceptance of the aforementioned briefcase filled with cash.

The most significant benefit that Schaefer reaped as a consequence of Golden Boy's "De La Hoya power" was a long-term output deal with HBO. That deal, signed in 2008, runs through 2011.

Output deals whereby a network commits to buying a minimum number of fights during a given time frame from a promoter aren't new in boxing. Over the years, Bob Arum has had them with numerous networks. Don King once had one with Showtime. For a fledgling network with little money to spend, they might make sense. But over time, output deals tend to work to a network's disadvantage because the promoter is guaranteed dates, which strips the network of a key bargaining chip in negotiations.

When Jay Larkin was in charge of Showtime's boxing program, he instituted a policy that encouraged contracts for one fight at a time rather than multi-fight deals. He called the policy "great fights, no rights." Golden Boy's output deal with HBO could have been called "great rights, no fights." In effect, HBO said to Golden Boy, "Don't tell us what the fights are. Surprise us."

Asked about the output deal, Schaefer says, "If you have the talent, you get the dates."

But another way of looking at it is, "If you have the dates, you get the talent."

HBO's output deal with Golden Boy wasn't based on fighters that Golden Boy had. It was based on fighters that Golden Boy was expected to sign in the future because it now had financial backing from the network and could tell fighters, "Sign with us. We can put you on HBO."

It's widely acknowledged within HBO that the Golden Boy output deal was a mistake and won't be renewed when it expires. Asked whether he would enter into the deal if he could do things over again, Greenburg answers, "That's a tough question. When we made that deal, it was a different time and boxing was in a different place than it is today."

Either way, there's a widespread belief that the HBO-Golden Boy output deal tilted the playing field in boxing beyond its contractual terms.

That's because HBO is thought by many to have performed additional favors for Golden Boy after the contract was signed in order to give value to the network's rights under the contract.

One common allegation among rival promoters is that, in recent years, HBO has steered fighters such as Amir Khan (who signed a three-fight deal with Golden Boy six months ago) to Schaefer and company.

"That's ridiculous," says Greenburg. "We've been adamant about never steering any fighter to any promoter. That's a nasty dangerous bad game. I take offense that anyone would suggest that. It just doesn't happen. I won't let that happen. And if it does happen on my watch, there would be severe ramifications."

"It has never happened," adds Kery Davis. "That's one hundred percent false. I'm a lawyer. I know where the lines are; I don't cross them. I would find it inappropriate for HBO to steer any fighter to any promoter."

But a promoter who regularly does business with HBO takes a contrary view, stating, "I'm afraid to say this on the record, because they'll retaliate against me if I do. But what Ross and Kery are saying simply isn't true. HBO was stuck with a bad output deal and a promotional company that doesn't know how to develop its own fighters. Kery steered fighters to Golden Boy to fill the slots that had to be filled, and there are a half-dozen promoters and managers who would tell that to Ross if he asked them. I'm not saying that Ross is lying. I'll give him the benefit of the doubt and say that he doesn't know. But Kery has steered fighters to Golden Boy."

The perception that HBO gives preferential treatment to Golden Boy is widespread throughout the boxing industry.

"Golden Boy gets advance notice of HBO's strategic planning," complains one promoter.

"Richard Schaefer tells managers and fighters about dates that the rest of us aren't even aware of," says another.

A refrain that rival promoters say they often hear from Davis is, "We don't have any open dates. Why don't you talk with Golden Boy."

There was no room at the inn for Zab Judah until Kathy Duva of Main Events (Judah's promoter) went to Richard Schaefer. HBO then agreed to televise Judah vs. Lucas Matthysse from the Prudential Center in Newark on November 6th, but insisted that it be paired with Robert

Guerrero against Vicente Escobedo. Matthysse, Guerrero, and Escobedo are all Golden Boy fighters.

"Look at the undercard for Judah-Matthysse," Duva says. "I wanted to work with Russell Peltz and put Mike Jones in the co-feature against another top welterweight. Mike is from Philadelphia. He's undefeated and has a big fan following. It would have given him a foothold in the Prudential Center and established him as a future opponent for Andre Berto. But Golden Boy had the date; so instead, we're stuck with two Mexican-Americans from California fighting in New Jersey in the first TV fight of the night. They'll sell no tickets and the crowd won't care."

Lou DiBella promoted Paulie Malignaggi from his first pro fight through July of this year. On September 28th, Golden Boy announced that it had signed Malignaggi to a three-year contract.

Anthony Catanzaro (Paulie's adviser) says that no one from HBO steered him to Golden Boy. "I called [Golden Boy president] Dave Itskowitch and asked for a meeting," Catanzaro recalls. "During the time that we were negotiating, Golden Boy never said they could get Paulie on HBO. Later, after Paulie had signed, Richard Schaefer told him, 'If we get you two wins, maybe we can get you back on *Boxing After Dark*.'"

Asked about the same issue, Malignaggi answers, "I'm not stupid. Lou was my promoter. But the last four times I was on HBO, Lou provided my services to Golden Boy and it was on Golden Boy shows. Golden Boy has a chance of getting me on HBO again. Lou can't. It's as simple as that."

After Kelly Pavlik lost to Bernard Hopkins, he was still middleweight champion of the world. But HBO turned down numerous proposed opponents, forcing Top Rank to put Pavlik on an independent pay-per-view card.

In and of itself, HBO's decision had a credible basis. Marco Antonio Rubio (who Pavlik finally fought) is a solid journeyman; nothing more. But Rubio and several other opponents that HBO turned down for Pavlik were as credible as the competition that Andre Berto has fought. And unlike Berto, Pavlik had earned a breather by going in tough against Hopkins, Edison Miranda, and Jermain Taylor (twice) in four of his previous five fights. Also, Pavlik had proven himself to be a far bigger attraction than Berto. There were those who thought that HBO was putting the squeeze on Top Rank to make it difficult for the promoter to meet its contractual obligations to Pavlik. That way, when the Pavlik–Top Rank contract expired, Kelly might sign with Golden Boy.

HBO also recently bailed Golden Boy out of a bad financial situation when it put its pay-per-view brand on the promoter's September 18th card featuring Shane Mosley vs. Sergio Mora.

In recent years, HBO has moved away from small pay-per-view events on the theory that they diminish the HBO-PPV brand and cut into enthusiasm for major pay-per-view cards. At the September 1, 2010, kick-off press conference in New York for Pacquiao-Margarito, HBO senior vice president Mark Taffet (who oversees the network's pay-per-view program) told the media, "At HBO Pay-Per-View, we're in the big event business."

Mosley-Mora was not a "big event." To the contrary, it was a predictably awful fight. Franklin McNeil's "Twitters" on ESPN.com as the bout progressed told the tale: "The fight has started . . . There was little action in the first round . . . Fans are starting to boo . . . It's only the second round, but this fight is boring . . . Mora is literally running from Mosley in the third round. This is bad . . . This fight had no business being on pay-per-view . . . This is one of the worst fights I have seen this year; maybe the worst, considering it's the main event of a PPV . . . This fight is so boring, I won't bother scoring it anymore . . . The fight still stinks . . . This fight is horrible. It's unbelievably bad."

By producing, distributing, and putting Jim Lampley behind the microphone for Mosley-Mora, HBO diluted its overall product.

Craig Hamilton sums up, saying, "Of course, HBO shows favoritism toward Golden Boy. Anybody who says they don't is lying or stupid. Let's see what happens when Timothy Bradley and Devon Alexander become promotional free agents next year. The truth is; neither of them needs a promoter. HBO has already made it clear that it wants them to participate in those big fights it's planning for the 140-pound division. So why should they give a piece of their share to a promoter? All they need is a manager and a good lawyer. Let's see if HBO pushes them toward Golden Boy."

HBO's tilt toward Golden Boy is now an assumption that's built into the business models of many promoters, who believe that the network has done a disservice to the sport by empowering one promoter. There are complaints that Gary Shaw enjoys similar favoritism from Showtime. But given Showtime's second-place status, that doesn't impact on boxing in the manner of decisions made by HBO.

"The way things are structured now," says Joe DeGuardia, "we're reluctant to invest money to develop fighters because, when the fighters are ready for the bigtime, they're incentivized to leave us. If you can't make money at the top, what's the sense of losing money at the bottom?"

"HBO and Golden Boy are destroying the farm system," adds Kathy Duva. "Most promoters are afraid to put money into the long-term development of a fighter, because they don't want to develop a fighter and lose him. HBO decides it's interested in somebody. Kery or someone else at HBO tells Golden Boy that it's interested in the fighter. Then Golden Boy offers the fighter a big signing bonus and high purse minimums because they know they'll get dates for him on HBO. It happened to us and it happens to other promoters all the time. Golden Boy has been in business for years and, even with everything it gets from HBO, it still hasn't developed a star of its own. Its main attractions have all been developed by someone else. But you get to a certain point and you almost have to look for a one-shot pay-off with your fighter instead of building him for the future because you're afraid that Golden Boy will come in with HBO's money and steal him."

"They're partners," Duva continues. "That's what Richard Schaefer says. 'We're partners with HBO.' Bob Arum didn't make them his partner. I didn't; Don King didn't. When Golden Boy came in; that was when this started happening."

Golden Boy shouldn't be blamed for extracting an output deal and other concessions from HBO. That's what promoters are supposed to do. The issue is whether Golden Boy's conduct in conjunction with actions taken by one or more HBO employees crossed over the line that separates lawful business practices from illegal restraint of trade and other wrongdoing.

In that regard, comments that Oscar De La Hoya made to Ben Grossman as reported in the September 27, 2010, issue of *Broadcasting & Cable* are instructive.

"I commend UFC for what they have done in such a short period of time," De La Hoya said. "They are the only real player in their category, the mixed martial arts world. They have been able to organize themselves, have all the TV dates, a pay-per-view every month. They are doing the right thing, and it's time for boxing to do the right thing, as long as we don't have those obstacles named Don King and Bob Arum."

Grossman then asked, "How does that actually happen? You want Golden Boy to replace them?"

"Absolutely," De La Hoya answered. "We need to sign all the talent and get all the TV dates. Then you can have your own agenda and have a schedule for the fans and the sport. You can do a monthly pay-per-view, a bi-weekly HBO fight. You can have the best fighters fight each other. When you have five or six promoters, it's very difficult."

"It's not my opinion anymore," Duva says. "It's fact. Oscar came out and said what he wants."

"What we're seeing here," adds another promoter, "is a classic example of how anti-competitive behavior hurts other competitors and the public. If HBO was giving preferential treatment to a promoter who was providing great fights, that would be one thing. But they aren't. Golden Boy is giving HBO a few good fights and a lot that aren't very good. I won't go on the record with you because we both know that, if I do, there will be retaliation. I'm in a dangerous position. My livelihood depends on the dates I can get from HBO. But if Bill Nelson or Richard Plepler called me in and asked me what was going on, I'd tell them to their face. So would a lot of other promoters."

Meanwhile, Golden Boy keeps rolling along. On July 12, 2010, it announced a three-year contract with Brooklyn Sports & Entertainment to promote twelve fights a year at the Barclays Center, which will open in Brooklyn in mid-2012.

The Barclays deal signaled Golden Boy's intention to move aggressively into the New York metropolitan area. Schaefer explains, "Making the deal now allows us to plan for the future. The situation is very fluid. But I would expect that we will have six club shows each year at Barclays that will be televised on an outlet like SportsNet, three Telefutura-ESPN-level shows, two shows on HBO or Showtime, and one pay-per-view event. The important thing is that there will be continuity. We'll lock in the dates and then we'll fill in the slots. It's an investment for Golden Boy in the New York market and it guarantees New Yorkers live shows."

The deal is "exclusive" in that it would allow Golden Boy to provide the services of fighters for other shows in New York, but Golden Boy cannot be the lead promoter on those shows. Similarly, other promoters can co-promote with Golden Boy at Barclays, but Golden Boy must be the lead promoter.

"We cannot force another promoter to go to Barclays," Schaefer continues. "I would assume, however, that co-promoters would want to go there, since the Madison Square Garden deal structure is about as unattractive as it gets and the Barclays Center's is about as attractive as they come."

On August 10th, Chris Mannix reported on SportsIllustrated.com that several industry sources "suggested that HBO was involved with brokering the deal with the Barclays Center." The most vocal among them was Brooklyn-born Lou DiBella.

"Golden Boy goes to venues," DiBella says. "They go to fighters, sponsors, and investors, saying, 'HBO is our strategic partner.' They give the impression that it will go on long after 2011 and that the deal will give Barclay's exposure on HBO. And HBO does nothing to rebut that. This is a contract between a hole in the ground and a promoter for unnamed fighters in fights that won't be made for years. The whole thing smells."

One of the questions raised regarding the deal between Golden Boy and Barclays is the role, if any, played by HBO senior vice president Mark Taffet. Brett Yormark (president and CEO of Brooklyn Sports & Entertainment) declined to be interviewed for this article. However, he told Mannix, "For me, everything is about gut. We [Golden Boy and Barclays] share the same vision. They want to grow the sport in Brooklyn. They have visions of going global. We do too. They were willing to make a commitment to us, help us grow this franchise."

Mannix further reported, "Both HBO and Yormark emphatically deny the network's involvement. 'Absolutely not,' Yormark said. 'I have some friends at HBO that date back a long way, but they never brokered [a deal] or interfered in it.' An HBO spokesman told SI.com, 'In no way did anyone at HBO Sports suggest or recommend to Mr. Yormark what promotional company he should contact, nor did Mr. Yormark indicate that he intended to approach any promoter as a potential exclusive partner or sponsor. Yes, one of our executives had lunch with Mr. Yormark once in the past year, but the conversation was general and no recommendations or endorsements were made."

Taffet elaborates on that theme, saying, "One of his [Yormark's] family members knows one of my family members, so there's a connection. In fifteen years, I've met him a few times at social functions. Five or six months ago, he asked to have lunch and we had a general discussion about boxing. I explained HBO's role as a broadcaster and HBO's role as a pay-per-view distributor, and that was it. He never expressed any interest in doing anything with any particular promoter."

Golden Boy can't be criticized for making the Barclays deal. As with the HBO output deal, it was in Golden Boy's best interest to do so. Barclays might have been unwise to limit itself to one promoter. Schaefer notes that, when Barclays goes into the market to sell luxury-suite packages, now it can tell buyers, "We're giving you twelve nights of boxing each year." But there are a dozen promoters who would have been willing and able to furnish good fights on a date-by-date basis for the individual dates that Barclays will be offering. Still, if that's bad judgment on Barclays's part, it's not Golden Boy's fault.

If Yormark were to leave Barclays before the arena is built and take a job with a company that has financial ties to Golden Boy, it would raise eyebrows. Otherwise, the agreement would appear to be what it is on its face; nothing more.

As for the allegations that something improper transpired, Schaefer declares, "I would say to the other promoters, 'Stop crying. Stop complaining. Get up, go out, and do something. No one said that Lou DiBella couldn't approach Barclays. I did, and he didn't. I've approached many people where nothing worked out. I didn't complain and stop trying. Lou DiBella complains that I came into Brooklyn. Fine. Let Lou DiBella come out to Los Angeles and make a deal with Forum Boxing. And don't stop with Los Angeles. Does Lou think that we're going to stop in New York? I'm looking now at monthly shows in England and to use our relationship with AEG [an equity partner in Golden Boy] to set up a presence in China. The New Jersey Nets [of the National Basketball Association] will play at the Barclays Center. The new owner of the Nets, Mikhail Prokhorov is one of the richest men in Russia. Don't you think that I will have conversations with him about a Golden Boy presence in Russia. Lou DiBella should go to England; Lou DiBella should go to Russia and other countries around the world and promote the way that Golden Boy is doing."

"I've had it with Lou DiBella and all the other complainers," Schaefer continues. "This is all just sour grapes. These other promoters cry all the time and don't do anything to build the sport. Why did I get every Friday night on Telefutura, fifty shows a year? Because I walked in with sponsor commitments. Why did I get ten dates with Fox? Because I walked in with sponsor commitments. Lou DiBella can complain all he wants. How many times has he walked into a network with a sponsor commitment?"

"I know what Oscar said about UFC, but I'm not following the UFC model. I'm following the Golden Boy model. Our output deal with HBO guarantees us three *Boxing After Dark* shows and one *World Championship Boxing* show each year. I would hardly call that a monopoly. Yes, Golden Boy aggressively pursues free agents. I like to surround myself with people who have deep pockets. The major shareholders in Golden Boy are Oscar, myself, AEG, and The Brener Group [which invests on behalf of a wealthy Mexican family]. That allows Golden Boy to aggressively invest in talent. That's why we get the fighters. Golden Boy doesn't steal fighters. If somebody is free, they're free."

"You know, it really is sad that so many people in boxing, especially promoters, spend so much time attacking each other. One thing Todd DuBoef says that I agree with is that we have to improve the brand of boxing. Not enough people care about the sport. There's a fight soon, Sergio Martinez against Paul Williams. Two of the best fighters in the world, fighters in the top five on almost everyone's pound-for-pound list, will be fighting each other. Everyone thinks that it will be a good fight. And no one cares. That hurts all of boxing. So stop complaining and help build the sport."

"I have November 27th on HBO. We agreed with HBO to do Juan Manuel Marquez against Michael Katsidis. Then I got a call from Kery. 'Hey, Richard; could you help us out and give Lou [DiBella] the two undercard spots on your show for Berto and Caballero.' I said 'no problem.' Then Lou sells HBO Berto against Hernandez and Caballero against Litzau. I would never have gotten away with those fights. If I made those fights, Lou would be screaming that they're horrible and HBO wouldn't have approved them. But HBO approved Lou's fights because he has scared them with all his complaining. So I gave up my undercard spots; Lou never called to thank me; and he's still talking shit about Golden Boy.

I'm really very tired of it. Lou does things like a mom-and-pop promotion company and then he complains when someone else tries to do more. And I'll tell you something else. Many people in boxing said that, once Oscar retired, Golden Boy would be gone. They were wrong. Now they're saying that, when the output deal with HBO is over, Golden Boy will be gone. And they're wrong again. Golden Boy isn't going to go away. All this complaining about HBO this and HBO that actually helps us, because it makes the fighters think that Golden Boy is even more powerful than we are."

So . . . where does one go to further explore the allegations that HBO gives preferential treatment to Golden Boy?

Possibly, the May 15, 2010, *Boxing After Dark* doubleheader at Madison Square Garden, featuring Amir Khan vs. Paulie Malignaggi, with Victor Ortiz against Nate Campbell on the undercard. Lou DiBella was Malignaggi's promoter at the time. The other three fighters were promoted by Golden Boy (the lead promoter for show).

HBO paid a $1,500,000 license fee for Khan-Malignaggi. Under the contract between Golden Boy and DiBella Entertainment, that license fee was to be divided 60 percent to Khan and Golden Boy, 40 percent to DiBella and Malignaggi. Golden Boy was to receive the entire license fee for Ortiz-Campbell. There was confusion in some circles as to what the Ortiz-Campbell license fee actually was.

New York law requires that anyone who promotes a professional boxing match in New York file various fight-related contracts with the New York State Athletic Commission. Federal law has a similar requirement. The federal and New York reporting requirements supplement each other. One does not negate the other.

Golden Boy failed to provide the contracts in question to the New York State Athletic Commission in a timely manner. As a consequence of that, the NYSAC made requests for the documents on May 19th, June 3rd, and June 10th. The requests were ignored. The commission then subpoenaed the missing documents. Golden Boy refused to comply with the subpoena. Its president (Dave Itskowitch) later told the *New York Daily News,* "We didn't want our contracts on the public record. We have confidentiality clauses in our contracts. We wanted to comply with what we needed to comply with; but at the same time, we wanted to protect our agreements."

Itskowitch is an honorable man, but his explanation ignored two factors: (1) Golden Boy can't pick and choose which laws it complies with; and (2) there's a confidentiality provision under New York law that Golden Boy could have invoked to protect the contracts from public disclosure.

On July 9th, the New York State Athletic Commission advised Golden Boy that its promoter's license had been suspended because of its refusal to file documents as required by law. The Notice of Suspension further alleged that Golden Boy had made false representations to the commission regarding the existence of certain contracts.

On July 12th, Golden Boy issued a statement acknowledging that "a number of significant, but innocent, mistakes were made in failing to make timely responses to legitimate information requests from the NYSAC." That same day, Judd Burstein (Golden Boy's lead attorney in the matter) told ESPN.com, "There was no willful intent or false statement made. The guy who usually handles it [Dave Itskowitch] went on his honeymoon, and the guy who handled it didn't know what the hell he was talking about."

Burstein further advised Michael Rosenthal of RingTV.com, "No one was minding the store. The commission made numerous requests for the documents, and no one really paid attention. The commission appropriately decided that Golden Boy was not responding and issued a suspension. I understand the commission was upset. The contracts should have been produced. It was an innocent error."

Skeptics pointed out that a honeymoon doesn't last for seven weeks.

On July 20th, Golden Boy and the NYSAC entered into a Consent Order, pursuant to which Golden Boy acknowledged "mistakenly" representing to the commission that all existing written agreements between Golden Boy and fighters participating on the May 15th card had been filed with the commission and, also, failing to file those agreements as required by New York law. In addition, it agreed to pay a $10,000 fine. The suspension was terminated.

Immediately after the Consent Order was signed, Golden Boy issued a press release headlined, "NYSAC Lifts Suspension of Golden Boy and Clears Its Name." In reality, the Consent Order left several questions unresolved.

The contracts filed with the New York State Athletic Commission confirmed reports circulated previously in boxing circles that HBO had paid a license fee of $750,000 for Ortiz-Campbell.

That $750,000 stands out like a sore thumb.

Ortiz-Campbell was the opening fight on a *Boxing After Dark* telecast. A $400,000 license fee would have been generous payment for that bout.

There were suggestions that HBO and Golden Boy had conspired to shift money from the license fee for Khan-Malignaggi to the license fee for Ortiz-Campbell in order to deny Malignaggi and DiBella their 40 percent of the amount that was shifted. But $1,500,000 was fair market value for Khan-Malignaggi.

Why did HBO pay a $750,000 license fee for Ortiz-Campbell?

Richard Schaefer says, "As with any *World Championship Boxing* or *Boxing After Dark* event, I negotiated the license fee with Kery. HBO really wanted that fight, and I needed that amount of money to get the fight done."

Davis explains, "I kept Ross in the loop with regard to the negotiations. He ultimately approved what we paid. I'm not going to confirm the license fee. I will say that we paid what I thought was fair market value for that fight. Ortiz had been in three fights on the network that had done well. Campbell was a former champion."

Greenburg notes, "I looked at it as one of the stars at 140 pounds fighting a rugged veteran, who was an ex-champion and had stymied the career of Juan Diaz."

The problem with that rationale is that Ortiz isn't a star at 140 pounds; not yet. He was knocked out by the only world-class fighter he faced. A lot of people have "stymied the career of Juan Diaz" lately. Diaz has lost four of his last six outings. Campbell has won one fight in the past thirty-two months. And Ortiz-Campbell was a lousy fight.

But the most compelling argument that Ortiz-Campbell wasn't worth $750,000 lies in what the fighters were paid. Victor Ortiz received a $100,000 purse. Nate Campbell was paid $125,000 plus an additional $25,000 for training expenses.

The value of a fight comes from the fighters. The idea that a fight can legitimately generate a $750,000 television license fee (plus a portion of the live gate) with the fighters getting only $250,000 might appeal to Don King. But it's not consistent with the stated mission of Golden Boy to ensure fair pay for fighters.

Moreover, Ortiz was managed by Shelly Finkel. There are people in boxing who like Finkel and people who don't. But one thing everyone agrees on is that Shelly knows the value of a fight. He could have been expected to get a purse well in excess of $100,000 for his fighter if Ortiz-Campbell was really worth $750,000.

Ortiz and Campbell were fairly paid. Golden Boy appears to have been grossly overpaid.

"A license fee of $400,000 would have been in line with reality," says Bob Arum. "Seven-fifty is ludicrous."

"It's not in my best interests to trash HBO for paying high license fees," says another promoter. "But $750,000 for Ortiz-Campbell is absurd. I've asked around, and everyone I've talked with says it's a joke. What really happened was, HBO subsidized Golden Boy's acquisition of Ortiz [from Top Rank] and Campbell [from Don King Productions]. Both of those guys jumped ship to be with Golden Boy, and HBO paid for it."

The $750,000 license fee that HBO paid for Victor Ortiz vs. Nate Campbell is an interesting entry point into the decision-making process at HBO. If enough people tug hard on that thread, the cloth might unravel.

III

"One of the things I hear all the time now," says Ross Greenburg, "is that everyone's problems seem to be HBO's fault. That's getting tiring for us. Most of what happens in boxing is beyond our control."

One of boxing's problems in 2010 is that the top promoters are fighting each other more often than the top fighters are fighting each other. The issues that HBO faces today are playing out against an increasingly ugly war between Golden Boy and Top Rank.

When Don King and Bob Arum ruled the roost, they disliked each other just as much as Richard Schaefer and Arum dislike each other. But the big fights between their fighters got made.

Pat English (who has served as counsel for Main Events since the 1980s) notes, "When Main Events promoted Evander Holyfield, Pernell Whitaker, Lennox Lewis, and others, we didn't have insurmountable problems making fights with other promoters. What has changed is that, in those days, promoters were promoters and knew how to build fighters and had to work together. Now most promoters are little more than packagers looking for a date and a big license fee from HBO, and HBO has trouble brokering the big fights."

Top Rank has been criticized for refusing to put its big money makers in against fighters controlled by competing promoters. To a degree, that's true. But Arum tried to make Manny Pacquiao vs. Floyd Mayweather Jr earlier this year. He co-promoted an April 17th fight in which Kelly Pavlik lost the middleweight championship to Sergio Martinez (a Lou DiBella fighter). On June 26th, Julio Cesar Chavez Jr (a potential cash cow for Arum) fought John Duddy (a promotional free agent). On November 6th, Juan Manuel Lopez (one of Top Rank's most promising young stars) will risk his elite status against Rafael Marquez (promoted by Gary Shaw).

Meanwhile, Arum and Schaefer have been sniping at each other for years. Their war escalated in late 2009, when Golden Boy supported the Mayweather camp in propagating the view that Pacquiao (Top Rank's flagship fighter) uses illegal performance-enhancing drugs. It heated up even more this July, when the latest round of negotiations for Pacquiao-Mayweather collapsed.

On July 19th, Leonard Ellerbe (Mayweather's friend and business manager) took issue with Arum's statements to the media regarding the failure of negotiations for the fight and declared, "Here are the facts. Al Haymon [who manages Mayweather], Richard Schaefer [who promoted Mayweather's most recent fights], and myself speak to each other on a regular basis. The truth is, no negotiations have ever taken place."

Four days later, Schaefer told Robert Morales, "You read the statement from Leonard, and I stand behind that statement. It's unfortunate Arum feels like that. But I tell you what; I would make myself available for a lie-detector test and let's see who's telling the truth and who's lying. If I say I stand behind Leonard's statement, it's because it's the truth."

That dialogue was troubling to Ross Greenburg, who recently told this writer, "Those talks were a difficult time for me. I was talking with Al Haymon, who was Floyd's representative, and I was talking with Arum, who was representing Pacquiao. I thought that everyone was negotiating in good faith, and then what happened happened."

On July 26th, Greenburg issued a statement of his own that acknowledged, "It's unfortunate that [Pacquiao-Mayweather] won't happen in 2010. I had been negotiating with a representative from each side since May 2nd, carefully trying to put the fight together."

That same day, Schaefer countered, saying, "I find it extremely unprofessional that the president of HBO Sports would issue this statement before this weekend's Golden Boy fights [Marquez-Diaz II]. My entire focus this week is on this pay-per-view card on HBO, and they would be well-served to do the same thing. I fully stand behind the statement I made. I have not negotiated with Ross and I am not aware of any negotiations that have taken place. If Ross or Arum wants to go through a lie detector test, we can arrange that. I can only tell you, I have regular contact with Al and Leonard and there were no negotiations going on. I don't know exactly what Ross is referring to or what he is talking about."

For good measure, Schaefer added, "Arum should just get a life and stop attacking me on a nonstop basis. This is really childish."

Dry wit that he is; Top Rank president Todd DuBoef countered, "Richard has always wanted to one-up Bob. Now he has: 'Yesterday, I was lying. Today, I'm lying.'"*

Arum saw less humor in the situation. Among the observations he offered were:

- "Richard Schaefer has prostituted himself to a place where he has almost no credibility. He has demonstrated a total lack of pride. He has demeaned himself to such an extent that he has to feel ashamed of himself."

- "Schaefer and Haymon and Ellerbe cling to the Mayweather boat because that's the source of their riches. For Schaefer to be part of this drinking the Kool Aid is really pathetic. Doesn't he have any pride?"

- "Schaefer saying the things he's saying might play well to the crazies, but it totally destroys his credibility with anyone who has a brain. And I'll tell you something else. This could put real strain on

* DuBoef was alluding to a statement attributed to Arum in the 1970s, when the promoter reportedly told Bob Waters of *Newsday*, "Today I'm telling the truth. Yesterday I was lying."

> the relationship between HBO and Golden Boy. First, Ross was burned by the output deal. Then Schaefer was totally powerless to deliver on what would have been the biggest fight in years. And now he makes that horrible insulting statement suggesting that Ross take a lie detector test."

In late September, Golden Boy fired back with a lawsuit in federal court in Nevada, alleging that Top Rank, Arum, and David Lopez (Top Rank's chief financial officer) are liable to Golden Boy for $3,000,000 to $5,000,000 in damages for racketeering and fraud. The suit is based on a June 2007 settlement between the warring promoters that provides (1) Top Rank retains promotional rights to Pacquiao; (2) Golden Boy is to receive a percentage of the promotional profits from Pacquiao's fights; and (3) when Pacquiao fights an opponent promoted by Golden Boy, Golden Boy is the lead promoter and in charge of the accounting process.

The thrust of the lawsuit is the allegation that, since the settlement, Top Rank has provided false accountings for Pacquiao's fights against David Diaz, Miguel Cotto, and Joshua Clottey. Golden Boy was not involved in the promotion of those fights.

"It's total bullshit," Arum says of the lawsuit. "It's a desperate act on Golden Boy's part, and it's going to backfire on them because, not only are they going to lose and wind up paying our attorney's fees; it's going to come out that Golden Boy is guilty of some of the same things they're accusing us of."

Golden Boy, of course, takes a contrary view. "The truth will come out in the courtroom," says attorney Judd Burstein. "Bob Arum will be my first witness and best proof that he and the other defendants are guilty of a scheme to commit massive mail and wire fraud."

And so it goes. Over time, the war between Top Rank and Golden Boy has become a proxy war, with other promoters quietly (and not so quietly) choosing sides. Meanwhile, the ripples emanating from their struggle are impacting on HBO and all of boxing.

"This dispute is damaging to everyone," Greenburg says. "It really hurts the sport. Schaefer and Arum don't have to throw dinner parties together, but they do have to find a way to promote fights together."

Schaefer voices similar thoughts. "I am sure that Bob Arum's feelings toward us are similar to our feelings toward him," Richard says. "I don't look forward to standing up on a dais with him, and I'm sure he feels the same way about me. But to make certain fights, for the good of boxing and the good of our companies, there are times when we should put our personal feelings aside and work together."

And Arum?

"I'd rather not co-promote with Golden Boy," Arum says. "I don't see how it could be anything but unpleasant. And they're so disorganized when it comes to the nuts-and-bolts work of actually promoting that working with them makes it harder to do the job right. What I'd be happy to do is enter into a provision of services contract with them where they provide a fighter, Top Rank promotes the fight, and we pay Golden Boy for providing the services of that fighter. Golden Boy enters into contracts all the time where another promoter provides the services of a fighter to Golden Boy, so they can't complain about Top Rank wanting to do it that way."

One assumes that Arum would co-promote with Golden Boy if that were necessary to make Pacquiao-Mayweather happen. The more intriguing question is, "What would HBO do if Floyd came back and wanted to fight someone other than Manny?"

"That would pose a problem for us," Greenburg answers. "The fact that we couldn't make Mayweather-Pacquiao cast a pall over the sport this year. Now we have to come to terms with the fact that the fight might not happen and move on. If Floyd came back and wanted to fight someone else, I'm not sure how we'd handle it."

But there's an issue at HBO that runs deeper than Pacquiao-Mayweather and the list of fights that the network will televise next year. For the first time, there are people inside HBO and the hierarchy at Time Warner (HBO's parent company) who are asking whether HBO actually needs a sports department.

In recent years, HBO has shed several seven-figure executive contracts and encouraged some lower-level employees to accept severance packages. All of Time Warner is looking to consolidate workload and cut costs.

Greenburg's contract expires in May 2012. If he chose to pursue other interests (such as producing feature films on a full-time basis) that might be an opportune time to restructure.

Sources say that talk of restructuring hasn't reached the level of strategic planning. But some key people are asking "what if?"

Most network sports departments deal with multiple sports. One of the questions being asked internally at Time Warner is, "Why does HBO have a sports department when it really deals only with boxing?"

Right now, talk of restructuring is just that. Talk. But it could become something more.

"If the past few years have taught us anything," one insider says, "it's that nothing in this business is inviolable or permanent. And restructuring would be easy because HBO Sports breaks down so easily into its component parts. There's boxing, documentaries, and the magazine shows."

Under one scenario, HBO's *Sports of the 20th Century* series and other documentaries would be placed under the purview of Sheila Nevins (who has been with the network since 1979 and is now president of HBO's documentary division). *Real Sports* would be phased out.

As for boxing; the Turner networks (which are part of the Time Warner empire) include inter alia TBS and TNT. TBS televised all four Major League Baseball divisional playoff series this year and the American League championship series. In May 2010, TBS and TNT acquired shared rights with CBS to the NCAA men's basketball championship tournament through 2024. TBS and TNT also televise NBA basketball, college football, NASCAR, and numerous other sports events. Turner has a huge sports production staff.

David Levy is president of Turner Sports. All sports in the Turner family of networks flow through him. There has been talk of putting HBO's live boxing program under Levy's guidance. The fights would still air on HBO, but acquisition and production would be under his umbrella. TBS or TNT might also televise fights to build synergy and provide a platform for young fighters.

When asked about this scenario, Bob Arum (who is not a source of the reports) says, "You'd save a fortune on salaries. You'd save a fortune on production costs. And you wouldn't be paying for all those first-class airplane tickets and all those rooms at the Four Seasons and Beverly Wilshire hotels. Forget all the planning and scheming and machinations that these guys go through. HBO has the biggest checkbook in the industry. Promoters will be lining up to sell fights to Turner or HBO or whoever. You're not reinventing the wheel here."

Like the rest of the media, boxing's media landscape is everchanging. HBO and Time Warner have to ask, "What programming is HBO Sports currently producing for subscribers that couldn't be produced at less cost under this new model?"

Of course, there's another alternative.

In less than a decade, Richard Schaefer has built Golden Boy into a powerful force in the boxing industry. He understands finance and media. And he bears listening to when he says, "If you're Time Warner and you see that ratings are down and there's criticism about this and criticism about that, at some point you will say, 'We really don't need boxing.' I can tell you from discussions I've had that Showtime is getting fed up with boxing too. People have to remember; HBO and Showtime don't need boxing. It's the other way around."

Warning lights don't come any redder.

When a friend dies, his memory lives on.

Jay Larkin (1950–2010)

I met Jay Larkin in the 1990s when he was riding high as the driving force behind Showtime's boxing program.

Jay wasn't a typical television boxing executive. In his twenties, he'd played the lead in *Hair* and been part of Broadway productions like *Sweeney Todd* and *Sunday in the Park with George.* TV soap opera devotees might remember him from his roles on *All My Children* and *The Doctors.* He'd also sung in a doo-wop group.

I got to know Jay by writing about him. Then we became friends. In early 2007, he was diagnosed with a grade-4 glioblastoma. That's an aggressive, fast-growing, malignant brain tumor in its worst form. Survival rates depend on which study a patient looks at. Jay was told that 85 percent of the patients with a grade-4 glioblastoma are dead within a year.

Jay underwent surgery to remove the tumor at Columbia Presbyterian Hospital in New York. When I visited him there, I told him that he was going to live to be a crotchety old man and, by the time he was eighty, I'd be one of the few people who liked him.

I honestly believed that Jay was going to make it. I suppose that was wish therapy on my part; also known as denial.

From that day on, Jay's telephone calls to me often began with the salutation, "Hi; it's the crotchety old man."

In early 2009, the tumor returned in the form of "a small isolated nodule less than one centimeter in size." Jay was accepted into an experimental vaccine program at Duke University Medical Center. For a while, the tumor grew smaller. Then it stabilized. Two months ago, an MRI revealed that it was burgeoning out of control. Absent a miracle in the most literal sense, there was no hope.

Last Tuesday (August 3, 2010), I visited Jay at his home in Sparkill, New York. He and his wife Lisa wanted to tape a video record of Jay's time in boxing told from his point of view to pass on to their children. Jay was having good days and bad days by then. There was no guarantee that he'd hold up on camera. I asked Steve Farhood and Steve Albert if they'd like to come with me. Jay was particularly fond of both men and they'd been cornerstones of his years at Showtime. If he was unable to articulate during the taping, the three of us would carry the ball for him.

I hadn't seen Jay for several months, so it was a shock to see him. His left side had been disabled by the tumor. He was in a wheelchair. He could push objects with his left hand but couldn't lift them. He looked twenty years older than he had in June.

We started taping. Jay expressed his thoughts in a linear manner rather than the free flow of ideas that once characterized his thinking. But he was lucid. He told old war stories, including a few that I hadn't heard before. He was in good spirits. I know I speak for Steve Farhood and Steve Albert when I say that it was a privilege to share those hours with him.

That night, Jay called to thank me. "Today was the first time in a long time that I had fun," he said.

We talked one last time on Saturday. "I guess I won't be a crotchety old man, after all," he told me.

The war had been lost. All that remained was negotiating the final terms of surrender. On Sunday night, Jay suffered a massive brain hemorrhage. He died on Monday morning.

Most of us have frozen at the thought of death in moments when we focus with clarity on the fact that we won't always be here. All of us in moments of truth hope that something good will follow the life that we know. I don't pretend to know what awaits us. I do know that Jay was a special friend and a thoroughly decent man. Good people will miss him.